Out of the Red

Critical Issues in Crime and Society

RAYMOND J. MICHALOWSKI AND LUIS A. FERNANDEZ,
SERIES EDITORS

Critical Issues in Crime and Society is oriented toward critical analysis of contemporary problems in crime and justice. The series is open to a broad range of topics including specific types of crime, wrongful behavior by economically or politically powerful actors, controversies over justice system practices, and issues related to the intersection of identity, crime, and justice. It is committed to offering thoughtful works that will be accessible to scholars and professional criminologists, general readers, and students.

For a list of titles in the series, see the last page of the book.

Out of the Red

MY LIFE OF GANGS, PRISON, AND REDEMPTION

CHRISTIAN L. BOLDEN

RUTGERS UNIVERSITY PRESS

New Brunswick, Camden, and Newark, New Jersey, and London

Library of Congress Cataloging-in-Publication Data

Names: Bolden, Christian L., author.
Title: Out of the red: my life of gangs, prison, and redemption /
    Christian L. Bolden.
Description: New Brunswick: Rutgers University Press, 2020. | Series: Critical
    issues in crime and society | Includes bibliographical references and index.
Identifiers: LCCN 2019037931 | ISBN 9781978804524 (paperback) |
    ISBN 9781978804531 (hardback) | ISBN 9781978813434 (epub) |
    ISBN 9781978813441 (pdf) | ISBN 9781978813458 (mobi)
Subjects: LCSH: Bolden, Christian L. | Gang members—Texas—Biography. |
    Prisoners—Texas—Biography. | Ex-convicts—Texas—Biography.
Classification: LCC HV6439.U7 T36 2020 | DDC 364.106/6092 [B]—dc23
LC record available at https://lccn.loc.gov/2019037931

A British Cataloging-in-Publication record for this book is available
from the British Library.

⊖ The paper used in this publication meets the requirements of the American National
Standard for Information Sciences—Permanence of Paper for Printed Library Materials, ANSI Z39.48-1992.

www.rutgersuniversitypress.org

Manufactured in the United States of America

For my mother, Debra. I promised to one day make you proud.

CONTENTS

PART III   REDEMPTION

Prologue

It was just another day in November, seemingly no different from the rest. My mom busied herself with her usual routine. She picked me up from kindergarten. I ran inside and plopped down on the couch, turning on the TV hoping to catch *He-Man and the Masters of the Universe,* but settling for *Looney Tunes* while I waited. I was a quiet, introverted child who preferred to do my own thing rather than interact with anyone. On this afternoon, my attention was focused on the television. The volume was abnormally loud and my mother had not made it into the house to tell me to turn it down yet.

My father was away, undoubtedly becoming alienated from the enlisted soldier working-class grind that was keeping the family afloat, and my older sister would be on her way home from school soon. As my mom walked into the house, the screen door began to close slowly behind her. It suddenly banged back open, and a tall man rushed her. He put a gun to her head and marched her through the hallway to the kitchen. A thin sliver of a wall between us, I sat on the living room couch, motionless, watching the roadrunner outwit the coyote. Perplexed and amused at the constant bumbling of this cartoon stalker, my five-year-old mind had no awareness or comprehension that a very real predator had invaded our home.

The man forced my mother to lay on the floor. "You better be quiet or I will blow your little boy away." With my safety in jeopardy, she could hardly fight back when he told her to take her pants off. He pulled her shirt up over her head so that she couldn't see anything. The whole time she was praying that this wouldn't happen to her. My five-year-old self, hearing the commotion, walked into the kitchen just as he began to rape her. I saw my mother naked on the floor with someone wrapped around her, and he saw me. "I'm not going to hurt you," he said and stopped what he was doing. My mother thought he was talking to her. She could not see and did not know I had walked into the kitchen. I walked back out and sat on the couch again, stock still, like an animal trapped by headlights. He got off of her and fled the same way that he came in.

The terror and confusion clouded my mind as the aftermath of the assault unfolded. The police came, but ignored my presence and experience as they took reports that never amounted to anything. The man was never caught. No one ever knew that I had entered the kitchen. No one ever asked. While I'm sure that my five-year-old mind could not fully comprehend abstract values like justice, whatever semblance of understanding I had of justice, safety, and security, was shattered that day. My mother was the guardian of my world and she was not safe. No one made things right for her. No one seemed to care about the horror that we lived through. The stark realization of personal violence and the societal indifference to our victimization sowed the seeds of resentment deep within me.

I struggled after that. As a kindergartner, at naptime I would run away from school to go home, only one street away. This infraction greatly upset the school administration. Either they were not very good at communicating with me or I was not very good at communicating with them. I only wanted to check on my mom to make sure nothing bad was happening to her. She was going through a spell of depression, which I did not have the capacity to understand. Running away from school was just the first step in a long road to delinquency. After that, my elementary school experience would be a roller coaster of destructive behavior, fed by emotional distress that created anger issues and mistrust of others' intentions. As I grew older, I approached the world with hypervigilance and wariness of everyone, as they all had the potential to harm me or someone I loved.

In the 1980s, psychologists began reporting that children who personally witnessed violence and traumatic events had a significantly increased risk for developing anxiety, depression, conduct disorder, and posttraumatic stress disorder (PTSD).[1] In a study of 100 uninjured children who witnessed violent trauma, psychologists found that 80 percent could clearly be diagnosed with PTSD, the symptoms of which include distorted patterns of thinking, as well as agitated, disorganized, and reckless behavior. A more recent study of 1,539 adult males found that gang members were more likely than gang affiliates and other violent men to have experienced severe violence and trauma, resulting in high levels of anxiety and implying an increased likelihood for developing PTSD and engaging in future violence.[2] Unfortunately for me, I would never be assessed, diagnosed, treated, or even counseled. In my family, like so many others who experienced trauma, the event was never discussed. Many people feel ashamed when they are victimized, and they hide it the best that they can. My mother coped with her depression through religious faith. No one even thought to consider the effects on the children. Using household victimization surveys, the same psychologists conservatively estimated in the 1980s that 25,000 children a year witnessed a rape in the home. How many of them had to navigate the trauma with underdeveloped cognition and no guidance? How many of them were also set on a path to destruction?

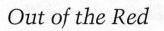

Out of the Red

Introduction

THIS BOOK DESCRIBES the events that shaped my life as a gangster, a prisoner, and an academic. They say hindsight is 20/20. I'm not so sure that any version of sight is that perfect. The various social frameworks we learn from our families and communities always color our perceptions. It is hard to be objective about one's own life history, and the people involved may recall these episodes differently. Most of the individual names have been changed to protect the people involved. Some names have been left unchanged, in which case, the individual's role was a positive one, and the person deserves acknowledgment and credit.

It is difficult to recollect the details of an entire lifetime, and I acknowledge the inevitability of events being colored by personal perspective. Save for those caveats, everything written here is true as I understand and remember it. My memory of these events is also supplemented by all that I have learned as a sociologist of violence and gang cultures, including forty-one in-depth interviews conducted with gang members in San Antonio, Texas. The autoethnography that follows is raw, intense, unsettling, and has been hard to deal with. It is hard to live with. I have included all that I can, even things that are unflattering and unseemly. Some of the events are very difficult to read about, but they were much harder to live through.

It is easy to assume that the behaviors described in this account are the result of personal pathology. The academic perspectives are provided to help the reader understand that the events related in this book are often influenced by social pathologies, have far-reaching consequences, and are much more widespread than is generally believed. This is not only an auto-ethnography; it also exemplifies the erased histories and sociological extrapolation of street gangs in San Antonio, and in Texas penitentiaries, which are a primary source of prison gangs.[1]

Prison gangs and prison societies are also woefully understudied in the modern era. Notably, as the United States shifted away from rehabilitation in the mass incarceration era, the seminal ethnographies on prisons dried up, as social researchers were denied access to prisons.[2] Thus another goal of this work is to reopen that world through lived experience. Just as important as all of that, this is a story that I need to tell.

Academic and popular debate about criminality varies from placing complete responsibility on the individual to finding fault in the social environment. My perspective is that both are correct. They feed each other in ever-growing layers that become so confounded that attempting to isolate a single reason as to "why" a person commits a criminal act becomes an exercise in futility. While individuals do indeed make choices, those choices are often influenced, limited, or opened not only by immediate personal relationships but also by authority figures and social forces that are far removed from the person. Some of these choices are major turning points that can result in dramatic shifts in a person's life trajectory, but those changes are often intricately bound to personal bonds and social opportunity.[3]

Most books on criminal behavior tend to be intensely academic or focused solely on personal perspective, each of which holds very important value. The issue is that books of either vein tend to be of little interest to the readers of the opposing genre.[4] In my fourteen years of teaching at various universities, I have noticed that students have little interest in an issue if they cannot humanize the subjects, as is the case when they read texts that are heavily based on statistics. While those data-centered volumes are important, their purpose is defeated if the intended audience does not latch on to the information. Behind each one of those numbers is a human story. Some of those narratives are very powerful. This work is an attempt to bridge the two worlds of academia and personal experience. The disconnect between the two has been detrimental to efforts aimed at resolving societal problems. To truly understand the behaviors of individuals, we must also understand how societal institutions affect those behaviors. This narrative demonstrates how academic knowledge found on a larger scale manifests in the life of an individual.

To be clear, this is in no way an attempt to justify my actions or mitigate my responsibility for the events that transpired. It is an effort to investigate how the road to those actions was shaped by ill-formed policies and decisions made by people in authority and social occurrences that influenced those personal choices. If the old saying that it takes a village to raise a child holds any merit, is it possible that it takes a whole community to destroy one?

The path of this book is split into three parts that take the reader through a life-course narrative journey. Part 1 is my developmental journey through childhood and into gang membership. This segment begins by providing background economic and racial context in chapter 1. The second chapter describes the impact of school bullying, school-to-prison-pipeline disciplinary procedures, and bussing on child development and gang risk factors. Chapter 3 provides an in-depth exploration of gang development in San Antonio, Texas, the process of joining a gang, and personal involvement with the gang. The fourth chapter explores criminal activity, police encounters, and gang-related behavior at school, at home, and on the streets. Chapter 5 addresses the school to prison pipeline, gang switching and gang expansion, guns, conflict escalation, and the cycle of violence. Chapter 6 includes pretrial events, the criminal trial, and issues with detaining juveniles with adults.

The narrative of part 2 follows my journey through the Texas prison system. The majority of the experience is re-created through 1,009 letters written between others and myself. Chapter 7 describes the Texas prison system and the induction processes experienced. The role of Texas in mass incarceration is examined as well as its relationship to the development of prison gangs. Chapter 8 describes gang desistance, prison society, religion, violence, and social support. Chapter 9 explores the next generation of prison gangs, prison riots, personal conflicts, and prison life in general. Chapter 10 discusses mass incarceration, constant transferring between prisons, and Huntsville, the heart of the Texas prison system. Chapters 11, 12, and 13 focus on college education in prison, work assignments, conflict avoidance, self-improvement, other prison groups, and preparation for parole.

Part 3 describes life postincarceration. Chapter 14 is about the lived experience of reentry—being an outcast from society, rejected by employers, awkward adjustment with family, and problems related to being a parolee. The final portion of the book takes the reader through the experience of successfully completing parole, finding a place through education, reaching achievement heights through earning a PhD, being chosen for a research fellowship with the FBI, and becoming a tenured professor of criminology. The goal of this manuscript is simultaneously to educate and connect personal experience to academic knowledge and to humanize those often viewed as folk devils,[5] who are people characterized as outsiders, deviants, or villains in media or story construction. They are used as scapegoats for society's ills as the audience can easily believe that the behaviors of the folk devil are malicious. The final goal of this work is to provide a message of hope in giving people second chances. They just might achieve what is generally thought of as impossible.

PART ONE

Gangs

CHAPTER 1

Poverty

As a child, I neither understood nor cared about poverty. Financial status was meaningless to me. Its impact on my family, however, meant everything. Financial status alone does not "cause" crime, but family poverty, transitions, financial stress, and low parental attachment are all risk factors for gang membership.[1] Along with a lower economic status comes substandard housing, lack of safe play environments, and less social capital. I would eventually find that I was no match for the socioenvironmental factors arrayed against me.

Not long after the home invasion and sexual assault, we left our house on San Antonio's West Side, moving to the Northeast Side. Known as Kirby, the area was not incorporated into the city and was officially its own jurisdiction. Overall, it was not a large area and, along with the other nearby municipalities of Converse, Live Oak, and Universal City, was considered little more than a suburb of San Antonio by the local populace. My parents had bought a three-bedroom mobile home and moved my sister and me into Kirby's trailer park. Although other people clearly understood that this was a poor populace and poor neighborhood, I had no conception of any of that. I approached the trailer park with wonder and excitement. The way the mobile home was long instead of wide and the way it rocked during thunderstorms were simultaneously thrilling and terrifying. I loved my new home, with all of its glistening white paneled glory. It took me far away from the lingering sense of pain and menace in our old house.

I would learn later what caused this sudden shift in our financial situation, but that can only be explained through the context of my family. My mother, Debra, grew up in New England, mostly in Massachusetts and Rhode Island. She was fair skinned, with light blonde hair that almost looks platinum. She spent her teenage years being bullied for her light complexion by the Italian girls with dark hair and dark eyes. Her home life was not much better. Though she got along with her father, an angst-fueled mother–daughter feud brewed endlessly, coming to extreme boiling points as a regular occurrence. My mother's rebellion would culminate with her running off to join the army. This was considered deviant for a young,

1-1. Christian as a child. (Bolden personal photos.)

middle-class, New England girl to do in the early 1970s, and such women who dared to enlist were put into a separate army branch called the Women's Army Corps. Debra's military service would land her in Germany, where she would meet my father in April 1973.

My father, Tom, is African American, with skin as starkly dark as my mother's skin was white. He was in Germany at that time through his own service to the U.S. Army. His roots go back to Tennessee, though his immediate family settled in Texas. He came from a sizeable household, having two brothers and four sisters, with him being the oldest male. Most of his siblings would end up doing very well for themselves, becoming solidly middle class with jobs in computers, information technology, and government, and raising families grounded in religious faith and custom.

My father, however, was very different. He was always unsettled, always searching. He would not stay too long with any one thing before moving on to the next. I never understood why his circumstances were so different from those of his siblings. The only explanation I was ever offered came from one of my aunts who conjectured that, as a youth, my dad was always in a state of transition. His father was also in the military, and they bounced from location to location, constantly switching schools. In most of these locations my father would have to fight in schools to earn respect or not be picked on.

In short, his youth, like my mother's, was also traumatic. His younger siblings, on the other hand, grew up in more stable conditions as the family settled in one place. I've asked my father about this and many other things, but he has never been very forthcoming. Perhaps he has not really thought these things through. Perhaps he doesn't want to. Perhaps he came from a generation that never learned how to process and communicate these things.

My mother fell for my father, and with her penchant for bucking societal taboos, they married in March 1974. It had been only seven years since the landmark Supreme Court case *Loving v. Virginia* (1967) had overturned state laws against interracial marriage. Despite the legal victory, outgroup marriages were still frowned upon in some areas of the country. This union destroyed the already tenuous relationship between my mother and grandmother, and they did not speak for a year, though they would begin a strained relationship after my older sister was born.

In Germany, my parents met and bonded with another interracial military couple, Sheila and Raymond, and their children Cheryl and Caleb. The families consider each other kin by choice and refer to each other as aunts, uncles, and cousins. By coincidence, both interracial families would eventually end up in San Antonio, which had five military bases at the time. Though typically conservative on most matters, the U.S. armed forces were progressively ahead of the rest of society regarding interracial marriages. International deployment, exposure to others on domestic military bases, and esprit de corps tended to supersede racial distinctions, increasing the rates of outgroup marriage among service members.[2] With all of its military bases, San Antonio provided abundant safe spaces for interracial families to live.

My mom was hopeful that my father would maintain his military career, and he made a promise to her to do so. He did not keep that promise. Citing a dispute with one of his superiors, he did not reenlist when his service contract was up, trying his luck with other types of work instead. This is what led to the dramatic economic downgrade to the trailer park. It was also the beginning of my mother's resentment toward my father, and my father's absenteeism. The older I got, the less I would see my dad. Nearly every day, instead of coming straight home from work, my father chose to whittle the time away partying in his favorite bars. The few times he took me to watch superhero movies are the only fond memories I have of my father as a child. I wish there were more. I have heard that he was a very jovial person when he was out drinking. On the rare occasion he was home, his mood was much darker. It was during this bleak period that my mother found herself unexpectedly pregnant with my baby brother, Ian.

Springfield Meadows trailer park was full of misfit families, not that I knew any different. I got along well with people, made lots of friends, and was completely content in my little trailer park world, unaware that people

1-2. Christian's parents. (Bolden personal photos.)

there were often shunned by those outside the neighborhood fence. Most of my friends lived in single-parent homes, with their fathers nowhere to be found. I was one of the very few kids there with an "intact" family, at least by official designation. I had friends with gay parents who masqueraded as roommates due to the fear of societal backlash. There were moms whose psychological and visible physical traumas had reduced them to seeking shelter in the lower rungs of society. There were homes that were so overrun with roaches that the carpet sometimes appeared to be moving, and there were kitchens with refrigerators that always seemed to be empty.

These things often created a sense of unease, though at the time I did not understand them as outward signs of poverty. There was a communal sense of caretaking from the adults that helped the children to look past the slow decay into poverty and ruin. Despite whatever skeletons haunted them, the kids in the neighborhood treated the parents with respect.

My two best friends at the time were Ace and Bret. Ace was mixed Black and White like me, though he had a much darker complexion and was most often assumed to be Black, and Bret was a redhead, which brought him no end of torment. My friends and I spent endless hours playing in ditches, catching the fish and crawdads that appeared during heavy rains and floods, and looking through the random bags people threw there, finding discarded *Penthouse* and *Hustler* magazines that kept us fascinated for days. I was fond of my trailer park milieu, never concerning myself with status or things of that sort. It would be my experience with the social institution of school that would upend my reality and degrade my self-esteem.

With a stamp of approval from the Supreme Court in *Swann v. Charlotte-Mecklenburg Board of Education* (1971), urban school districts throughout the nation began addressing desegregation through mandatory busing. This practice of ensuring racially mixed student bodies would go on for decades, but self-interest and old racial attitudes would eventually win out. After the Supreme Court case *Dowell v. The Board of Education of Oklahoma City Public Schools* (1991) provided a way for districts to opt out of busing, many schools rapidly and publicly desisted from the practice.[3] In the meantime, I would be one of countless kids subjected to a busing scheme without the slightest inkling as to why. Though part of the same large school system, Judson Independent School District, kids in our neighborhood did not attend Kirby Elementary, which was less than two miles away, but instead were bussed more than four miles to Woodlake Elementary. The experience of going to a middle-class school is what taught me that I was poor.

I remember gawking out the window of the school bus at homes that were unimaginable. While in reality the area was only middle class, in my mind and limited perspective, I was seeing wealth and opulence for the first time. I had never encountered two-story homes before. Everything looked so clean and new. It was like I had entered a different world, and for all intents and purposes, I had.

Some scholars will argue that delinquency is not caused by poverty. Indeed, in many rural communities in the United States, despite endemic poverty, crime rates are relatively low. But relative deprivation is something different. The state of being poor and having people with wealth right next to you, constantly showing you what they have and you don't, can cause problems. Negative feelings about self-worth can arise when a person self-compares to peers.[4] These adverse feelings become more severe when other people consistently emphasize their higher economic standing. The economic and emotional punch of realizing I was in a lower social stratum inspired feelings of shame.[5] Gang involvement would be one way to manage those emotions, but it would be some time before I came to that conclusion.

Those of us from the trailer park were the only poor kids that went to Woodlake, and the middle-class kids there made sure we knew it. Our clothes and mannerisms easily set us apart. Though the teachers were good, the curriculum was great, and most of the other kids were friendly, there were just enough kids with a commitment to bullying us that we knew we didn't really belong.

Renowned criminological theorist Robert Agnew explained that there are certain negative stimuli which increase the likelihood of individuals coping through criminality. Those negative strains are things that feel unjust or unfair, are attributable to the intentional behavior of another, are perceived to be of great magnitude, and are beyond one's ability to control.[6] Agnew was spot on. A pool of anger over perceived injustice would plague my life, boiling over into a series of aggressive acts that would each create a turning point leading deeper into delinquency. At Woodlake, there was one kid in particular who was a source of intentionally malign injustice. Brian was a sixth-grader who reveled in degrading us. We found his bullying intolerable, but there was nothing we could do about it. His harassment never let up until finally our anger exploded. One day, without any planning, the first-grade trailer park kids, en masse, cornered Brian on the playground. Bret disabled his legs by getting down on all fours behind him, while I jumped up and hit him in the face and someone else pushed him. He fell down, hard. He never came near us again. That victory over Brian provided an extreme sense of satisfaction and relief. It was also the initial development of a clique mentality.

First, second, and third grade came and went. Over time, we became more comfortable and accepted at Woodlake. It seemed as though we were on a conventional path, and everything would be all right. But it was not to be. "Experts" enjoying powerful positions, both in our immediate social realm as well as in much higher levels beyond our community, would make decisions about what was best for us that would dramatically and traumatically affect our life trajectories.

CHAPTER 2

Adultism

CHILDREN DO NOT have free will in the way most people understand it. Adults make decisions about where to live, where to go to school, and what social relationships are acceptable. All of these things constrain the possible choices that children can make. Decisions about the life and welfare of children are made not only by adults in the home and at school but also by adults far removed from the lives of the people they affect. Though a variety of factors may influence those decisions, feedback from the children who will be affected is not considered, and they are left to deal with the consequences. Rather than being listened to or understood, these children instead receive harsh punishment for their maladaptive responses to these choices. Adult decision making is not perfect, but seeking guidance and communication from those affected by their decisions would prove beneficial. The resulting physical and mental violence meted out to children as corrective punishment does not build resilience, but instead may breed deep resentment. Although these circumstances are not deterministic in causing delinquent behavior, they do sharply narrow the choices available, making criminal behavior a more likely, prominent, and viable option. In my case, adult decisions would set the stage for a life cycle of violence and punishment.

Judson High School has been a football powerhouse since the late 1970s, holding the state record for thirty-nine consecutive winning seasons, and winning six state championship games. The Judson Independent School system seemed to redistrict on a semiregular basis. There were always rumors that gerrymandering occurred for the purpose of obtaining football players, but there was no evidence that validated those stories. Still, the redistricting never made sense to those it affected. The first redrawing of school zones that mattered for me happened in the fourth grade. We were bussed four miles in a different direction to Park Village Elementary School.[1] Park Village was nothing like Woodlake. Gang graffiti covered the outside walls of the elementary school, creating a sense of unease that I feared but could not comprehend.

Though the Spring Meadows trailer park kids had no experience with gangs, the young people at Park Village were a different story altogether. Gang activity had intensified in their area, and many of their older siblings had already enlisted in these street wars. The kids at Park Village idolized their older siblings and attempted to mimic them as best they could.

My initial experience with gangs came inadvertently in my first weeks at Park Village Elementary, when I made the mistake of liking a girl. Audra had pale skin, long black hair, dark brown eyes, and a sweet and playful demeanor. Unfortunately for me, she had a boyfriend—whatever that means in the fourth grade. Her boyfriend, Max, fancied himself a Crip. Though undoubtedly a wannabe gangster, he might as well have been a kingpin for the amount of hell he rained down on me. Max and his crew would catch me every day and beat the shit out of me. Every single day! There was no way out: every morning, kids were kept outside on the playground until the doors opened to start the school day. There was no admission into the safety of the building. The absurdly long morning bus commutes were fraught with dread, as I knew an ass kicking was waiting for me as soon as I set foot on school grounds. Despite the agonizing length of the journey, I always prayed for the bus to be late so that I could avoid the morning playground. Once I arrived, I would try to escape by camouflaging myself among other kids—I was pretty small—but Max would find me every time. Though I couldn't hide myself from his crew, they circled around me and hid me from the rest of the playground. Inside the circle, they would take turns beating me up one at a time, mostly dishing out painful leg and gut punches so that marks would not be visible on me, until a teacher came near or the bell rang. The attacks would last only a few minutes at most, but a minute of getting beat on felt like an eternity. The irony of violent victimization being inescapable for me and yet somehow undetected by adults left me feeling bitter. The torment occurred for weeks.

Still, I didn't stop talking to Audra.

The inability to deal with particularly noxious stimuli, such as bullying, piles on feelings of injustice.[2] At some point, the strain of it all would no longer be contained by social constraints, and I would lash out at the cause of my stress.

T-NOTE (3-5-7 CRIP): If you can spark some violence in a child, then he is already recruited without knowing it.

One day during recess, I had retreated to a far corner of the athletic field when Max and his crew caught me again. I had a feeling that this time the level of danger had intensified, as recess had just started, and no one was around but them and me. This one short kid, named Mark, was especially vile. Because of his little man complex, he would always try to increase his torment by adding humiliation to my beatings, either through words or wedgies. I held a particular hatred for Mark. In this instance, in this corner of the field, Mark was the first to step up and confront me. Something about this time and it being Mark who started in with the insults, made me feel a keener sense of danger, but also that I was ready to put an end to the ass beating. I snapped. The pain of being consistently tortured, the humiliation of being constantly picked on, and the injustice of no one coming to my aid had turned my vision to a ferocious red. Understanding that I was completely on my own and there was no way out of this, I disregarded the fact that I had no chance against all of them, and I flew into a rage. I slammed Mark to the ground and began choking him with all my might, yelling "I WILL KILL YOU!" Even though the seven of them could have easily pulled me off of him, they didn't. Instead they yelled at me, begging me to stop. I finally relented and Mark scrambled away with shock and fear in his eyes. The other kids backed away from me as I trembled with fury. Some of them issued halfhearted threats as they left. They never bothered me again. I was wary of them and didn't want further trouble, but I knew if they attacked me that I would respond with all of the ferocity that I could muster. It wasn't as if they gave me a wide berth, they just did not harass me anymore. I had learned my first lesson in the code of the street—people respect your capacity for violence.[3]

CAJUN (DOPE OVERTHROWING GANGSTER/DOG): Being a criminal, being a gang member, something like that is a lot different because I guess if you are capable of violence and you are capable of not having a conscience you know a lot of time fear entails respect and if you can instill fear in people then you are definitely respected.

It has become almost cliché to say that "hurt people, hurt people," but I imagine that some of the people who were bullying me were doing so as a result of their own traumas. Max suffered a terrible fate. A few weeks later, his stepfather went on a rampage, killing everyone in the family except Max, who was at school at the time. He was sent away to live with extended family. Audra would also move away very shortly thereafter. I remember an announcement being made about the event and little else. I wondered if anyone ever helped him through the trauma or if he was also set on a path to devastation.

I would have many more fights at Park Village. Win or lose, I learned that people would respect me once I fought back. I was skinny and short, something that would plague me most of my life, but I was a determined scrapper. When you are small and unskilled in a world of potential predators, you show your sharp edges in any way that you can. For some people that meant setting traps;[4] for me, it meant persistence and doing the unexpected, like going up against kids twice my size. This earned me a reputation as a fighter. I did not see much of my friends at school because we were on different schedules. But I would see them on the bus and in the neighborhood, and I could tell that they were going through the same socialization process. Fights and verbal conflicts on the bus became routine. We learned to not back down and to respond to all affronts with violence. All of the prosocial ways of dealing with conflict, like constructive communication, that we had learned in Woodlake and before, had eroded. We were becoming hardened.

One morning, I was running around the playground when I was snatched from behind and slammed against the wall, my head banging into the bricks. I immediately retaliated by swinging my backpack, which had been in my hand, and striking my assailant, who turned out to be a teacher. She had been chasing a particular kid who was wearing a hoodie the same color as mine. When she saw me running by, she confused me with the other kid and went after me. None of the adults involved—my parents, the teacher, the principal—seemed to care that the teacher assaulted me and actually hurt me. The only thing that mattered was that I struck her back. I could neither fully understand nor explain my conditioned response, so in fourth grade I was given my first out-of-school suspension.

Fifth grade came, by which time we had fully adapted to our new environment. Fights would occur on occasion. They were bloody, painful fights, but as long as I stood my ground and dished out what I could, my opponent would either shake my hand or just leave me alone afterward. Not fighting back would mark me as a target for bullies and other predators. Peaceful existences seemed nearly impossible, and trailer park kids seemed to forget what that was like. And then, without warning, the mysterious adults in their infinite confidence in their own decision making, and lack of regard for repercussions, chose to redraw the district lines again. Never being told why the change was occurring, the trailer park kids were going back to Woodlake Elementary for sixth grade.

Though it is logical and expected for those of legal age to have complete power over children, societal bias that favors the attitudes and ideas of adults can also be detrimental. The assumptive wisdom of adults, without regard for input from children or concern for ultimate consequences, is referred to as adultism.[5] Indeed, much of what those of mature age do is intended to be beneficial for the child, but when those adult decisions are ultimately harmful, there is often no accountability for their actions. Eventually youth begin to stop viewing adults as allies. Mistrust and lack of communication create a volatile mix.

The school didn't know what hit them. Woodlake Elementary, in all its callow middle-class privilege, was not ready for the lot of us. Middle-class kids are raised with the values and standards that situate them for success in middle-class schools and equip them to directly seek help from teachers. Working-class kids like us, who often lacked supervision, learned not to trust authorities when they were around, and since we had always been expected to figure out the world on our own, we were unaccustomed and unable to communicate our need for help to the teachers.[6] Add to that the posttraumatic stress disorder from the rough-and-tumble socialization we had gone through and we were beyond the scope of what teachers, administrators, and the middle-class kids were used to dealing with.

My beginning foray into the sixth grade would foreshadow a rocky experience. I came to school with glasses that year, and the first day I wore them, a kid named Gordy laughed hysterically at me. After I landed a flurry of punches on his face, he and everyone else around stared in utter shock and silence. There was no more laughing about my glasses.

The conflict resolution strategy of the trailer park kids consisted of outbursts and violence. It is not that we thought we were cool or had any type of swagger. We were well aware that we were outsiders. I actually performed well academically and was put into the Gifted and Talented Program. The kids in there were alien to me, though, and their attempts at getting me to play Dungeons & Dragons with them ultimately failed. I just did not connect with them.

The trailer park kids were trouble for the school from the start, but the administrative responses only ensured we would travel farther down the path to delinquency. Aggression, conduct disorders, negative labeling by teachers, low school commitment, and low attachment to teachers are all risk factors for gang involvement.[7] Our poor relationships with the educators meant we were well on our way. We were a nightmare for the teachers, as we refused to tolerate disrespect. If we felt we were being talked down to, we would yell at them and tell them off. The principal's solutions to our behavior only made things worse.

Texas is one of nineteen states that allows for corporal punishment in schools, which is defined as "deliberate physical pain by hitting, paddling, spanking, slapping, or any other physical force used as a means of discipline."[8] The principal at Woodlake believed in the philosophy of physical punishment, and his immediate response was to paddle us. I still remember the swooshing sound from the air going through the paddle holes as they spanked our behinds. No one seems to grasp the irony of trying to dissuade people from violent behavior by hitting them. Despite all the research showing that the more corporal punishment is used against someone, the more the person will aggressively respond to others,[9] adults still cling to the idea that harming a child will work a positive change in the child's behavior.

The next solution was to incarcerate us in school. We would each be locked in a room, alone. It was usually an abandoned office or storage room with no windows, or windows with closed blinds on the opposite side of the glass. Nothing else was in the room but a table, a chair, and dim lighting. We would be given our homework, our lunch, and left alone for the entire school day. These stints of solitary confinement would typically last a week, but on one occasion it lasted an entire month.

Back in the 1950s, criminologist Albert Cohen described the status frustration that occurred when male children in the working class ran up against the middle-class measuring rod of school teachers.[10] The teachers would interpret the children's lack of fidelity to and adoption of middle-class values as malicious delinquency and obtuseness. The consistent obstacles of disciplinary punishment and tracking into "slow learner" classes could create a reaction in which the youth rejected what they believed they could not achieve. One of the ways of dealing with this status failure was to become an entity antithetical to the middle class—a gang. Cohen was not too far off. For my friends and me, school had become a hateful place that we were forced to go to. However, gangs were far from our realm of possibility. There was a bridge of time and circumstance that still needed to be crossed before we got there.

Cohen's theory seemed to have been forgotten or ignored as educational systems were beginning a phase of harsh punitive measures. The disciplinary philosophy of the time would be disastrous for kids like me. Consistent exposure to school discipline has destructive academic consequences and creates a negative turning point toward involvement with the criminal justice system.[11] There were people who believed that there were other ways, but they were fighting a losing battle. Some of the teachers disapproved of what was later known as the school-to-prison pipeline approach and began to develop their own solutions. The one that was most effective for me was the simplest. I had a teacher who requested that anytime I felt like I was about to blow up, I could simply raise my hand, walk out of the room, and cool off before returning. I appreciated her effort and understanding. This worked for me. I only needed to use it a few times, and I never abused it.

Discipline at home was also harsh. The only time I could expect to see my dad was when it was time to dish out my punishment. He was built strong, a stature he had developed playing football in the military, and he was scary when angry. He had a way of holding my arms behind my back and lifting me off the ground with one hand while whipping me with a belt with the other hand. I know there are people who believe in spanking, but it did not work for me. Every time an authority figure hit me, I seethed with resentment and fury, internally vowing to do something worse in retaliation for the assault on my body.

Harsh discipline was common among the trailer park kids, and we avoided it in any way that we could. It was simple to do when the adults were barely around to witness anything. If not in school, we spent sunup to sundown roving the neighborhood unsupervised, fighting with each other, roughhousing in the lifeguard-less swimming pool, or trekking through Kirby.

Our violent behavior was not limited to school. Though the neighborhood was generally peaceful, the end of the sixth-grade school year culminated in a series of fights revolving around Ace and me taking on people who were much older and stronger than either of us. The events of that day made us legendary in the neighborhood, and it was all people talked about for several months. This event was significant for us because the accolades we received were focused on us as a group, a tribe, and, for the first time, our fighting exploits generated respect from all the kids in our neighborhood. It felt like a good end to the year. It was also an end to that era.

Over the summer, all of my close friends moved away, either to places similar in status to Springfield Meadows, or to greener pastures. As I traversed junior high school alone, gang activity became pervasive throughout Kirby. The suburb bordered the East Side of San Antonio, which was full of gangs, and they had begun to spill over. Kirby became a new battleground.

The next important adult decision for my life was a move made by my parents. Though the intention was for the betterment of the family, the relocation would create the conditions that eased my transition into street gangs. The beginning of the 1990s coincided with a better financial situation for my family, bringing us out of poverty as I entered my eighth-grade year. My father was working a steady job as a postman. We moved to the Converse suburb, settling into the economically diverse neighborhood of Crownwood.

As I moved into ninth grade at Judson High School, DJ moved into the neighborhood on the corner of my street. DJ was a White boy with a long, shaggy mullet, who came to Texas from Florida, bringing some of the Miami gang culture with him. We hit it off immediately, and though we would have some ups and downs throughout the years, he remained one of my best friends. DJ's mom was very sweet and always cared for the neighborhood kids when they were in her presence. I did not get to know DJ's dad very well. He was a disgruntled military veteran, and shortly after they moved to Crownwood, the ghosts of war got to him and he ended his own life with a .357 magnum.

Over time, the friends I had made were wearing red with increasing frequency. Most of them were from a nearby neighborhood called Miller's Point. A contingent of Blood Stone Villains (BSV) had emerged there. The BSV were a Blood gang out of California, and they were soon everywhere.

My wardrobe also became increasingly red. The progression was insidious in that I was aware of the changes in my style and demeanor but not fully cognizant of the implications. The adaptation to wearing the color red and adopting gangster regalia seemed natural, not forced. My history of violence and the pain of my friends who lost their fathers through violence or abandonment had primed me for a brotherhood of anger and despair.

CHAPTER 3

Neighborhoods

As I entered ninth grade, I was overwhelmed with the sheer number of students at the high school, and how easy it was to feel insignificant as a freshman. I came in with a few friends, but we were all generally in the same boat. We had no real social capital, street credibility, or place in this new environment. We were each suffering from the lack of a father's presence in our lives due to abandonment, suicide, or, in my case, absenteeism, which only compounded the sense of being lost amid the adolescent chaos. I did not have the wealth, skills, mannerisms, material belongings, social savvy, or any of the other cultural capital necessary to fall in with the Preps, nor the athletic ability to fall in with the Jocks.[1] But there were several social cliques that burnouts who were prone to bad behavior, and who had no interest in school or its activities, could end up in.[2] One possible avenue of climbing up in the social hierarchy and finding a place in the world was joining a gang, and it just so happened that right at the time DJ and I entered high school, gangland exploded. Now gangs were all around me.

I reunited with almost all of my old friends. Just about everyone I knew had been independently associating with Bloods, and the pros and cons of joining was a constant topic of conversation. Both of my best friends from the trailer park were once again in my social sphere. Ace was back, as he now lived near Woodlake, and he had been hanging around Big Time Player Bloods. I also found Bret again. Though he went to Roosevelt High School, in the adjacent school district, his neighborhood, Oak Crest Pointe trailer park, was less than a mile away from Crownwood. Bret was associated with the Blood Stone Villains (BSV) and some remnant West Side Varrio Kings (WSV).

All my friends being Blood associated, combined with my distaste for Crips (stemming from my fourth-grade experience of being constantly assaulted by them) made my decision of which group to hang around with relatively easy. I had always heard that people wanted to join gangs for the material economic benefit, but that did not fit my circumstance or that of many of my friends. People also joined gangs to camouflage their other activities, to garner protection in dangerous neighborhoods, to resist the working-class life path of their parents, as a commitment to their community, or simply to have fun.[3] None of these reasons resonated with me. I was searching for a place to belong. I was looking for identity and support. It also seemed like a natural progression. I agonized over it nearly every night for weeks, until I decided I was tired of floating in the adolescent sea of anonymity. At age 14, I became the first of my friends to officially join a gang.

Some gangs continue to grow by creating feelings of community obligation or in rare cases by coercing new recruits through fear or violence. Other gangs simply rely on the reputation they have gained, drawing a fraternity-like pool of people who want to enlist.[4] Gangs on the Northeast Side had not existed long enough to create obligatory sentiment, and any attempt at coercion would likely drive a person into one of the many opposing gangs. This left reputation as the primary source of recruitment, and since I decided to commit, the group I was going into needed to be hard core. I chose to join the Rigsby Court Gangster Bloods (RCG). There were too many BSV, and their large numbers had caused them to lose quality control, due to wannabes claiming their set. Gang members were preoccupied with the issue of legitimacy, always challenging the validity of each other's gang membership, spurring those being challenged to respond with violence or to commit greater criminal acts to demonstrate their legitimacy as gang members.[5] Picking BSV would also mean inviting many more challenges to credibility. Plus, the BSV originated from California, which I knew nothing about, and I would feel disingenuous and illegitimate joining such a gang. The Rigsby, on the other hand, were local, small, selective, and fierce. If I was going to make a name for myself, I wanted to be associated with something that had a hard-core reputation. It would have been too easy to get overlooked among the numerous BSV. Rigsby Courts was an East Side neighborhood that I had never actually been to at that point, ironic given my then teenage logic about being disingenuous. But I didn't care about the place; I cared about the people. I was in awe of them, and I wanted to be one of them.

Dax and his brother Dave were the preeminent RCG at Judson. I approached Dax, with whom I had gym class, and told him I wanted to be down. Dax never tried to recruit me, but his charisma was one of the reasons I chose RCG. He tapped me on the knee with his knuckles and told me "tomorrow morning." When I made the decision, a sense of calm resolve came over me. There is something freeing about deciding. I knew what it meant to be initiated, even if there was no way I could fully understand what I was getting into. I did not fear the beatdown I was going to get, as my life had prepared me to face that form of violence. I was ready for it.

I met up with the Bloods the next day in a dark, hidden corner of campus. The RCGs approached me. I was surrounded by Dax, L-Dog, a Mexican Blood named Big Moe, and Half-Life. "Are you sure about this?" Dax said. "I wanna be down," was my only response. The initiation began. The "beat in," "roll in," or "jump in," was the most common of gang initiations, and it meant being assaulted by gang members from all sides.[6] A fifth gangster, Andrew, moved in on me. Andrew was a White guy, a member of the allied BSV. He was notorious, and not to be trusted. I was annoyed by his presumptiveness of participating because he wasn't an RCG, but it didn't matter. A kick to my stomach and heavy black fists raining down on my head rattled me out of my preoccupation with his role in my initiation. I was determined to hold my own, lashing out wildly, hoping to connect with one of the five, all of whom were bigger than I was. Dax's fists felt like stones, but I kept standing. I have no idea how long it lasted, but someone yelled "teacher coming," and everyone fled. I ran too, but during my escape I slipped and fell forward. My hand instinctively went out to catch my fall and my wrist fractured. A friend helped me up. Somehow, we made it to an inside bathroom as the doors were opening for classes to be let in. As my adrenaline subsided, I collapsed against the wall, racked with pain. I could no longer move, no longer think, and no longer breathe. I don't remember how long I stayed there, lost in a pain-induced fugue. I don't remember going to the nurse's office or my mom being called. I only remember getting the cast on my wrist at the hospital. It was done. I was a Blood.

When I returned to school, they gave me the baby gangster name of "Lil' Man." Andrew went around saying that they broke my wrist during the initiation. This annoyed me, but several people were upset with him for jumping in without permission, and that was satisfaction for me.

Outside of school, I mostly spent my time as a baby gangster in Bret's trailer park. I got drunk for the first time in that trailer park, off of an entire bottle of Strawberry Hill. I puked endlessly and woke up on a bed with a girl that I had a crush on, Jillian, sitting next to me. She had made me a sandwich and coached me through the hangover. I never did get with Jillian. I did have sex for the first time in that trailer park though. Age 14 was a banner year for me. My first real girlfriend, Kandice, was White, with mousy brown hair. She was 17. Somehow, I had convinced her of my prowess, when in fact my only "experience" consisted of the *Penthouse* magazines I would find in the ditches behind my old neighborhood.

I hung out with Bret and Coop in the trailer park. They were both BSV, under the tutelage of Original Gangsters (OGs) Tommy, who was a

WSV King, and Cadillac, who was BSV. Tommy and Cadillac were in their
mid-20s, and both had been gang banging in the 1980s. The whole lot of
them were White boys, but that didn't matter. They would bang just as hard
as anyone else when it came down to it. The trailer park was a safe haven as
enemies never came into that neighborhood. We would often sit by a bon-
fire while Cadillac would teach us, lecture us, berate us, or regale us with
stories. We would watch the movies *Colors* or *Boyz n the Hood* on repeat,
soaking up any aspect of gang culture we could, but always upset that
Bloods got short shrift in the films. Although we understood that the movies were not trying to promote gang culture, we did not care and preferred
to be selective in what we paid attention to. We would move on to *Menace
to Society* and *Bangin' in Little Rock* in later years. Gang knowledge was
inculcated in me, and through fireside stories, I would learn about the history of gangs.

Between the 1920s and 1940s, early Chicago School sociologists discovered an ecological pattern to crime in larger urban locales, and San Antonio
would turn out to be no exception to that archetype. Outside of the central
business district or "downtown" existed a circular "zone of transition" that
had the highest rates of crime in a city, regardless of the population that
lived there. This was due to poverty, residential instability, culture conflict,
class isolation, and lack of commitment to communities. By the 1950s San
Antonio had about sixty barrio gangs and 1,300 known gang members,[7]
most of which were restricted to the West Side and the housing projects,
usually known as courts, that circled downtown in the zone of transition[8]
(e.g., Alazán-Apache Courts, Cassiano Homes, Denver Heights, Lincoln
Courts, Menchaca Courts, Mirasol Courts, New Light Village, Rigsby Courts,
San Juan Homes, Skyline Park, Sutton Homes, Victoria Courts, Villa Veramendi, and Wheatley Courts).[9]

ROYAL (BIG TIME KINGS/BTK): You know gangs have always been around in
    San Antonio. My best friend, his dad back in the sixties, used to live on
    Menchaca Street, you know the Menchaca Street Gang or whatever you
    know what I'm saying. Wherever there was Mexicans back '50s, '60s,
    '70s, there has always been gangs.
AZTEC (ALAZÁN-APACHE COURTS, 1960s): Right here in San Antonio, in the
    Westside- Guadalupe St., Brazos, Zarzamora, anything on the West-
    side, it all used to be gangs. De la Cruz, the projects, the Alazánes and
    then there used to be other projects, so we would break down. El Alto,
    Alto was up here, it's the projects. Then the mountains down there was
    the Ghost Town. And there was the Cassianos. Then there was the
    Tigers and then the Alazánes. There were so many others, La Trista, La
    Crepa de Brazos off Brazos street.

The barrio gangs of the 1950s and '60s were no strangers to violence. Between 1959 and 1967, the notorious gang Varrio Ghost Town racked up an astounding 886 shooting and stabbing incidents reciprocated with twenty-seven enemy gangs.[10] The difference in the violence at the time was the lack of sophisticated weaponry and the low likelihood of lethality. In all of those incidents, only four resulted in fatalities. Gang warfare flared up intermittently every couple of years until sociologists implemented an "indigenous" gang worker program, to help barrio youth navigate the social spaces and expectations of middle-class teachers, police, and business owners. The gang workers also helped institute a neutral war council, where members of eight major gangs, El Alto, La Blanca, the Cassianos, Chicago, El Detroit, Ghost Town, the Lake Boys, and the Tigers, could come to negotiate peace.[11]

Between the late 1960s and the early 1970s gang warfare in San Antonio all but ceased. Though the specific reason for the calm was undetermined, it was likely due to a confluence of factors, including the draft and enlistment into the Vietnam War, the influence of gang worker peacekeeping, the crackdowns of police, the dissolution of segregated boundaries, and the rise of the Chicano civil rights movement.[12]

Politically savvy college students recruited and co-opted barrio youth, educating them on issues of racial and social justice. Mirroring the Black Panthers, the first cohort of San Antonio Brown Berets comprised politically and socially aware former gang members, many of whom were returning from the Vietnam War. These former members of the Ghost Town, La India, El Detroit, and Lake gangs used their old gang war council contacts to recruit heavily from the barrio youth, and the energy that used to go into street warfare was now redirected toward civil rights causes. The Brown Berets addressed food insecurity and job placement for barrio residents, all while brokering peace treaties between gangs and protesting police brutality.[13] Like many of the other militant organizations of that time period, their heyday did not last. As civil rights organizations became more legitimized, they distanced themselves and cut off funding for factions with sordid histories, and the influence of the former gang members began to wane. After the major legislative victories of the civil rights era, the reign of the Brown Berets was all but forgotten, and a new generation of gangs began to rise.

By the late 1980s, the pervasiveness of Los Angeles and Chicago gang culture had begun a rapid march throughout most sectors of San Antonio. Gang violence had been ramping up for the last several years, but it had been mostly stable in San Antonio through the 1980s, due to the prevalence of large gangs, such as Dawg Pound, Fly Riders, Nova, Powerheads, Town Freaks, Varrio Ghost Town, and Young Country. Three large gangs would usher in a new era. The West Side Varrio Kings (WSV), a gang that wore black bandanas, amassed an army that seemed endless. They were initially at peace with a large South and West Side gang called the Klik, whose members wore red flags, but that relationship would eventually sour. The WSV and the Klik both hated the Klan, which wore white and spanned the North and Northwest. There were several smaller gangs, but the numerical strength of the WSV, Klik, and Klan kept them at bay or forced them into alliances. The power garnered by the three groups would put them directly in the crosshairs of law enforcement, the result of which would make the gangs in San Antonio spiral out of control.

Gang interventions, such as removing leaders, have repercussions beyond the target. The result may be a disruption of the social ecology of gangs and an increase in violent conflict.[14] In San Antonio, the equilibrium would be disrupted when law enforcement captured the leader of the Kings. He was sent away for twenty years. Though I'm sure the police patted themselves on the back for that achievement, all hell broke loose in the streets, and the Latino gangs went wild. The WSV were reported as having over a thousand members.[15] The top echelon of WSV splintered over leadership succession and warring King factions emerged: Big Time Kings (BTK), Ruthless Kings (RK), Under Ground Kings (UGK), Purple Kings (PK), and Grand Theft Auto (GTA, who wore red).

ROYAL (BIG TIME KINGS/BTK): There was a little kid walking down the street and most likely he was a shorty Ambro, because back then you knew better not to wear all A's. He had an A's hat on he had an A's shirt, he was all A'ed out dude. Okay, they rolled up on him, popped his ass. The head King happened to do it, [name redacted]. He got locked up. He's locked up, structure just [makes crumbling sound] everybody was fighting for leadership, you know everybody was like, fuck that no more Kings. WSV dropped their rags, and then there was two gangs that everybody went into, well I take that back, there was a gang called the Purple Kings, which were Crips, basically. There was GTA Grand Theft Auto, which were red raggers, and there was BSV, WSV–BSV, kind of one letter difference, well they were Bloods okay. Basically everybody joined the Bloods. Well, [name redacted] and them started the BTK, well everybody who was a WSV kind of had not a free membership, but we were able to come back to the King organization. BTK started and I was, I was fully on that, I was like hell yeah BTK! So we started banging that. . . . I don't know if you ever heard of Ruthless Kings, there were Ruthless Kings . . . UGK, there was the UG's the Underground, which was Northeast Side San Antonio, MacArthur High School and then Poteet was the UGK.

The Latin Kings from Chicago tried to send representatives down to get a handle on the situation, but it was too late. The Almighty Latin Kings (ALK) became just another faction.

ROYAL (BTK): As we got to high school there was a shitload of ALKs and for a second when ALKs started coming down from Chi they were cool with us. But then they started going, we used to have problems with them dudes all the time, like if you ain't from Chi, you ain't a Latin King, then you ain't a real King. And we're like who the fuck are you to come down here and tell us that. I mean I don't understand that, we come down here, we show you respect and you turn around and say fuck you.

All of the Kings' enemies as well as every other startup crew decided it was time to take a piece of the pie or try for glory. Gangs seemingly popped up everywhere, and nearly every color bandana imaginable was represented.

The homegrown San Antonio gangs, known as 210, after the area code, now had to contend with influence from Chicago. In the 1970s, as street gang members were increasingly incarcerated, the four largest Chicago gangs became more organizationally sophisticated in prison.[16] By the end of the decade, the four gangs would orchestrate nearly all-encompassing alliances with the other gangs of Chicago. On one side was the Black Gangster Disciples, led by Larry Hoover, who created the Folk Nation. The three other large gangs, the Black P Stones (El Rukns) led by Jeff Fort, the Vice Lords, and the Latin Kings, countered with their own alliance called the People Nation. People and Folk gangs comprised various racial and ethnic groups and were represented by a multitude of gang colors. Although the alliances still exist, their influence is stronger in prison as their ability to maintain control of Chicago's numerous street gangs has deteriorated. Their legacy outside of Chicago, however, has been far reaching.

In San Antonio, the People Nation and Folk Nation allegiances were predominant among the Hispanic gangs. Other Chicago area gangs, such as Two-Six (Folk/beige) and Ambrose (Folk/baby blue) started to show up. San Antonio–area King sets began using three-point crowns to be distinguished from Chicago-area Kings. The Klan sprouted the subsets of Culebra Park Klan and West Side Klan.[17] The Klik also splintered, and the break-off groups of the Kin (People/green), and the La Raza Bloods (red) took sizable portions of the gang along with them.

OSO (ROMOS KLIK): The Kliksters, Klanners, a lot of people. How can I explain it to you? Families—black circle, blue, and red circle. The Romos were a little older than that. They grew up. They were bigger

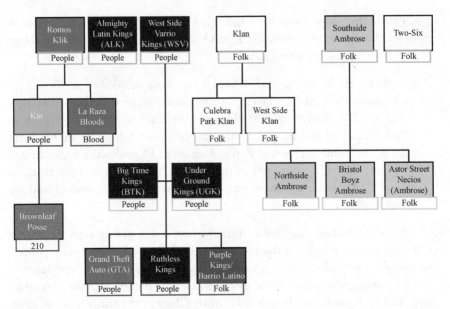

3-1. Latino gang family tree, 1980s to 1990s. (Data by Christian L. Bolden, graphic by LukePruettArt.)

gangs with bigger money. Allies would be the black and blue circle. They stay together. The Romos are a little older. They got incarcerated then started growing up. Some went to military and some left the state of Texas. Generations of younger people had nothing to do, different allies. The Kingsters, LA Boyz, Ambrose, gangs everywhere really. They didn't like a lot of people. They say they have grudges against other people.

In California, Latino gang affiliations were delineated by region, with northerners designated as Norteños 14, southerners as Sureños 13, and Bulldogs occupying the central part of the state. Though area animosities may have existed, juvenile penal institutions practiced forced sorting and segregation by region, which created, reinforced, and solidified these regional identities.[18] As cultural dissemination of gangs began to occur, Sureño gangs like Sur 13 (blue) and Lil' Watts 13 (LWS X3/black) started showing up in San Antonio as well. The South and West Sides of the city became major war zones. With so many little armies, it was hard to tell who was friend and who was foe. Some people tried to make sense of the madness by creating coalitions based on gang color—Black Circle (Kings, Bad Boyz, Lil' Watts, and other non–black rag allies), Red Circle (Bloods, Klik, Grand Theft Auto, Midnight Colors, Suicidal Locos), and Blue Circle (Crips, Folks, Ambrose, Damage Inc., LA Boyz, Wrecking Crew), but they would all break apart as gang leaders and founders were eliminated through homicide and incarceration.

P-MA (LADY WATTS x3): It is a saying that we would say. Kings, carriers of black rags, horses, spears, forks, and they go up and they go down. Black circles are down—Kings, Bad Boys, PMG, Little Watts, those are the main black circles. That is just a saying. Black circle, you got red circle. It just depends on what the slang is where you are from. Everybody knew that when you say black circle, you are a black ragger.

In 1993, San Antonio would record over 1,200 drive-by shootings, which were only the ones reported to police, averaging 3 to 4 per day, earning the city the dubious distinction of drive-by capital of the country.[19]

While the wars between Latino gangs were going full force, the African American gangs were not idle. The Crips, started by 15-year-old Raymond Washington, primarily wore blue, and had arisen in the area of Los Angeles, California, in 1969.[20] One theory of the Crips' emergence is that it resulted from the vacuum of role models caused by the exile, incarceration, and wholesale assassinations of civil rights leaders. Even though civil rights legislation had been passed in the legal realm, it had come at great cost, and its promises were far from realized in daily life. Ultimately, this left a young generation of Black men without faith in society, hope for a future, or charismatic guidance.[21] Hypermasculine peer role models and a subculture of violent behavior enhanced by racial segregation and volatile relations with law enforcement provided a perfect storm to whip up a new version of gang culture that would last into the modern day.

The Crip phenomenon steamrolled over rivals, forcing them to become a part of the Crip affiliation, while others latched onto to the bandwagon of Crip fame. By 1972, the remaining rival gangs, such as the Bishops, Brims, Bounty Hunters, Denver Lanes, Athens Park, and Pirus, created an alliance of red flags called the Bloods, and a never-ending war was begun.[22] During the late 1980s, Crips and Bloods started popping up all over the United States. Though it was initially blamed on purposeful migration of gangs for criminal intent, the reality was that most locations with Crip and Blood emergence already had local gangs, and migration was due to social motivations, such as families moving for job opportunities or to escape crime-ridden neighborhoods, rather than for purposeful criminal expansion.[23] San Antonio's East Side African American neighborhood gangs, which already had competitive rivalries, were no different, and they easily adapted to the Crip and Blood affiliations. The long-standing neighborhood feuds amplified as a result, and violence became steady. The street wars quickly boiled over into a tidal wave of gangs flooding the Northeast Side, where I lived. By the time I reached high school, most of the neighborhoods surrounding

Crownwood had succumbed to gangs, and their reputations were rising rapidly.

STICK (SA TOWN BLOODS/STB): Certain neighborhoods were more infamous than others. You hear about the dudes from those neighborhoods. The neighborhood next to mine, Camelot II Townhomes, there were a few dudes who everybody talked about, names ran through the streets.

PRANX (WHEATLEY COURTS TEXAS/WCT): It's just how San Antonio East Side is broken up, you have all these housings, and then from the housings is poverty, so that is why the East Side is so bad to this day because all the housing is just broken off into sections, you know you have East Terrace, you have Rigsby, you have Sutton Homes, you have Victoria Courts that used to exist but then they tore them down. So you have all these hoods and then from the hoods they started cliquing, and then, hey man, you know we should be called this. And they feel the best and then the other people feel the best and then from that went on to gangs, they became gang members, from how San Antonio was sectioned, that is how it led up to gangs to me. Because, they put all the minorities on the East Side, and then the ones who was able to have money went to the other side of town, so all the gangs was right there in the inner cities and all that shit so, just branched off and they became gang members and that is when the violence started.

SHUGA (23RD ST. HOOVER CRIP): [the years] '89, '90–'97, '98 were the most crucial times. All types of madness going on. Everybody! You could not go through any kind of hood, and not find some kind of people cliquing in some kind of way. It was everybody from the age of 15–18, 19, 20. It was everybody. There was nobody out there not involved in some kind of gang. It was how it was going down. It was fucking crazy. It was fucking crazy to see that shit!

Appendix A provides lists of San Antonio gangs in the early to mid-1990s.

Though I was insulated when in the BSV trailer park, conflict, violence, and danger gradually increased everywhere else. The social arrangement at Judson's campus consisted almost entirely of cliques. In the mornings and at lunch, groups had specified locales where they could be found. Crips, Bloods, and Kings would line up on separate walls of the cafeteria, while Jocks, Preps, and Kickers took the tables. Smaller gangs like Barrio Latino and Murder, Inc. held the courtyard with other social cliques like the Goths and Punks. Earning my post on the Blood wall felt great. I felt like I was somebody.

On days that the Crips chose to stand inside, they would leave first, walking past the whole line of Bloods. We would mad dog each other with hard stares, and if someone said something on either side, people would go

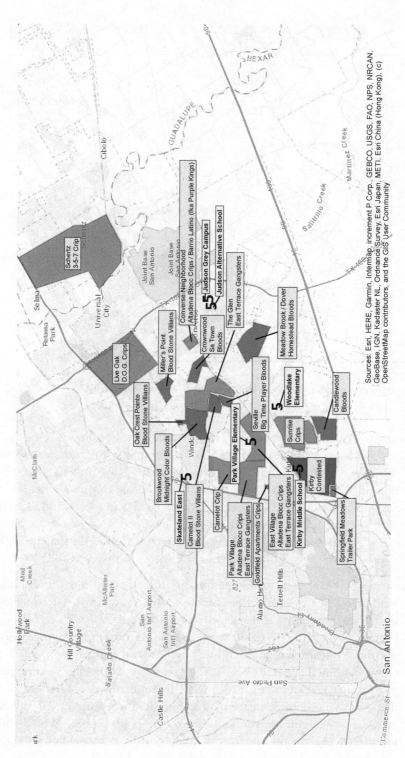

Sources: Esri, HERE, Garmin, Intermap, increment P Corp., GEBCO, USGS, FAO, NPS, NRCAN, GeoBase, IGN, Kadaster NL, Ordnance Survey, Esri Japan, METI, Esri China (Hong Kong), (c) OpenStreetMap contributors, and the GIS User Community

3-2. Northeast gang territory map. (Data by Christian L. Bolden, graphic by Melissa Tetzlaff-Bemiller.)

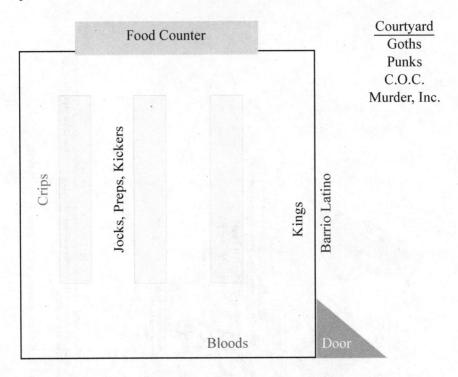

3-3. Cafeteria social map. (Data by Christian L. Bolden, graphic by LukePruettArt.)

to scrapping. We were mostly fair, letting people fight one on one. One day, Andrew, who was still peeved that he was taken to task for participating in my initiation, began riling me up, demanding that I prove myself. I was still wearing my cast and unsure of what he expected me to do. We had four separate lunch periods due to the large student body, and I was in D lunch that day, the last lunch. None of the gang members I was close to were around, so I was stuck with Andrew and a few other Bloods that I didn't really know. I was new, so I couldn't back down; I just went with it.

CAJUN (DOG): Yeah, there is definite qualifications, because if you are not willing to listen to an older person or you are not willing to do some of the things, you know that you need to do to prove themselves, I mean I remember pulling up to the store and telling the youngsters, hey get out and go steal me a uh, each one of y'all's steal me a quart and some blunts or something like that. And if you didn't do it, then you might just get smacked and not get to ride along tomorrow or something like that, so I would say definitely you know there is requirements. If you got heart when you are young, then you are going to be accepted and when I say heart it means, basically, you got the ignorance or you got the balls or whatever you want to call it to just do some dumb shit and try to get away with it.

Andrew pointed to a new kid about my size standing on the Crip wall and told me to go "check him," to see what he represented. I walked up to the Crip wall to challenge him and starting yelling at this kid until he trembled and a tear dropped out of his eye. He did not speak a word back to me as I threatened that I better not hear that he was claiming Crip. I had no real quarrel with this kid, nor did I get any satisfaction out of checking him. I fully expected one of the other Crips on the wall to start wailing on me, but nothing happened. I walked away, Andrew was satisfied, and I had proven to the other Bloods that did not know me well that I wasn't afraid. The retaliation for what I did would come later on when I wasn't expecting it.

The next day, several Bloods and I were walking out of the gym. Right before we were about to exit, the door flew open and in slithered Blacky, who pushed me. I was so startled that I pissed my pants a little bit. For real. Blacky was the clear shot caller for the Altadena Blocc Crips (ABC) at school. He was much older and taller than I was. His lankiness, streamlined cornrows, and the sinuous way he moved always made me think of a black mamba snake. He was careful not to disrespect the Bloods, but made it clear that he was threatening me over the incident of the previous day. He was giving me warning that he would not tolerate my harassment of that kid. I said nothing. Partially because I was still startled, partially because I felt a semblance of fear, and partially because I actually felt I deserved this berating. I was also still wearing a cast. Afterward, the older Bloods that were with me told me not to worry about it and that they would handle it. My fear of Blacky would fade, but our animosity for each other would grow. From that point forward, Blacky had it out for me.

The posting up on the wall routine would be disrupted soon after my initiation with the return of Manny. He was a skinny, Black Blood with really big hair, who had gone off to juvenile prison and returned as a Crip. In conversation, gangsters had very severe things to say about gang switching, but in reality, it happened all the time. Usually the switch was between allied or affiliated sets.[24] Completely switching sides was much rarer and more complicated. Whatever happened to Manny during his incarceration really messed him up. The mere sight of a Blood would send him into a rage. The first day he came back, as the Crips marched past the Blood wall through the cafeteria door, he began screaming all sorts of insults at us. The moment he stepped foot outside, some Blood took him to task for it, but that wasn't satisfactory enough, and several other Bloods jumped in. I was also caught up in the moment and took some swings on Manny with my one good arm. All the Crips saw what was happening but did nothing at first. I think the whole thing caught them by surprise. Their collective anger began to mount, and they screamed that it was "on" as the non-gang populace fled into the classrooms.

Judson had an ineffective way of dealing with gang riots called lock-outs. All the conventional kids would go into the classrooms, and the teachers would lock the doors. The campus police and security volunteers would attempt to round up the people outside the classrooms and lock them in the cafeteria. While the police and security searched for us, we hunted each other. On the occasion of my first gang riot, I was all but useless, having only one functioning hand, yet I was out in the hallways with the rest of them.

On the second floor of the main building, I encountered Manny. He was surrounded by a cadre of Crip girls, who were simultaneously trying to protect him from others and trying to keep him from going after anybody. He saw me and screamed, "Are you a Blood?" "Hell yeah, I'm a Blood!" I shouted back. His rage was palpable, his eyes bulging out of his head. Cast or no, I was ready and wanted to take him on. The attack came unexpectedly from two of the girls that were with him. They scratched my face with their long nails as I used my cast as a shield, while the other girls whisked Manny away. Dax had arrived on the scene, and he was mad at me for the way it went down, but I wasn't going to hit girls.

We heard security coming and people ran. Dax fled down the hall the way he came, and I ran up the stairs to the third floor, not realizing that two DOGs were hunting me. The Dope Overthrowing Gangsters were technically a neutral gang, but in reality they had a strong bias toward Crips.

The twin-brother DOGs caught me on the third floor balcony. "Let's throw him over the rail." I was screwed. Just as they grabbed me, Prophet, a Blood Stone Villain from Camelot Deuce, showed up and pulled them off of me. I did not know Prophet very well, but this was only the first time that he would end up saving me. While we were tussling, security finally caught up to us. We were tossed into the snake pit of a cafeteria. I'm not sure what the administration was thinking, but putting rioting gangsters all in the same room was a bad idea. Trying to keep us from going after each other was virtually impossible. Being tossed into the cafeteria with the Bloods felt like a sense of accomplishment. We believed that we won that day, and I felt intoxicated by the camaraderie and excitement of it all. It rapidly cemented my involvement with the gang.

There would be more gang riots over time. Sometimes we would be involved, sometimes not, and we would sit in the cafeteria whooping and hollering as we saw which people got tossed into the pit with us. Though the whole scenario was dangerous, it was also exciting. Being the first to be initiated inspired the rest of my friends. One by one, they would join other Blood sets or factions.

DJ (SA TOWN BLOOD/STB): [Violence]. At least once a week, but more like once a day [*laughs*]. I mean, a very slow week, something would happen on the weekend, but for the most part it was pretty much every day at school, maybe even several times a day at school. I mean, I can remember being class, I'm sittin' there tryin' to learn [*laughs*] and opposition gang members are actually entering my classroom to come get me. Yeah, I remember one time there were three gang members, two were brothers, they almost look like twins and then the same Hispanic dude who I always had problems with, they all come into my classroom ready to start you know jumping on me, but I was in GMR, which was a mechanics class, and I had a tire iron [*laughs*], so other than the mixture of that and my teacher, they dispersed and went ahead and left the classroom but then I had the same run-in with the cats later on that day, so you know you can, it was so much action at that time, I mean pretty much to go through a whole day without nothing would be a surprise.

Though everything was new and exhilarating for me, the realm of social science had been discussing since the 1950s what I was just now feeling.[25] The focal concerns of lower-class male delinquents, particularly those involved with gangs, had been described as including "toughness," which entailed a hardened facade and a willingness to fight others, no matter the odds. My participation in the riot while wearing a cast fit that description. "Trouble" and "excitement" included conflict over women and prowess, adrenaline seeking, rioting, and evading capture by the authorities. A belief that my life course had been mapped out for me, which in my case was being reunited with my friends who were all affiliated with the Bloods, fit the category of "fate." My resistance to and distrust of authority figures easily fulfilled "autonomy." And though I had not yet demonstrated streetwise "smartness," if my experience up to this point indicated anything it was that my participation in gangs was not special at all. It was classic. My initial gang activity would seem to match this older description of gangs, but in reality, it would only scratch the surface. As later researchers would find, the theory of focal concerns did not have enough depth. It did not go far enough in explaining why these behaviors occurred. In my case, lashing out at perceived injustices and the stinging slap of the middle-class measuring rod solidified my involvement more strongly than any temporary thrill. And it was only going to get worse.

Back in Crownwood, Bloods were slowly gaining momentum. It started with DJ and me, but more and more people were becoming Bloods. Even

3-4. Baby gangster "Lil' Man." (Bolden personal photos.)

still, there were some scattered Crips throughout the neighborhood, which resulted in erratic fighting after school and on the weekends. Blacky would also send Altadena Blocc Crips on occasional infiltrations into our neighborhood, hoping to catch us slipping alone. His odious henchman, Nolan, would jump out of a vehicle and chase us with a long-bladed knife in his hand. Lucky for us, he was too heavy and slow to ever catch us. On one occasion, Blacky rolled up on me while I was waiting for the bus. He was in a car full of East Terrace Gangsters and I was completely exposed. "I heard you been talking shit," he said, as he laid the barrel of a pistol across the rolled down window. I, of course, said nothing. Then they drove off.

The tide turned when Knockout (KO) moved in across the street from me. KO came from Hawaii, where he said African Americans were Bloods and Samoans were Crips. He adapted easily and was all in. Tall, lanky, and skilled in martial arts, KO was legendary for knocking people out with one punch.

DJ (SA TOWN BLOODS/STB): Well, let's see, I ain't going to say no names but there were several cats, one cat you know, martial arts cat, you know what I'm saying. We used to watch this dude kick the tops of the garage doors and kick the stop sign dead in the middle. Man, my homeboy, I remember one time before school started, this cat was standing in the group and just out of nowhere he knocks this cat out man! He hits him square in his grill and ol' dude just falls on the floor, like he must have flew a few feet.

With him at our side, we began to aggressively overpower the Crips that came into our neighborhood. No one living there was representing blue anymore, and at some point they stopped coming in. Crownwood was all Blood. The excitement and risk of danger served to unite the neighborhood, building trust and loyalty. The hood became our identity, and our reputation was added to the endless list of street soldiers in San Antonio.

CHAPTER 4

Bangin' in San Antone

IN THE MOVIES, gang life appeared to be glamorous or action packed all of the time. The reality of gangbanging was far from that. Theorists have argued over whether gangs select people who are predisposed toward delinquency or if joining a gang increases delinquent behavior, with an overwhelming amount of evidence favoring the latter.[1] In my case, gang involvement created a spiraling effect that slowly took over all aspects of my life.[2] Though some of the deviant activity was real, the resulting assumptions about gang members and the lack of understanding by authority figures led to false accusations and miscarriages of justice that bred resentment and intensified my downward spiral. Street culture was being reinforced by my peers, and I learned the methods, techniques, and attitudes of gangsterism,[3] but it was adults with legitimate oversight who eliminated any alternative influence. School authorities had already written me off, and the gangster label meant that they had an easy scapegoat, often holding me responsible for offenses I didn't commit.[4] I did not blame them for my behavior; that was all my own. I also did not subscribe to the notion that I would behave according to their expectations. They were, however, some of the primary catalysts of my fury, and I wanted to lash out at the world because of their treatment of me. Their relegation of me to the status of a degenerate and the negative strain of feeling unjustly punished for things,[5] effectively marginalized me from the educational system.[6] Unable to live up to middle-class standards due to consistent obstacles, failures, and rejections in school hastened my involvement with delinquent subcultures.[7] Between the pull of brotherly love and excitement from the gang, and the barriers and rejection from legitimate society, my identity as a gang member and involvement in criminal activity became solidified.

Between the ninth and tenth grades, my academic progress was going in reverse. It wasn't that I was not capable. I typically breezed through my schoolwork with ease. Gang life was beginning to take its toll on my time and energy. There were some caring instructors, like my history teacher, Ms. Wynn, who was great at de-escalating conflicts, but generally my relationship with the teachers and administration continuously worsened.

Gang members actually believe in and practice conventionally favored values, such as honor and loyalty, but are ill equipped or unable to do so within conventional contexts. Instead, these values are manifested within the gang scene and in street reputations.[8] I was as obnoxious as any other young gang member, but I had my own honor code. I wouldn't lie about anything. I'm not sure where that came from, but I found lying to be too difficult and troublesome. All lies led to more lies, and you would eventually get caught. And it typically went badly for me if I attempted to tell a lie. What I could do was keep my mouth shut or lie by omission. I did that quite often. I would also own up to any wrongdoing that I was caught for and willingly accepted my punishment. The problem was that half of the things the school administration punished me for were things that I had not done. This made me seethe with resentment toward them. Once someone gains the label of delinquent it becomes a master status, and it is hard for people in authority to see them any other way.[9] All behaviors of the delinquent person are assumed to be criminal or deviant, and it becomes easy to lay blame at their feet. Many actions of gang members came from a moral code of the street subculture and were not intended to be malicious. Agents of social control, such as teachers and principals, refused even to discuss the causes or complexities of these actions, choosing instead to immediately vilify people they viewed as criminogenic.[10]

I was once pulled out of class and taken to a vice principal's office. The campus police were waiting for me there. They slammed me against the wall and searched me head to toe. The vice principal said that a certain kid had accused me of stealing his wallet. I had not, but of course the cops and principal did not believe me. They searched the classroom I was in and my locker and found nothing. The principal gave me a Saturday detention for "not returning the wallet." The kid who accused me was a shit kicker. His wallet had gone missing during gym class, and I was one of the people behind him in line for class, so he assumed I was the culprit. I searched for the guy at lunch and found him among the other country kids. I confronted him about his accusation, and he maintained that I had stolen it, so I slapped his face. I imagine it is hard for people to maneuver in cowboy boots and impossibly tight jeans. He took a swing at me, missed and fell. It was over for him. I put my knee on him to keep him down and pummeled his face and head with a barrage of fury. A crowd had quickly emerged to witness his thrashing. When the authorities started coming, someone pulled me off and blended me into the crowd. It was Prophet, saving me again. Security grabbed Prophet instead of me, and I escaped. I don't know if Prophet got out of that or not, but given the authorities' penchant for making people pay for things they didn't do, I doubt it. A teacher in the gym had already found the kid's wallet, where the kid had dropped it.

The following year, as violence between gangs escalated, Prophet would be "caught slipping," off-guard, alone, and unprotected. No matter who you were, if rivals caught you alone, it was their chance to turn you into a victim.[11] Prophet was murdered. His loss was a gut punch that never went away. Though I had heard about street soldiers falling throughout the city, Prophet brought the reality of death much closer. It was chilling at first, but as things worsened, I expected that it would eventually happen to me as well. It was a common belief among gangsters. The harsh realities of our existence would eventually instill mental acceptance of a very short life expectancy.[12]

Another time, I was pulled out of my algebra class. Since math was like a foreign language to me, I had long since given up trying to understand it, and I slept through class. When security came to get me, I figured my snoring during the lecture had finally gotten me in trouble. Turns out, the teacher said I wrote graffiti all over her classroom, so the principal was giving me Saturday detention to come and clean it up. I was livid, I knew that I had not somehow sleepwalked and graffitied the classroom. When I got back to class, I looked at the tables that had been marked up with representations of Latino gangs that certainly weren't mine, and then I lit into the teacher. I yelled at her that she was a liar and that she was wrong and should be ashamed for accusing someone without investigating. When I was done, I sat back down in my chair, at my table that had no graffiti on it. She stood trembling for a few moments, her back pressed against the chalkboard, and then she inched her way along the chalkboard toward the door, eyeing me like I was a rabid wolf just waiting to pounce on her. When she got close enough, she dashed out the door. The campus cops came back to arrest me. That Saturday detention turned into alternative school.

In 1995, the Texas legislature mandated the institution of disciplinary alternative schools in all districts throughout the state, although by that time, many school districts, like Judson, already had them well entrenched. Originally meant to be alternative education for students who committed criminal offenses, the schools became a dumping ground for children who were in any way problematic. By 1996, Texas would have almost seventy-one thousand students in alternative schools.[13] With teachers that were unqualified to teach and the lack of a unified curriculum, education seemed to be the lowest priority at these institutions.

Our alternative school sat in the middle of the field that separated Judson's Gray and Red campuses. It consisted of a modified mobile home building filled with student desks and a couple of offices. Unruly kids who were sent there were made to sit in the desks and do their homework, never speaking. There was no instruction and no interaction. We would sit at our desks all day long. We would even eat lunch at our desks. I would breeze through my homework, and then be bored for the rest of the day, so I resorted to writing raps and making lists of my favorite things. I had some bizarre obsession with making lists that helped occupy my mind. We would occasionally get a short recess outside where we could interact. Gangsters serving time in alternative school would limit their conflict to rap battles, which was a respected alternative for demonstrating street authenticity and aggressive competitiveness.[14] I would work all day preparing for these verbal contests. Recesses were uncommon though, because the privilege was taken away if any one of us was caught talking, which almost always occurred. Any fight in alternative school meant expulsion. Remarkably, I made it through without fighting. Most of the kids there were sentenced to specified time periods before they could return to regular school. Any infraction could get time added on to your sentence. My sentences were always six weeks or more, so the Gray campus would sometimes become a distant memory. True to Texas disciplinary philosophy, our education was training us to be prisoners. Instead of critical thinking skills or creativity, the focus was on making us docile, controllable, and isolated, all while normalizing surveillance and disciplinary procedures that were almost identical to those in prison.[15]

There was one principal, Mr. Alfred, an African American man in his early forties, who seemed to be more understanding than the others. He was more likely to be reasonable when talking to me. He didn't always assume I was guilty; he appreciated my honesty when I was guilty, and he was more likely to show leniency. Though I felt more comfortable speaking with Mr. Alfred, his outreach would be ruined by personal failings. He started flirting with my mom when she was with me in his office. "How can you look into her beautiful blue eyes and still do the things you do?" Puke. Whatever! My trust in his intentions began to reverse.

He and the other administrators also had several blind spots that prevented them from truly understanding gangs and the gang members they were dealing with. Mr. Alfred had a strange notion that I was some kind of gang leader. He would often stop me in the mornings to ask me about some specific happening or killing in gangland. I almost never knew what he was talking about. I don't think most authority figures had any conception about just how many gangs there were or how dynamic the gang scene was. He came to this notion of leadership because, whenever I was walking, there were a lot of people following me. The reality was that, other than to get food, the only time I ever came off my post on the Blood wall was to go fight someone. People knew this, and when they saw me come off the wall, they started following me to see what would happen. I was quiet, deliberate, and action oriented. I spent very little time talking but often struck out against my enemies, and I had a long list of them. It wasn't just the Crips.

Kickers and Jocks were also on my shit list, so fights were a regular occurrence.

I was no leader at all. More accurately, I was, in effect, some sort of social nexus. I brought people together from different gangs and different neighborhoods. They converged at Crownwood, and our own crew began forming. Alliances with people from different neighborhoods created an unintentional expansion of the gang network. As the influence of Crownwood spread, the group included more people who did not actually live in the neighborhood. The presence of these "fictive residents" would inevitably create more conflicts.[16]

DJ (SA TOWN BLOODS/STB): Converse mostly, Converse, San Antonio, but Crownwood, neighborhood seemed to be the heart of the beginning of it. You know, everybody seemed to hang out there, you know centralize there. Shit, I lived in the corner house, so we would hang out like 20 something people on the corner sometimes. It was just something else.

At the core of it were KO, Ace, and me, though Ace lived quite far away. DJ was down with us, but his time had become dedicated to making music, and we were often recording raps together. He had also discovered a consuming affinity for marijuana and his Blood-affiliated girlfriend, Isla, which probably mellowed him out more than the rest of us. For Ace, KO, and me, the gang was our life and our identity. Bret and Coop would pop into the hood and we began rapidly picking up more people.

When gangs become larger, they tend to splinter and reassemble as smaller groups.[17] As the squad got bigger, we realized that we were, in effect, our own gang, and a new formulation needed to occur. We experimented briefly with the name Juvenile Blood Mafia (JBM) but abandoned it. We eventually became the Sa Town Bloods (STB). Initially, it was simply a coalition where people still represented their original gangs, but eventually STB would become primary for most members. It grew rapidly. We picked up Stick from Seville. Stick was part Haitian, very tall, and stocky. He walked with a cane and an uneven gait, but it all looked cool and natural. There was Chubbs, D-Rock, and Jag (a twin) from Miller's Point, though they largely remained on the periphery. KO, DJ, and I initiated Remington and Special, a Black and White best-friend duo, in one of the Crownwood ditches one day. When we returned to my house, I went inside to bring back out a tray of orange juice for everyone. As I exited, someone kicked my legs out from under me. I face planted into the ground with orange juice splashing all around me. It was the police. They had come to arrest us for fighting in the ditches. No one pressed charges, so they eventually let us go. Special's parents immediately shipped him off to another state.

DJ (STB): I remember one time we were rolling this cat in, in a drainage ditch and police came because neighbors called and when they got there we told them we were playing rugby [*laughs*]. They didn't buy it, they rolled us to the dude's house and asked his parents, asked if they wanted to press charges, they said no and that guy matter of fact ended up telling the cop, [*in a mocking voice*] "yeah, they are rolling me into the gang" [*laughs*]. Messed us up [*laughs*].

K-Dog, who was the only Mexican kid among us at first, came out of an intact upper middle-class family in Universal City. He also played football for Judson. K-Dog only came to the hood on the occasional weekend, earning the title of weekend warrior, but he loved to get into trouble when he did come around. He spent most of his time adoring his girlfriend, a non-gang-related, blonde, preppy young lady. One weekend, when his girlfriend was "off to see her grandmother," K-Dog was driving back through the hood with us when we saw his girlfriend sitting on another guy's lap, kissing him. What a stroke of bad luck. K-Dog beat up that kid, who I am sure had no idea what he had gotten into, and that relationship ended. This severed a major connection he had to conventional life, and he was down to roll with us much more often after that. K-Dog added Shorty, a White, middle-class kid, who would drive us around in his nice car. His sister, Blondie, would usually come along for the ride.

We mostly got around through Tommy, Cadillac, and Tiger, another 20-something-year-old head from their crew. Tiger was an Asian dude who literally never talked, but drove us around in his van. I use race and ethnicity to be descriptive, but we honestly didn't give a shit. In fact, many of us were mixed, like me. Most of the other gangs were primarily of one race with a token person of another demographic thrown in every now and then. I think some people were attracted to STB because we didn't care and had people from all groups.

I dropped my baby gangster name Lil' Man. I began growing my hair, which would eventually be in braids that went past my shoulders, and I grew the nails on my left hand over one inch. Some people used long nails to sniff cocaine, but I was clueless about that connection and just grew them to contribute to my image. Blondie liked to take care of my nails and cuticles whenever I was rolling with Shorty, so they stayed well kempt. My appearance could sometimes be frightening, so I gained the moniker Wicked. The enhanced gang persona plus the acquisition of guns for several members of the STBs was enough to send people fleeing, thereby avoiding the need for any conflict.

The proliferation of gangs in the 1990s also coincided with the mass availability of guns. Gangs had always been violent, but the damage they

TABLE 4-1

Sa Town Blood Gang Members and Allies

Sa Town Bloods	Original/Other Set	Allies	Ally Gang
Lil' Man/Wicked	RCG/AVL	Andrew	Blood Stone Villain
Ace	Big Time Player	B-Loco	Blood Stone Villain
Bret	Blood Stone Villain	Big Moe	RCG
Caleb		Cadillac	Blood Stone Villain
Chaps		Dave	RCG
Chubbs		Dax	RCG
Chuckles		Dizzy	Blood Stone Villain
Coco (F)	Almighty Vice Lord	Half-Life	RCG
Coop	Blood Stone Villain	L-Dog	RCG
Daisy (F)	Almighty Vice Lord	P-Ma (F)	Lady Watts X3
Devil	Almighty Vice Lord	Prophet	Blood Stone Villain
DJ		Ricky	Blood Stone Villain
D-Rock		Tiger	Blood Stone Villain
Isla (F)		Tommy	WSV King
Jag		Vincent	Blood Stone Villain
K-Dog			
KO	Almighty Vice Lord		
Remington			
Shorty			
Snappy (F)	KAP Crip/AVL		
Stick			

caused had been historically mitigated by their limited weaponry, which consisted of knives, bats, brass knuckles, zip guns, and then, ultimately, pistols. In the late 1980s and early 1990s, all types of sophisticated weaponry became available. The majority of gang members either owned a gun or knew where to go to immediately obtain one. With Texas already having a pro-gun culture, a firearm became one of the easiest commodities to obtain.[18]

🌿 My gang identity also influenced my home life. My mother was in denial about me being a gang member for the first year or so. My sister would show my mother my monochromatic wardrobe and scream at her, "Open your eyes! It is all red!" My mom would finally accept what was going on, but I don't think she knew what to do about it. I would try to hide my activities from her as much as possible. She would occasionally find guns that I had hidden around the house and go throw them in some nearby large body of

TABLE 4-2
Foes

Altadena Blocc Crips
A-Dog
Blacky
Chip
D-Town
Duck
G-Rocc
Killian
Kyle
Laces
Nolan
Other Crips
Manny
Marvin
Zilla (F)

water, or at least that is what she told me. My dad's response to my gang involvement was to pick me up by the neck with one hand, punch me in the face with the other, and tell me, "You don't need to be down with anybody but me!" KO wanted to kill him over that. I once found my brother, seven years my junior, and one of his friends, tearing up a blue bandana, stomping it, and smashing it with a rock. That image haunted me. I never wanted my brother to be like me. I loved him dearly. I tried to make sure to bring him new toys whenever I could. Thankfully, he never did gangbang. Years later, he would tell me that my reputation saved him from getting beat up on different occasions.

I'm not sure what the other Blood sets thought about STB. I suspect that they didn't like the phenomenon, but they couldn't deny our popularity. Our numbers kept growing. This also caused issues with quality control, as we would encounter wannabes everywhere who were getting into messes and creating new enemies for us that we didn't even know about.

DJ (STB): Well I was in a specific set, STBs, which we had created, me and my friends in school, which, uh, there were probably, I mean in the beginning it was say ten friends, and then from there it went, boy it skyrocketed quick. I say by the end of one year we had already accumulated a good thirty or so and I swear by next year we heard about them in different schools and everything that we didn't even know these people. You know but they were claiming our set, so we had already blown up to that status where people would copycat, which was cool.

✳ Gang territory was generally delineated by neighborhood, but it wasn't limited to that. Territorial spread occurred ecologically or by happenstance, but rarely by intention. Other than Crownwood and the trailer park, our territory was Skateland East, which occurred early on and by coincidence.

K-DOG (STB): I was at Skateland and these guys were part of a group called COC and I was the only Blood there and there was a lot of Crips there, so I was just like well, I went up to them, I told them hey man, if y'all need to fight with anybody, I am going to jump in with you guys and they were like OK, man alright, OK well we got your back right now or whatever. So I was skating out there and rocking talking or whatever, and then didn't care.

Initially, Ace dragged me to the skating rink to mack to some girls. The Crips there were not happy about our presence, and Killian, a White Altadena Blocc Crip took a particular disliking to Ace, asking him where he was from, which was a common gang challenge and prelude to conflict.[19] They let us know that they were going to beat our asses once we were outside. That didn't occur, for two reasons. Surprisingly, another gang that was there, the Crusaders of Converse (COC/Folk/white and gray), took our side. We didn't even know them, but they were tired of the shit that the Crip crew was dishing out to people. With the COC on our side, we significantly outnumbered the Crips. Secondly, the police officer assigned to Skateland was watching all of us intently and called for backup when the place closed, so that police presence prevented anything from happening. Even so, Killian's decision to check Ace that night would cause him a lot of pain in the future.

The STBs didn't like what happened, and Stick in particular was furious, so he and some others went with us the next weekend. The COC were in reduced numbers, and Killian and his boys were there. Stick let him know that he was in for it. Killian seemed strangely confident, even though he was only half Stick's size. The fight took place outside, in an alley behind the skating rink. A large crowd circled them, and, as expected, Stick began easily beating Killian's ass. Two of Killian's allies jumped in. One picked up a wooden board and broke it on Stick's back. Another pulled out a whip and threatened the rest of us with it. Everyone was stunned. In what was either a moment of brilliance or a genuine belief that they were coming, someone yelled "Five-Oh" (police) and people scattered everywhere. There were actually no police coming, and the only ones left were Bret, Stick, and me, all surrounding Killian. He was doomed. We beat the ever-living shit out of him. Stick threw him through a wooden fence and we ran around to stomp him. Random people on the other side of the fence also kicked him just because he was an asshole. We left him there coughing up blood and barely able to move.

After that, the skating rink was ours. The COC were cool, but they stopped coming around after a while. Any friendly gang could come in, but we would chase out enemies who ventured in there. The cops that regularly moonlighted as security there hated us, and we were officially banned; but we would just hang around outside or wait until a cop that didn't know us was working. Shielded from surveillance, the unlighted areas on the sides and behind the building became our alternative set space.[20]

Most of our time at Skateland was fun, but there were a few exceptions. One time, only Ace and I were there when two unknown Crips, one Black and one White, came in. We checked them, and they didn't represent. Later on, at the nearby 7-Eleven where all the kids from Skateland would go, we ran into them again. I was carrying a slushy that I had just bought when I walked out and saw them. I started running my mouth off at the White one, dissing Crips, and he slapped the slushy out of my hand. I took a swing at him but slipped on my slushy and went down. He had the advantage and could have taken me but he never touched me. Ace was right there boxing with him in the street. I had on baggy pants and when I fell, the long bar-reled .22 Ruger I was carrying slipped all the way down my pants and was at my ankle. I stood up, picked it up, and pointed it at him. "Get off my homeboy, Blood!" The gun went off. He fell down. I didn't know the gun was a hair trigger, and did not mean to shoot. This was my first time using a gun, and I had no idea what I was doing. Gang members tend to be noto-riously bad shots. Thankfully, I didn't hit him. He popped back up and ran behind a car, screaming, "Don't shoot!" He and his partner kept running, using cars for cover. Ace and I fled in the opposite direction. We ran through the wealthy neighborhood of Windcrest for miles, hiding behind bushes and jumping fences. We finally reached the trailer park and told Tommy and Cadillac what had happened. Cadillac rounded up the boys in the trailer park and gave us a very stern lecture. "Never, ever, pull a gun unless you intend on using it." I wished I hadn't done it. The cost of that mistake would be very high.

On the streets, affronts are often responded to with imperfect retalia-tion. Emotions are strong motivators, and the anger felt by someone who has been disrespected limits that person's rationality. Impulsivity and the lack of cognitive sophistication in young gang members meant that the force of anger was often felt by someone other than the primary foe. Due to the uncertainty of locating the person that was the source of provocation in a timely manner, gang members might satisfy their anger by lashing out excessively at targets that they perceive as related to their quarry.[21]

A few weeks later, Ace and I were headed to Skateland on foot, coming from Windsor Park Mall. It was quite a distance so we were going to get there later than usual. The trailer park BSV were already there in force. When Ace and I were about halfway there, walking across an empty parking lot, we heard gunshots in the distance. We began running toward Skateland. There were police everywhere. We found Bret on his knees, tears streaming down his face. He hugged me with all his might when I arrived.

Bret told us that the unknown Crip that I shot at had shown up looking for me. He walked up to the BSV standing on the wall. "I'm looking for Wicked." "You found us instead." They started chasing him. At first he ran, but then he turned around with a .380 and fired. The bullet hit B-Loco in the stomach. It was pretty bad.

BRET (STB): There was other activities that came up just by hanging out and that is when somebody crossed the path you know wearing the wrong color, you know what I mean. That would engage in a confrontation, sometimes worse, you know watching, something simple like hanging out at the skating ring back then turned into one of my friends getting shot. So, it was, it was six or seven of us against two other people and then one pulls out a gun and starts shooting. So, the day-to-day would range from very simple to very, very crazy man. It was something else.

The surreal array of feelings I had at that moment was dizzying, both in the magnitude and the variety of the emotions. Cadillac's words haunted me, and I felt very guilty about causing this. My guilt was accompanied by pangs of hollow horror eating at my stomach in a way that I imagined was like the bullet punching through B-Loco's gut. On the outside though, I did not show my shock, both from needing to be a strengthening presence for others and from actually becoming hardened in that moment. I was cradling Bret as he was wracked with tears. He had been one of my best friends since first grade, and I loved him. I felt no shame at all letting him cry on my shoulder. I barely even knew B-Loco, but he and Bret were close. Ace and I were looking at each other and knew that not only had we been the cause of this but that this was now the way things were going to be. We had reached a violent tipping point, and we knew that we weren't coming back. Bret noticed our hardened faces, and I think it terrified him. That event broke Bret inside a little. It began a slow progression of him pulling back from the gang. B-Loco would survive the gunshot, thankfully, though a colostomy bag would now be a constant reminder of what happened. Both he and Bret were the first in the mental tally I began keeping of people's lives that I had messed up.

Bret (STB): My reasons for starting were something else, you know, it was a group of friends, and then I realized that it was more than that, more than just a group of friends to other people. So, I became that temporary. I kind of distanced, became more distant with the people that became stronger and stronger in their gang affiliation and it became more than what I really wanted to be a part [of].

We decided to chill on Skateland for a while. When we came back several months later, we would find none other than Killian, trying to bully the little wannabe Bloods. It could not have happened better if it had been a scene choreographed for a movie. Killian and the kids he was picking on were standing on a hill right next to the street. We pulled up in a pickup truck full of about ten people. The little kids screamed with excitement, pointing fingers at him. We jumped out of the truck and stalked up the hill. His eyes widened, and I could see the fear in them. Chuckles, who had picked up a rock, reached him first. One punch to the face and he was flat on his back. The rest of us never had a chance to get to him. The little kids swarmed him like hyenas going after animal scraps. We would have many a laugh remembering all of those little kids beating up Killian.

Chuckles was one of the more sinister additions to the STBs. Half Black, half Korean, Chuckles grew up mostly with Crips and had many Crip friends. We met him through our exploits at Skateland. Despite his upbringing with Crips, he chose to hang around us. He associated with us for quite a while before actually joining. I never really understood why he chose us, although the nature of gangs forces people to negate their neutrality eventually.

T-Note (3-5-7 CRIP): One time, I was chilling in a house with a bunch of Crips, listening to Brotha Lynch Hung and this is the first time that I came across the rapper, and he has a line in the song that was like "if your homie is a Crip, you're a Crip." Basically, saying that whatever beef goes down while you're there with your man, you know it is going down with you. You know, so if you are in a situation where Bloods and Crips are fighting and these Bloods see you, they are not going to recognize you as a possible civilian with some Crip homies. They gonna look at you as a fucking full-fledged Crip no matter what color you got on.

Chuckles wore purple every single day, which the other Bloods gave him hell about. Some Crip gangs, like Grape Street Watts, and other gangs that we weren't friendly with, like Barrio Latino, wore purple. Chuckles was going to wear what he wanted. He very much became a part of the core group, but a lot of people didn't trust him and did not want to be around him. Stick, who was friends with him at first, would quickly find Chuckles intolerable, and for good reason. Chuckles was ultraviolent and unpredictable. Coming from a Crip background and not being originally from the neighborhood, he would respond to constant questioning with aggressive overcompensation.[22] He would shoot at random, and not only at rival gang members. His actions were disconcerting to the rest of us, and whenever he was confronted about his behavior he would just giggle hysterically. Many of us thought Chuckles was insane. Whether he was or not was anyone's guess, but his psychopathic behaviors were tolerated and sometimes useful in the gang scene.[23]

In my own lapse in sanity, I still attempted to bond with Chuckles, in whatever way it is possible to bond with someone who has unusually volatile characteristics. Every time I was hanging out alone with Chuckles, the shenanigans that ensued would land me near death. Very soon after Chuckles officially joined us, he and I were at a major bus transit hub fairly late at night. There was no one around, and we were slipping with no weapons. A car rolled up and out hopped Duck and Laces, two notorious Altadena Blocc Crips in the MacArthur Independent School District, known for shooting people. Duck, tall and Black with a large Afro that made him look even taller, and his Mexican sidekick, Laces, who seemed to be a third of his height, were inseparable. "Chuckles is that you?" Laces tucked a black 9mm back in his waistline. "Man, we saw red (my Chicago Bulls hat) and you were about to get blasted. Why is your friend wearing red anyway?" Chuckles giggled. I guess they were used to that response from him, as they grew up together. They had no idea who I was. Our respective stomping grounds were very far removed from one another. I knew that they could put a bullet in us at any moment, but Chuckles seemed to be amused by my discomfort and kept chatting with them about asinine things. Finally, Laces said, "We gotta bounce," and off they went. When they were gone, Chuckles fell to the ground and rolled with laughter for several minutes. Fucking Chuckles.

"I got an idea," he said. That was never a good thing, but I went along with it anyway. I knew he wouldn't tell me what it was, so I didn't bother asking. Instead of catching the bus home, we got on a bus going to a destination only known to him. We got off by an apartment complex. It was the last bus of the night, so we were stuck there. It turned out to be his old neighborhood, the stomping ground of Duck and Laces, and it was crawling with Crips. We stuck to the shadows, as all the gangsters were hanging out in the courtyard. Chuckles knocked on several doors looking for girls he knew. Some took us in and visited with us for a while. One even kind of liked me and gave me her phone number. None of them were going to let us stay with them though. We ended up at his old friend Chip's house, where we stayed. Chip was a Crip. Fucking Chuckles.

Chip eyed me suspiciously for the first few hours, but the idea that an enemy gang member would walk through his neighborhood and into his apartment was preposterous. And plus, I was with Chuckles. I tried to keep a poker face on, but Bloods and Crips each have their own language identifiers (Bloods avoid using the letter C and Crips avoid using the letter B while speaking). I was sure that some of mine would slip out, and my reactions to his were noticeable. At some point, while we were playing dominoes, he said, "Are you a Blood?" "Yeah, I'm a Blood." We stared at each other. Chuckles giggled hysterically. The staring match and giggle fit lasted an inordinate amount of time. Finally, Chip said, "Fuck it" and went back to playing dominoes.

We stayed up all night. I was partially afraid that if I fell asleep, I would wake up dead. Something about the absurdity of the situation and delirium caused by lack of sleep caused us to regress to acting like children. We had a beanbag version of a pillow fight and pranked each other by putting toothpaste on someone's hand then tickling their face if they dozed off. In a potentially lethal situation, the need to be goofy kids is what saved us. We survived the night without incident and snuck out of that hood in the morning before anyone was up. I thought that I had had enough of Chuckles for a lifetime after that night, but that wasn't the case.

He would often come to my house to get me. My window faced the street, and people constantly came to my window if they needed me for something. I was perpetually grounded, but I would just sneak out of the window. I probably left through the window just as many times as I walked out through the front door. Whatever adventure Chuckles would take us on usually left us stranded far from home in the middle of the night. We would go into random apartment complexes, find the neighborhood laundromats, which were usually left open, and fall asleep on the folding tables.

The criminality of the STBs began to increase, likely a result of increased mobility and cooperation with allies. There always seemed to be a guest with us, anytime we went on a criminal excursion. Spoils were kept by the individuals who went on the outings, and each person who went had their own motivations for doing so. We were opportunistic, not having any criminal specialty, but we would take advantage of whatever was available to us. We were like most gangs, not specialized, engaging instead in cafeteria-style offending, sampling any criminal opportunity that presented itself.[24] We would burglarize houses. We targeted the middle- to upper middle-class homes in the Madison school district, far away from us. We didn't touch anything in our own neighborhoods, which was a result of being admonished by one of the residents. One day when we were walking through Crownwood, we broke into a car. We only used the "check if the door is open" method, and never broke windows. When we were scanning the car, the

owner, a Black man, probably in his late thirties, came running out. "Come
on man," he said, "why do you have to break into my car? Why don't you
break into rich, White people's cars?" "Sho, you right!" we said and gave
whatever we had snatched out of his car back to him.

Some of the guys became proficient at burglary. I hated doing it. Something about the thought of going into someone else's home repulsed me. On
the occasions I was with the burglary crews, I would insist on being the
lookout or target spotter. It was easy to know which houses were unoccu-
pied by the amount of mail or newspapers that were accumulated outside.
Other than guns and musical equipment, there was not much in the way of
big scores. Nearly all our firearms came from burglaries. Gun enthusiasts
were gold mines. I wouldn't know how ironic this was regarding the debate
on gun control until I was much older. I didn't know of anyone who got
their weapons on the black market, though I am sure some people did.
There was also some buying, selling, and trading between gangsters. The
.22 Ruger I had during the Skateland trouble was sold to me by Chuckles
for twenty dollars. In retrospect, that was probably a foolish purchase. The
local flea market also catered to the underworld. They had those crafty tri-
angle display cases. When gangsters were around, they would display Tech-
9s and Mac-10s. When police were around, they would flip the cases to
display only revolvers. By and large, the STB arsenal consisted of guns stolen from someone's home.

We also got into "jacking." We would drive around at night searching
for people who were out by themselves. It was amazing how many people
you could find skulking around alone outside after midnight. We wouldn't
even have to hurt them. A truckload of gangsters jumps out on a skulker
and he is quick to hand over money, weed, or whatever he has of value.

The STB did not deal drugs, nor did the vast majority of gangs that we
knew of or encountered.[25] Not that we had any restriction against it. We
just didn't care about it. Though I had smoked weed several times out of
solidarity with my homeboys, I didn't care for it. It made me paranoid or
sleepy, so I often opted out.

With our wide array of involvement in both major and minor criminal
activities, and our low levels of drug dealing or drug use outside of social
settings, we were what is known as a serious delinquent gang.[26] We did not
have many adult criminal role models to teach us to commit crime for
profit. We had to come up with our own avenue of esteem. Our real MO
from the beginning was conflict.[27] Ace, KO, and I would always go off to
some other part of town looking to cause trouble. We knew where to go
because in the gang world there was a system of electronic voice mailboxes
from remote answering machine services that everyone used to call up to
deliver news, messages, or gang pronouncements. Once someone hacked

into a voice mailbox, the code would be given out and everyone would start chiming in. We would also have our own personal voice mailboxes that allies would call to say what's up, enemies would call to talk shit, and girls would call to try to hook up.

DJ (STB): I remember we used to do a lot of stuff like the telephone mailboxes and stuff and we would figure out the codes, get into a mailbox and leave messages like crazy. I don't even remember how exactly that worked but I remember a lot of gang members used to do that, make threats, and see if we could get the other gang members to show up at a spot and you know, we was definitely, we was using the technology of the time.

K-DOG (STB): There was even like the phone numbers that we would call that were boxes, people would just be talking shit straight up on these boxes that were on the telephone, I don't even know where they came from but we would get ahold of these numbers and we would call them and then there would be like all kind of gang members just talking shit. We would be setting up fights and just everything you know what I mean, and it was like, it was weird, there was stuff online and there was also stuff on telephone lines [*laughs*].

We would go downtown to the teen clubs to flirt with girls from the Notre Dame Posse (NDP), pick fights, or make allies. One time a new friend we made offered to drive us home. He was supposed to take us to Windsor Park Mall on the Northeast Side, but he dropped us off at a mall on the Northwest Side instead at three o'clock in the morning. San Antonio is massive. It was the tenth-largest city in the United States in the 1990s. We were screwed. Starving, we climbed through the drive-through window of a closed fast-food restaurant and ate as much soft-serve ice cream as we could handle, as it was the only unsecured food. We hopped back out of the window and trotted toward the sidewalk that followed a main street, when sirens appeared from the other direction as police came to investigate the silent alarm we had tripped. They never had a clue. We walked that main street until daybreak, passing neighborhoods with "Blood Killer" spray painted on the outside fences. The insanity of walking in enemy territory so far from our turf made us feel powerful. When the sun came up, the buses started running, and we were able to make it home.

The three of us decided to go back to the Northwest and West Sides whenever we could, looking for trouble. We were always outnumbered but were undaunted by it. It would send us into frenzy. Latino gang members would call it La Locura.[28] It meant aggressively wild and unrestrained behavior.[29] The audacity, intensity, and craziness of the three of us was often enough to make people back down.

DJ (STB): People would gain leadership through willingness to do whatever it took, because part of being in a gang was bringing the attention to people in your set to let people know that your set is the roughest, so you needed those couple people that was just off the hinges and that would just snap and just do whatever without caring about nothing except for making their mark in history.

On the streets, being crazy earned you the highest level of status.[30] Acts of extraordinary violence or bravery got you the respect and admiration of others. It also reduced the number of people willing to challenge or harass you. Very few gang members successfully fulfilled this role. Most were content to hold their own and be violent only when and if it was necessary. Of course, everything in the street was tentative, and roles could shift instantly depending on the situation. Being the wild ones was a dangerous game, but once we achieved that status, most things worked in favor of maintaining that reputation. Even if we got jumped, the fearlessness of taking on so many would only contribute to our persona. It usually didn't happen that way though. Our opponents would sometimes back off, taking our bold behavior to mean that we must be packing considerable firepower. Our targets were also calculated. Take down the core members of groups, and the peripheral ones who ride their coattails will want none of it. Our favorite target in the Northwest was the Grape Street Watts Crips. After several of our incursions into their territory, fighting them in their own mall, even when they outnumbered us significantly, and having their loudmouth figurehead back down from fighting us, their respect dwindled, and our social capital rose. Word spread fast in gangland through the voice mailboxes. Above and beyond all of the other delinquent opportunities, exploration for new conflicts was like a fetish for Ace, KO, and me.[31] The status of fearlessness and stripes (accolades) earned from ever-crazier capers was everything in a conflict gang. The West Side would be much more difficult to infiltrate, as we would learn to our chagrin. They had been banging a lot longer and a lot harder over there.

Ace had a hooptie (old-style gangster car) that he cherished. It was how we got around for these adventures. Our first time rolling through the West Side, we were finding no game, which was strange to us, as we knew that side of town abounded with enemy gangs like Wrecking Crew (WC), LA Boyz (LAB), Indian Creek Gangsters (ICG), and Damage, Inc. We were fools. An unknown group was stalking us the whole time. We pulled into a corner store to get gas. I was riding shotgun. As soon as I opened the door and stepped out of the car, tires started screeching and a car came at me full speed. I dove back into the hooptie and the car crashed into the open door and kept on going. We never expected anything like that. The car door was now barely hanging on, and I had to hold the heavy door closed for the whole drive on the highway home. It was humiliating and hard. Ace was mad at me because he had expected me to jump back out of the car and shoot at the culprits. I knew he was just upset because he really loved that hooptie. There were no more forays into the West Side.

I did finally make it to the Rigsby Courts at some point. A formidable place, it was gated with a single, large cul-de-sac. It had one way in and one way out, with extremely slow-moving gates on both sides. Any attempt at causing trouble in there would mean certain death. I had been hanging out with Dax and Dave when I ended up there. Some people knew of me. I was the Rigsby who wasn't from Rigsby. This caused some of them to give me hard stares, but most didn't care. I wasn't offended. STB had really become my identity anyhow.

Identity was a tricky thing in the world of gangs. Many if not most people operated on the outskirts of street life, choosing to invoke gang status or hide it, when and if it was necessary to navigate through dangerous and questionable territory.[32] They had other things to live for, and the gang was only a portion of their identity performance, albeit one that was a required survival tool in a gangland era. Most of those kids were just trying to make it through somehow and orbited around core gang members who had reputations that were significantly violent enough to carry the gang.

T-Note (3-5-7 CRIP): It just happens to be, because no one wants to be alone in the hard ass street, and not have anyone to clique up with and shit, in case something really goes down. And no one wants to have all they shit out when no one else is watching them, so it is like you automatically become that.

Conversely, the more known you became as a core member, the less ability and desire you had to turn gang identity on and off. Save for the occasional distraction of girls, for the violent core members like KO, Chuckles, and me, the gang was all there was.

Of course, it didn't matter how hot your street star was burning, there was always something more dangerous when you were roaming outside of your gang set space, and the seemingly random chance of police encounters that could either hurt you or help you. In that same trip to the Rigsby, we ended up at Dave's house in a Crip neighborhood called Jolly Time. It was a small hood consisting of a cul-de-sac and the Jolly Time store, where all the gangsters and people from the hood amassed. In Dave's house, there was a paranoid intensity. He sat in a chair holding an SKS assault rifle with a banana clip across his lap. Everybody else had small arms at the ready. Every odd sound would have people scrambling to the windows to check things out. I couldn't get out of there fast enough, but the transportation that had brought us there was already gone. The only way home was the bus stop across the street from the Jolly Time store. Eventually, KO and I decided to go and went to the bus stop. Decked out in red and black, we stared at the storefront full of Jolly Time Gangsters and they stared at us. We were going to get eaten alive. Just then a cop car pulled up. "You are in the wrong place, aren't you?" "Yes sir, we are." They stayed with us until the bus came, chatting about things in a friendly manner. I was taken aback that police would do something so benevolent. My other experiences with them were far different.

I was chased and arrested once when I came back on Judson's Gray Campus after being suspended. I picked up a criminal trespass charge. It was the only time I ever went to the juvenile detention center, and I was there less than an hour before my mom came to pick me up. I received probation and community service for that. My recompense was to get on a boat and clean trash out of the San Antonio River. I actually enjoyed it, though the people in charge of supervising all these gang kids on probation would often make us wait while they stopped at different places to buy and sell drugs.

A cop also assaulted me once. The incident started at Windsor Park Mall (a place that would be so plagued by gang violence that it would eventually close down). We ran into Blacky there. We would have loved to provide Blacky an ass kicking, and he was running his mouth nonstop asking for it, but he was also holding his baby in his arms. He kept taunting us, saying if we were so hard, we wouldn't care about the baby. What an asshole!

Later, we ran into some Camelot Deuce BSV in the mall who said that they had seen Blacky without the baby and wanted to get him. Outside, seven of us piled into Ace's hooptie and began roaming the outskirts of the mall. Seven was too many though. Mall security stopped us, and police were soon on the scene. In my possession was the same long-barreled .22 Ruger that had fallen out of my pants and gotten me in trouble before. The BSV were telling me to run, but I knew it was too late. The cops pulled us out of the car and made us assume the position to search us. As I leaned against the car, my baggy shirt camouflaged the outline of the gun and only the long thin barrel was in my pants close to the middle. The police found bullets in the car, and an officer searched me twice, missing the gun both times. Vincent, a Mexican Camelot Deuce BSV kept mouthing to me to run. I knew I wasn't going to make it. I stood stock still in the same exact position, praying that my shirt would not shift to reveal the pistol. "We know you have a gun. Where is it?" No one said anything. They finally let us go.

We were all dazed and could not believe what had just happened. Vincent was pissed. He was yelling at me that I should have run and demanded that I give him the gun. I gladly handed it over to him. The police were not done with us though. They waited a few blocks and pulled us over again. I immediately said, "Man, you JUST pulled us over. Why are you harassing us?" All I saw was sky. An albino gorilla of an officer had picked me up and slammed me on the hot hood of his police car. His nightstick came crashing down on my neck. I couldn't breathe, and my neck was being crushed. My legs began flailing, I started seeing colors swirling in my eyes, and I began to black out. He finally relented, laughed, and said, "You got something to say now?" I rolled off of the car onto the ground, choking and gasping. Vincent got arrested for the gun, I got a citation for not having my seatbelt on, and all of us got tagged as gang members. Needless to say, I did not find the police very endearing.

We mostly loved to gangbang closer to home. We weren't the hardest set by far, but we also were not soft. There would be gangs that we terrorized, and there were gangs that hunted us. One of our favorite targets was the Tray-Five-Seven (357) Crips in the Universal City/Schertz area. It was a large gang, as every African American gangbanger at Samuel Clemens High School was a Tray-Five-Seven. We wreaked havoc on the 357, catching them slipping or in groups at car washes, parks, or fast-food restaurants. We would put them in check, push them around, or beat them down. We always came out either in force or with our most hardcore contingents. They never claimed a victory on us.

But things go both ways. On one occasion, we were at the Wendy's next to Windsor Park Mall. It was in the afternoon, broad daylight, and the restaurant was full of conventional people. A car came screeching up, and out poured four East Terrace Gangster Crips. They ran up to our table and immediately began talking crazy to us. We stood up, and then the younger one pulled out a gun, and put it up against KO's head. He yelled at KO, "Say something else! Say something!" He slapped KO, and then they all ran back to their car and drove away. The entire restaurant was appalled and concerned for us, but that was the way it went in our world.

In the neighborhood, there were people who thought of us as trouble, but there were also those that appreciated us. You never heard about a house being burglarized in our hood. Some people would even tell us that if trouble came to the hood, they would bring their guns out and defend the place right along with us. We were far from all-knowing though, as a major tragedy hit the neighborhood right under our noses. On a summer night, I was talking on the phone with my girlfriend Daisy when I heard a gunshot followed by a car screech. The shot was so loud that I was momentarily certain that I was the victim, as I was standing near a window. I recovered my senses and ran outside, as did all of the neighbors. A couple of houses down, there was a guy lying face down with his brains and blood scattered all over the street. He was much older than us, so we didn't know him. He had a

4-1. "Wicked." (Bolden personal photos.)

beautiful red Cadillac decked out with nice rims. Someone had killed him and stolen his car. I questioned all of the neighborhood STB and our BSV allies, but no one had anything to do with it. The rumor mill traced the event back to the Wheatley Courts, but we never found out for certain.

Despite all of the antics I have described, most days were uneventful. Malcolm Klein, the premier researcher on street gangs once said, "It's a boring life. The only thing that is equally as boring is being a researcher watching gang members."[33] In a sense, that is true. The vast majority of time was spent sitting around playing dominoes or spades, drinking Strawberry Hill, Mickeys, Mad Dog 20/20s, or Thunderbird with Kool-Aid, all of which were either stolen from a corner store or bought from unscrupulous cashiers who did not care that we were underage.[34] Ace, Stick, and I would spend most nights having three-way phone calls, laughing about everything in the world, or prank-calling people. We also spent a lot of time rapping or making music.

On occasion I would drop acid with DJ, and we would find ourselves wandering through tunnel systems that ran under streets. We would talk about the problems of the world and how they could be fixed. I, like many other gang members, suffered from status anxiety. The reputations we had built prevented us from voicing opposition to gang behaviors, even when we disagreed. In one-on-one contexts, like the times I hung out with DJ, it was easier to admit vulnerabilities, discuss misgivings about our own involvement, and discover the shared delusion of believing that others were more committed to the gang lifestyle.[35] It is easy to think that gangsters would be callous, but when it was just one on one, we would bond over our vulnerabilities and talk about how we wished for a better life. The real problem was that we had no hope.

CHAPTER 5

Escalation

THOUGH MORE DELINQUENT than other youth, gang members did not spend all of their time engaged in bad behavior. Like other adolescents, they tended to drift between conventional and deviant behavior.[1] Contact with the criminal justice system, marginalization from both family and school pushing a person away from legitimate society, and the gang simultaneously pulling someone toward it with its promises of inclusion, work as a trifecta to solidify an individual's underworld identity. The person then has the perception that there is no option left but the hood.[2] The more time spent on the streets, the more conflict occurs, and violence only begets more violence. Affronts are answered with retaliatory violence, which is then reciprocated more severely, and so on.[3] My individual spiral away from school and into the gang was about to reach a tipping point from which there was no return.

Through the 1990s, the media-fueled panic on juvenile crime combined with the prevailing crime-control ethos and the school accountability movement championed by Texas governors Bill Clements and George W. Bush, spurred legislatures across the country to implement zero-tolerance policies in schools.[4] This new regime gave schools an easy tool to excise youth that were viewed as irredeemable, allowing the schools to focus their efforts on students that they thought showed potential for success. Blacks,[5] Latinos, and poor kids would feel the brunt of this disciplinary whiplash, as they were kicked out of school for any infraction, regardless of context, and primed for encounters with the criminal justice system.

I only made it through the first four days of my junior year before being expelled. Judson Rockets' football had been in peak form, and the night before games there would be a large pep rally. The first one of the year, called Meet the Rockets, was held at the huge football stadium Pepsi Cola had bought for the school. That school year, Converse Judson would win the state championship against Odessa Permian, the team that inspired the book, film, and TV series *Friday Night Lights*. But I wouldn't be around for that.

That night, I was roaming around with a contingent of various Bloods. As we walked through one of the corridors under the bleachers, two Crips attacked Dizzy, a BSV who was walking in the front of the group. He fought back, and other Bloods rushed to his aid. Someone tapped me on the shoulder. I turned around and Blacky sucker punched me square in the face. I landed on my back. I popped back up to see Chuckles and Blacky go toe-to-toe, and I went after him also. Blacky fell to his knees and desperately tried to shield himself from our retaliation. Other fights were going on all around us. Someone shouted that "po-po" was coming and everybody fled except for Chuckles and me. I was enraged and wanted to make Blacky pay for all the years of shit I had gotten from him. We were arrested and taken to the Converse police station. For some reason, no charges were brought against us, and the school said that they would handle it internally.

Dizzy would later become best friends with Stick, but he held an eternal grudge against me over that incident. He faulted me for ruining his life because he believed I snitched on him, which, in essence, I unintentionally did. I had to come back to Judson with my mother to face a tribunal of four principals. I was subjected to a half-hour of them questioning me and berating me, "You are nothing but a troublemaker," "We will not tolerate you on our campus," "The school colors of red and gray are the only colors representing this campus," and so on about what worthless human beings my loser gang friends and I were. After wearing me down with the tirade, I was ambushed by the one principal playing good cop, with the question, "So what happened to Dizzy?" "He didn't do anything wrong. He got jumped on by several people. He was only defending himself," I said. Shit! They had caught me off guard.

In the mid-1990s, schools en masse shifted to harsh disciplinary policies like zero tolerance, in which students were suspended or expelled for any infraction. Black and other minority youth were the primary recipients of this form of discipline. Once they were caught in this net it would land them out of schools, into the streets, and ultimately into the criminal justice system.[6] Judson had moved toward zero tolerance, contributing their piece for the school-to-prison pipeline. According to those policies, self-defense was not even allowed when a person was being attacked. Dizzy would face consequences for that. Though I highly doubt my slip was the cause of all the grief in his world, he seemed to blame me for it. It did not matter that this incident started with both of us defending ourselves; the result was that we were just two more people being flushed down the school-to-prison-pipeline toilet. I was 16, which meant most places would not even consider me for employment. My exile from school ensured that my life would be headed for disaster, as I would be spending all of my time in the streets . . . and the streets were becoming deadly.

Gangs have less control over the actions of individual members than what is portrayed in the media. Rather than attacking rivals, the volatile nature of individual gang members might lead them to kill allies or members of their own gang.[7] I wouldn't see Blacky again. Crips had the tendency to cannibalize themselves and fight other Crip groups. Blacky and some East Terrace Gangsters would commit a drive-by on the Wheatley Court Gangsters. The Wheatley Courts was another very large and formidable East Side Crip neighborhood. Blacky's drive-by would kill a little kid and land him in prison with a fifty-year sentence. The kid was the younger brother of a prominent Wheatley Court Gangster. That event would lead them to transition into Wheatley Court Texas and change their color to red, though they initially identified themselves as neutral. Seeing this large, powerful group of former Crips show up everywhere wearing crimson was surreal.

PRANX (WHEATLEY COURT TEXAS/WCT): Because my hood was, at first they was Crips and then they went to Bloods, I don't know the whole deal behind it, but then they went to Bloods. And it was WCG [Wheatley Court Gangsters] and then it became WCT and then you know it just, they became Bloods and then they didn't like other Crips, that is just how it go, you don't, you don't affiliate with Crips. But a lot of the OGs [Original Gangsters] were Crips but a lot of the people were Bloods so . . .

Other Crip groups would implode. The most renowned member of the DOG would march one of his associates into the woods behind their neighborhood and put à bullet in the back of his head. The other DOG [Dope Overthrowing Gangsters] succumbed to disillusionment and quit banging, or they bounced to other gangs.

CAJUN (DOG): The one that touched my heart the most was uh, you know I was young, I was 15 and my best friend was murdered. I say best friend loosely you know, we were roll dogs, we were companions, we spent quite a bit of time together when we were young, and we lived right down the street from each other. And one of our friends murdered him, right here where we are sitting doing this interview, in this park. You know and they were friends, you know shot him in the head.

Two of the three leaders of the Tray-Five-Seven would get into an argument with each other at a card game that ended with one of them dead and the other in prison, leading to a rapid disintegration of the gang.

T-Note (3-5-7 crip): You know [redacted] and [redacted] and shit. Two
niggas in the same gang; they were roommates. Get into some little
bullshit argument, they gonna kill each other over a game of fucking
Spades. Then whatever the fuck happened, [redacted] being little and
[redacted] being bigger and shit. He scared, don't want to take the ass
whooping, don't even want to try to talk with his partner, so he just
dump on that nigga.

Conflict on the streets had escalated to the point that people were
considered lucky if they only received a beatdown. Retaliation was always
expected, so gangsters opted for finalizing confrontations on the first encounter. Shooting had become the name of the game. Being caught slipping
could likely end your life. Everyone started carrying guns, either for protection, identity formation, or impression management to ward away opponents.[8]
The previous ten years had seen a 79 percent increase in juvenile murder
nationwide, peaking in 1993 with 2,880 juvenile homicides.[9] Between the
wholesale abandonment of youth by school systems through zero tolerance,
the proliferation of street gangs, and the easy availability of guns, violent
escalation seemed inevitable. I needed to be prepared for the street, but I
had learned the hard way, from carrying that long Ruger, that a big gun was
unreasonable for someone of my small stature. I carried a two-shot .38 Der-
ringer, a forty-dollar purchase from someone's burglary loot, that was easily
concealable.

DJ (stb): I mean our streets got flooded with guns in the first place, that was
part two of the reason why people bang, cause hey, shit people all got
guns, we may [as well] gang bang you know what I'm saying, I remember guns were fifteen, twenty dollars a pop.

The gang continued to expand outside of the neighborhood. The city
was large and dangerous, which made it increasingly important to have allies
and satellite members. Kinship was another way in which gangs expanded.[10]
My cousin, Caleb, joined STB, becoming the youngest member.

Caleb (stb): Well, I figured I wanted to follow in my cousin's footsteps,
cause I wanted to be like him, I wanted to do what he was doing.

He was in his last year at Krueger Middle School, which was in the
Roosevelt school district, fairly far away from the rest of us. There were
only four other baby gangster Bloods at Krueger but many Altadena Blocc
Crips. Being outnumbered meant searching for more delinquent peers to
bolster safety.[11] The Bloods there survived by being allied with the Latino
gangs, particularly the Lady Watts and Lil' Watts X3 (LWS 13). The LWS

13 was a Sureño gang that had migrated from California and was initially on friendly terms with the Blue circle. The leader of the Lil' Watts was killed by the Ambrose at a party, which effectively ended the LWS alliance with blue, and they represented the black rag from there on out. P-Ma was the leader of the Lady Watts, and it was her brother who had been murdered. She did all she could to keep the Watts together. P-Ma was a force of nature like I had never seen. She was big in both size and heart and she would barrel through anyone in her way, male or female. She took care of her people and would not tolerate disloyalty.

Chuckles and I would stop in occasionally to check on Caleb and his crew. Chuckles had attended school there and was somewhat known in the area. The principal of Krueger Middle School hated Chuckles and me passionately, and if someone said our names, it would drive her into a fury. She had no power over us, except to make sure that we did not set foot on her campus, and that fact seemed to enrage her. Any student at Krueger that she suspected of being under our influence would face her wrath, however, and they received harsh punishments if she caught them talking to us through the fence.

For the most part, Caleb seemed to do fine, even under those conditions. When his enemies started getting out of line, I took one of his homeboys with me to a party I had heard about, that the Crips and Ambrose were having in Caleb's neighborhood. There were a bunch of them outside that saw me coming. I pulled out the .38 and they dropped to the ground. I aimed above their heads and fired, knowing that I wasn't going to hit anyone. They knew who I was, and the warning shot was effective enough. People didn't mess with Caleb for a while after that.

CALEB (STB): I remember one time specific, I was across the street or actually down the street and two of our guys were walking up to a party that was hosted by Ambrose and I knew what they were going to end up doing and words were being thrown out in the street and the next thing you know gunfire. . . . I looked up to my cousin because basically it was everything, the way I looked at it everything revolved around him. If something was going to happen, he was involved with it, if there was money to be made, he was involved with it, if guns needed to be there he had them, so basically, you know a lot of people looked up to him, a lot of people still look up to him and that's where I wanted to be when I joined the gang; I wanted everybody to look up to me just like him. And another couple of cats [names redacted], they looked up to him cause he was big, if there was any problems they could call him and then they would all get together to hang out with, and he was a crazy motherfucker because he would, if someone needed to be shot, was right there asking who.

The dynamic of gang members and guns includes posturing and impression management. Fear of a person's perceived capacity for violence was an important strategy used to sidestep having to actually use violence.[12] There is a common misconception that, on the street, people feel invincible with guns. For me, that couldn't be further from the truth. People got dropped all the time, and guns were easily accessible to anyone with a desire to get one. I did feel that without a gun I was likely to be the one getting dropped. Willingness to use a gun also boiled down to a simple calculation—how much of my teeth do I need to show to get other predators to back off? It is not something I wanted to do, as my heart would race and airways would constrict anytime I had to use one, but that is how I got my point across in gangland. Guns did not make me strong; the people in my gang did that.

Gangs have a way of propagating themselves, and Caleb was not the only younger recruit. With new people come new dynamics. I found Devil in one of the baby gangster groups in the Roosevelt district. I immediately saw that he was too advanced for the group he was hanging around with and plucked him up for STB. Devil was a soldier. Other people thought his loyalty to me was stronger than his loyalty to the gang.

I also found my girlfriend, Daisy, in a neighborhood of the Roosevelt district, occupied by Crips and Lil' Watts X3. A Latina, she was loosely affiliated with the mixed-race Altadena Blocc Crips in the area. She wasn't much interested in hanging around with a Blood at first, but my persistence won her over. I would spend every moment I could with her, and falling in love would dramatically reduce my gangbanging activities, which annoyed Ace to no end. It is amazing what prosocial turning points like starting a relationship can do to one's behavior.[13] Unfortunately, it would not be enough to pull me out; instead, I pulled her in.

KO went to Detroit for a while, and when he and his sister, Coco, came back, they were claiming Almighty Vice Lord (AVL). The Vice Lords arose in the St. Charles Reformatory for Boys and the North Lawndale neighborhood of Chicago in the late 1950s. They would become one of the four largest gangs in Chicago and be one of the three architects of the People nation alliance. The history of the gang included attempts at being prosocial, neighborhood cleanup, civil rights activism, and various alliances before completely abandoning their attempts at legitimacy in the early 1970s. As a result, the Vice Lords had a much more sophisticated ideology incorporating spirituality and leadership structure.[14] I didn't care about any of it though. KO was one of my closest homeboys. If he was going to bang Vice Lord, I would bang it right alongside him. Their colors were red, black, and gold so it did not take much to add it to my repertoire. I had another initiation, but this time it was just one on one with KO. True to his name, he knocked me out cold.

The Vice Lords had yet to make an appearance in San Antonio; so as far as we knew, we were the first. KO, Coco, Devil, and I would be viewed as the Vice Lord contingent of the STB. Daisy also joined the Vice Lords, as did her friend Snappy, who crossed over from the Killing All Problems (KAP) Crip gang. Although most of the STBs did not approve, it ultimately didn't matter.

DAISY (VICE LORDS): It was just me and one other girl, her name was [redacted] and her and her brother are the ones that brought the Vice Lords here to San Antonio. And they asked me if I wanted to be a part of it, because of course my boyfriend was and I said yes! So, she just pretty much knocked me out [*laughs*] and that was it, we hugged and that was it.

Dangerous streets called for more dangerous allies. Each addition made us feel safer, but, in reality, they just added new dimensions to our problems. Another Blood had emerged, named Ricky. Technically a Blood Stone Villain, he spent most of his time hanging out with STB. Ricky was exceptionally hard core. He came to us out of California, and his identity was purely gang banging. We knew very little about him, other than that he did not seem to care about anything but the gang. He had a hair trigger temper, and people he thought were looking at him wrong would get knocked out. Though Blood to the fullest, he always wore head to toe blue, with a neatly ironed red bandana hanging out of his pocket. We would jokingly call him Flu Time Piru ("flu" being Blood lingo for the color blue). He would use his blue uniform to walk up to unsuspecting Crips and sneak attack them. Ricky often carried around a small duffle bag, and inside it he kept a sawed-off shotgun that he had named Tasha.

Gang violence was rarely planned and was mostly the result of random encounters. It would be one of these chance meetings that would ensnare me in the cycle of violence and bring my whole world crashing down. On some day in March 1995, Devil, Daisy, and I were hanging out at my house when Ricky came by. Bored and with no transportation, we decided to hop on a bus and go to the movies. The closest movie theater at the time was the Galaxy, which was near Windsor Park Mall. We got off the bus at the stop nearest the theater but still had quite a distance and a highway to cross.

As we walked through the parking lots and alleys behind various businesses, we encountered someone wearing all red. It turns out the guy, Marvin, was a Crip that Devil knew from Roosevelt. He was in all red because he had been working at Rally's and was wearing their uniform. We stared at each other, tense, and unmoving. Though Marvin was outnumbered, he was emboldened by being on his own territory. Knowing that he only had to turn the corner to be in his own neighborhood, he broke the silence,

"Oh, y'all think y'all hard." Devil hit him up with gang signs in response, "Sup Blood. STB! Almighty Vice Lord! Fuck Crabs!" The set tripping and disrespect got everyone's adrenaline immediately pumping." Crab" is a disrespectful name for Crips; "Slob" is a disrespectful name for Bloods. It was Marvin's move, and he wasn't backing down. He responded, "Rollin' 60s, Cuz! I ain't scared of you Slobs!" Ricky pulled the sawed-off out of his bag. Marvin's hands shot up while he backed away. The look on his face was both fearful and furious. Everyone knew that this was going to end badly. "Oh, oh, it is going to be like that, it is going to be like that?" he kept saying. "Damn, right it is going to B like that," Ricky responded in a level voice. "Nah, it is going to C like that," Marvin said as he got close to the corner and turned to run. The repeated boom of the 12-gauge firing was deafening. Marvin was bent over and his movement was erratic. The ringing in my ears enhanced my confusion as to how he was still running. He rounded the corner and made it into his neighborhood.

Most of the situations I had been in with Ricky up until this point had resulted in fighting, but those had been mitigated by the location of events. People rarely went beyond fistfights at school. We all knew that when it came down to it, though, Ricky was a shooter. Contrary to popular belief, most gang members are not shooters, although a gang's reputation often relies on having a few people who are willing to use a gun.

T-Note (3-5-7 CRIP): You are trying to be a part of that, and you don't really know what it takes to be that tough guy, or to be that nigga who is carrying guns and got bodies and shit like that and ain't even sweating it. It is easy to look up to 'em and want to be like that but it is hard to walk in his shoes and shit and carry out those duties.

There is no way to tell what triggered the gunfire in that moment with Ricky. It could have been that Marvin's return to his neighborhood would pose a significant threat to us, or it could just have been the way Ricky handled things when not under conventional restraints. Either way, the situation had gone from minor to severe in seconds, and I had not been expecting it.

We dashed in the other direction and played real life *Frogger* as we ran across the highway. Cars were not stopping, but the adrenaline and impending doom at the hands of the police or the Rollin' 60s, spurred us to brave the danger in front of us instead. When we got to the other side, we didn't know what to do. There were no accolades or celebration. The gravity of what had just occurred was incomprehensible. We were swirling in panic, confusion, dread, and breathlessness. We had nowhere to go, so we just went to the movies. We didn't care which one, we just bought tickets and sat down in one. Full of adrenaline and unable to process what had just happened, the pictures in front of my face made no sense. Everything played back in my memory on endless repeat. I only had the presence of mind to nervously kick my .38 under the seats.

The police came in like we were America's Most Wanted. They were all over the theater, and there were so many guns pointed at our heads that I was afraid to breathe. We were arrested, and when they brought us outside, the news media were everywhere. They focused on me, probably because my braids and nails made me look the most threatening and interesting. The cameras stayed in my face, flashing and filming. Family and friends would see me all over the news.

The police took us to Marvin's neighborhood where they made sure to parade us in front of his homeboys. Once they got a good look, we were brought into the ambulance for Marvin to identify us. He lay on his stomach with his back exposed while the paramedics worked on him. He was bleeding from lots of tiny holes in his back. It turns out that Ricky had loaded his gun with buckshot.

At the police station we were all kept separate, but Daisy, Devil, and I were in the same general area. We would never see Ricky again. During the holding pattern while we were interrogated, I was with two cops who threatened me the whole time. The Hispanic one kept telling me how he couldn't wait to cut my nuts off and how we were going down for attempted murder. I was tense and wary and did not respond in any manner. They finally left me alone, and another person, Officer Pink, came in to talk to me. He was a gang investigator, and he was very friendly. He kept making jokes about gangs that were my enemies, and I eventually cracked a smile. He just seemed interested in chit chatting about gangs. He was a clever hunter, waiting patiently for his moment to strike. When he finally did, I wouldn't see it coming.

They would eventually let both Daisy and Devil go under the recognizance of their parents. I was 17, so they sent me to the city's detention center over the seat belt citation that I had never paid. I served a few hours, and the magistrate released me with time served. It was my face that was all over the media, so everyone thought I had shot Marvin. My phone rang nonstop. My street credibility had just been dramatically enhanced, but so had the list of people wanting to take me out. A new cycle of violence had begun, and retribution was coming my way. Marvin would survive his injuries, but he walked with a limp afterward. Ricky was 17 and already had fourteen felonies under his belt. He was sentenced to thirty-five years.

Two months later, in May 1995, I had plans to get my mom a gift for Mother's Day. I had seen those aquariums with fake plastic fish swimming around and wanted to get one for her because she loved the oceans and sea creatures. Daisy and I were walking to the flea market in her neighborhood to buy it. Daisy lived in Altadena Blocc Crip territory, but I had always walked around with impunity there because I wasn't afraid of that crew, and Daisy knew most of them. The flea market was on Eisenhauer Road, about a half-mile from her house.

A hooptie full of the neighborhood ABC rolled by, and they started screaming out the window at me, "Fuck you, Cuz!" I threw up my gang signs and gave them the middle finger back. They kept rolling, but I had a bad feeling about it. I was slipping. They made a U-turn at some point and caught back up with us as we reached an empty parking lot. It was broad daylight, and we were in plain sight of many people across the street in the flea market parking lot.

The Crips seemed to flow endlessly from the hooptie, like it was a clown car. Heading up the pack was Zilla. I was a bit surprised to see her, because she was much older than the others and usually hung around older, more sophisticated Crips involved in drugs and heavy crime, and with harder reputations, like the gang Marvin was from. Her younger brother, G-Rocc, seemed to be the central member of this group of Altadena Blocc Crips. Some of the Crips rushed me, grabbed me, and immobilized me. Zilla, who was a sizeable person, and some others went to work on Daisy. My girlfriend had always been dainty and she never stood a chance. They beat her senseless. Another car of Crips pulled up and out popped more of G-Rocc's people, including his two main partners, A-Dog and D-Town, and a Crip that I didn't know, leading them toward me. I would immediately understand that he was one of Marvin's homies, "I heard you shot my homeboy, Cuz!" He said, as he snatched my herringbone necklace off of my neck. The people holding me had momentarily loosened their grips, and I took the chance to break free and connect my fist with the guy's face. He fell underneath me from the momentum of my hit. All of the Crips began pummeling me. It felt like a hundred fists raining down on my back and head. It was all I could do to dish out some punishment to the guy beneath me as well. I could not see what was happening to Daisy.

It finally stopped, and they left us lying there, bloody, pulpy messes, as concerned bystanders from the flea market parking lot came rushing over to render aid. The police came to take a report but didn't seem very concerned. "Yeah, we know those guys" was all they said. They didn't even offer to take us home.

When I finally got home, I took a bath. Soaking my wounds, I thought about nothing but revenge. It was a cold, pure anger that I had not felt before. I did not care that the attack was in response to the assault on Marvin. In gangland, their affront could not go unanswered. My friends called me nonstop. When I finally walked out of the house, they were all there in force. "Tomorrow," I said, "We will get them tomorrow."

Gangsters are not morning people. Only five homies showed up the next morning. We rolled over to G-Rocc's house where the ABC crew was known to hang out. I knew some of them were there. The six of us took positions around the yard and I knocked on the door and called them out. "I'm going to give you this chance to come out and fight me one on one. If you don't come out, then you know what it is going to be." They didn't come out, and we left.

That night, all the boys were back over in my yard getting drunk, high, and riled up. Alcohol often provided the liquid courage that enabled acts of violence.[15] "Let's make it a Crip Killer summer," they were saying. "Let's take out our enemies." Guns started coming out and people began loading up. Some went into a car and the rest of us into a pickup truck. I sat in the back of the truck with a .22 rifle. People were silent. People were angry. People were scared.

We drove the distance to G-Rocc's house. The ABC Crips were having a party, and a lot of them were outside in the yard. The car went up first to scope the scene and gave us the signal. When they saw the car, they began running inside. "You want me to do it?" Chuckles asked, and I knew he would have done it. "No, this is on me," I said, trying to block out the fear to steel myself for what was about to happen. The truck crept by at a snail's pace. Everyone else in the bed of the pickup truck laid down flat.

Pop-pop-pop-pop-pop-pop-pop-pop. Eight shots. Someone fell down in the doorway. The truck picked up speed but before we could round the corner, there were flashing red and blue lights everywhere. Not even thirty seconds had passed, and we were completely surrounded by police.

Drive-by shootings are a distinct and common mode of gang violence in spread-out cities like those in the southern and western states. They are used to hunt particular enemies, elevate a gang or gang member's status, or retaliate. Rapid mobility allows for a surprise attack and a quick return to a gang's territory.[16] Police in San Antonio had a lot of experience with drive-bys, and this time they seemed to know what was going to happen and were just waiting for it.

Cops were everywhere, but there was no sense of urgency with them. They knew they had this one in the bag. As they were running the Q-tips over my hands to look for gunpowder, the same albino gorilla cop who had choked me before walked up. "Hahaha- HA! Hey, Wicked, you remember when I bounced your ass off of the top of my police car? Haha-HA! We got your ass now." And I knew that they did. I had been caught red-handed for a drive-by shooting. It was surreal, being surrounded by police lights and see-ing the glee on the faces of some cops. I forgot all about my target and why I had attacked them. My main concern was that I didn't want my homeboys to go down with me. Others have claimed that the connection between

gangsters is false, but that was not my experience. We were certainly mis-
guided and foolish, but I did love them, the only way I knew how to.

All of us were booked into Bexar County Jail. Everyone was keeping
their mouth shut, except Chaps, who was willing to snitch because he had a
severe probation violation hanging over his head. Chaps was the driver of
the truck, a peripheral member who mostly hung around with DJ. I barely
knew him. It didn't matter, though. I admitted to the crime so that the
others would be released.

DJ (STB): Yes, I had two best friends basically at the time. They were both
involved in the same situation. They were both involved in several
other situations, but this was the main situation you know where one
went to prison for quite a while, and the other went to county jail for
almost a year and when he got out cops wouldn't stop messing with
him, so he just went ahead and jumped state. I ain't heard from him.

One by one, Dax, KO, Ace, Chuckles, and the rest were let out of jail, leaving me there alone. No one else was hit in the shooting except the person in
the doorway, who was G-Rocc's stepfather. For some reason, while everyone else was hitting the floor, he chose to stand in the doorway. He fell when
a bullet grazed his neck. Thankfully, his injuries were far from life threatening, but it had been too close to being something catastrophic. A violent crime
at age 17 in Texas meant that I would be adjudicated as an adult. My charge
was aggravated assault with a deadly weapon.

CHAPTER 6

Purgatory

I ONLY SPENT a few days in jail before my mother posted the $25,000 bond. I'm still not sure how she raised the money to do it. I would later learn from her that my father wanted no part in it and preferred to leave me inside. I was given a court-appointed attorney who spent most of his time lecturing me, scolding me, and treating me with contempt. "That was stupid and you will face the consequences for it!" I learned very quickly that just because he represented me it did not mean that he was on my side. I was going to face judgment with a false ally. Ideally, everyone hopes for a zealous advocate in a defense attorney, but in reality, the defendant is often paired with someone who is overworked, underpaid, or not interested in putting forth the effort. With my life on the line and my "defender" having no respect for me, I knew I was in trouble.[1] If anything was going to work in my favor, it would be of my own doing. Over the summer, my gang banging stopped, and I spent every moment that I could with Daisy, with whom I was completely in love.

For the first time, I began to contemplate having a life beyond the gang. I was fully into my relationship with Daisy and realized that the gang and my upcoming court date were obstacles to any real chance at a future. I did not know if I could turn it around, but I started taking steps in that direction. I finally cut my nails, and the braids came off. I started getting haircuts to look like a square kid. I went to take the tests for my GED, and though I hadn't studied for it or attended much school the last two years at Judson, I passed with ease. I was awarded the GED and was even automatically enrolled in the National Adult Education Honors Society. I was shocked at this development and extremely proud of it. Things seemed to be going well, though there was the lurking shadow of my crime and upcoming trial.

Unexpectedly, I got a summons to court that September. This wasn't my trial date, and the hearing was a complete surprise to my attorney and me. The district attorney (DA) was asking the judge to revoke my bond because I had been threatening the victims. This wasn't actually true.

Though I was not factually guilty of the accusation, the prosecutor still had the power to hold me legally guilty.[2] The DA's motion to revoke was based on two things reported by G-Rocc's family. At some point over the summer, while Daisy was with me, she was talking on the phone with one of her friends. G-Rocc and A-Dog came to the friend's house, and when they realized the girl was talking to Daisy, they grabbed the phone and started threatening her. I got on the phone and sternly told them that under no circumstances would I allow them to disrespect Daisy. "What are you going to do? Shoot at us with a .22?" they mocked. "Would you like me to try with something larger?" I responded. They stayed quiet. "I'll tell you again, DO NOT DISRESPECT DAISY!" and that was the end of the conversation.

The other thing the DA used against me was my own rap.[3] There was a greeting message on one of my voice mailboxes where I was rapping about the shooting that had occurred. Though I was insulting them in the rap, the song was about the prior incident, not a new threat against them. It is common to tell street stories through rap, and since it is a form of artistic expression, it is often filled with hypermasculine braggadocio or made-up statements that help it fit a rhyme scheme. Sometimes threats in the lyrics were real, sometimes they were not; it was difficult to say.[4] Rap occupied an integral part of the street subculture, serving as an artistic outlet for indi- viduals and a recognizable reflection of the struggles and experience of that life. In the criminal justice system, however, prosecutors sidestepped the concept of rap as artistic expression, relied on negative stereotypes, and argued that an individual's rap lyrics are a confession, indication of a threat, or evidence of a malicious character. Despite a lack of contextual analysis or real understanding of lyrics, several convictions have been obtained based on an individual's rap lyrics. Several convictions have also been overturned based on the improper use of rap lyrics in court.[5]

My public defender was completely unprepared. I asked to represent myself but was shut down by my attorney. I wanted to bring up how both instances had been initiated by the other gang members, not by me. They had started threatening Daisy first, and they had searched out and called the mailbox to hear me rapping because it was not a message that was left for them. My attorney did not bring up either point. His defense was paltry and virtually nonexistent beyond a promise that I was doing well and would behave myself. The judge approved the motion to revoke and raised my bail to $75,000. The bailiff took me back to Bexar County Adult Detention Center.

I was put in a general population wing that was nothing like my previous experience. The first time I was in, my wing had very few people in it, and everyone had their own cell. It was quiet. This time, the wing was completely full. The noise was so loud that everything was indistinct. There were people everywhere, so finding a place to sit was difficult. Everyone there was an adult, and most were large in build. I knew how to navigate the streets and all of its predators, but I was a foreigner here, outclassed in size, supporters, and savvy. I was vulnerable. I did the only thing I could do, which was to keep my mouth shut and observe. There were a few funny stares, but for the most part, people did not seem to pay attention to me.

The person sharing a cell with me was Ghoul. He was a Black man with an impossibly squeaky voice, though he was gargantuan. He was easily over three hundred pounds, and his insistence on being on the top bunk worried me to no end, as I thought I would be flattened at any moment, should the tiny bed frame fail to support him. I didn't know how right I was to be afraid. Ghoul introduced me to his friends, who let me sit with them to eat and play cards. Ghoul asked me a ton of questions about my family and the letters I would write. He always seemed friendly and interested.

On the third night, I made the mistake of sleeping on my stomach. I woke up as my body was being crushed. Ghoul was on top of me and the weight was unbearable. He rammed my face into the pillow. "Don't make a sound!" he said. His childlike voice now sounded sinister. Between his weight and the pillow, I couldn't breathe. He pulled down my boxers. I felt a sharp pain and heard him panting as he forced himself inside of my body. It was probably over in seconds, but it lasted an eternity. "I know where your family lives. If you say anything, something is going to happen to them," as he climbed up the ladder to his bunk. His threat did not bother me. I was too in shock over what happened to even consider it. My insides felt shredded, and I immediately ran to the toilet to defecate. It seemed to never stop coming out, and when it did, I wiped myself for hours. I sat on the toilet the entire night, tears streaming down my face, while Ghoul watched me silently. I felt so much physical pain, humiliation, anger, frustration, helplessness, and horror. I'm certain I went temporarily insane sitting on that steel toilet.

I didn't come out of the cell for breakfast. I did not come out for lunch. "You have to come out of the cell," Ghoul said to me angrily, "people are going to start wondering." I came out of the cell for dinner. Ghoul and all of his friends looked at me. Some of them snickered and pointed while Ghoul shook his head. I couldn't handle it. I turned to sit somewhere else, but then I saw that Blinky was in the guardroom.

Blinky was a Bexar County sheriff who had been kind to me for the short time I had been in the detention center. I had given him his nickname because he blinked incessantly to the point of distraction. My feet carried me to the guardroom. I motioned for Blinky to come out. When he opened the door to ask what was up, I could not find my voice to respond. Tears fell uncontrollably from my eyes. He told the other deputies that he would be back, and then took me out of the wing. He sat me in a room and asked me what happened. I couldn't speak. My throat and my heart felt like they were constricting, and I couldn't breathe again. I couldn't stop trembling. He waited patiently. Blue eyes staring at me. Blinking. Blinking. It took all my might to say it. "He raped me." And my voice gave out again. I curled my head into my lap and sobbed uncontrollably.

They took me to the medical ward, which had ten large cells with single beds. Almost all of the other inmates were psych patients or suicide attempts. I spent a long time on my stomach while the medical staff conducted a rape kit on me. I had probably shit away or wiped away most of the evidence, but I was torn up. I would have severe hemorrhoid problems for a long time after that.

One of the deputies told me that the word was out that Ghoul had raped a 17-year-old kid, and that he was conveniently left in a place where some of the more privileged inmates could have their way beating him down. I don't know if that was true or not, and I didn't care. I never again heard about Ghoul or what happened to him.

There was no real way to know the commonality of sexual assaults in jails and prisons. Just a year later, 18-year-old Rodney Hulin Jr. would commit suicide in a Texas prison after being sexually assaulted. Hulin became an icon in the fight against prison rape. In 2003, the federal government passed the Prison Rape Elimination Act (PREA), which held zero tolerance for sexual assault in prisons and began tracking statistics on the crime. To date, Texas remains as one of four states that are in noncompliance with PREA.

The medical wing of the detention center felt like a mental asylum because the inmates walked around in hospital gowns and had color-coded armbands indicating why they were there. The staff was very nice. There was always a little something extra with the meals, like a cookie or a brownie. Inmates in the medical wing were also allowed more phone calls.

My mom was hysterical over what happened to me. She said she would move mountains to get me out, and she did. She scrambled to get money from everywhere and took out a loan. I think my father's unwillingness to assist in trying to get me out was the final straw in the deterioration of their relationship. After two weeks, my mom had raised enough money and bonded me out.

I waited in trepidation for my trial. The DA had been offering me a plea bargain of ten years, and my public defender was pushing me to take it. After the horror I had been through, I wasn't going to be bullied into the plea bargain.[6] Though people generally thought of a plea bargain as a better deal for the defendant, I knew in my gut that it wasn't true. After learning about all my options, I chose to plead guilty but to take it to a jury trial for sentencing. That annoyed both the DA and my attorney. Public defenders get paid the same whether the case ends in a plea bargain or continues, so there is no incentive for them to want to go to trial.[7]

The three-day trial began in early December 1995, and weighing all of the options presented to me, I asked for it to be a closed session, which probably helped me tremendously. A closed trial meant that, during proceedings, only my attorney, the prosecution team, the judge, and the jury could be in the court with me. No one else could watch what happened, and witnesses would not know about each other's testimony.

I had already pleaded guilty to the crime, so the defense strategy was to convince the jury that the attack against Daisy and me should mitigate the punishment they handed down. He also emphasized my youth and lack of sophistication, pointing out that since the scope was put on the gun backward I could not have been using it to aim.

On the first day of the trial, when I was entering the courthouse, I ran into Officer Pink. It took me a moment to recognize him as the funny gang investigator. "Hey buddy," he said, and smiled. "It's all right, you can shake my hand." And we shook hands. He was two-faced. In the trial he was called as a witness for the prosecution. "Wicked is a menace to society and needs to be incarcerated for as long as possible," he said. It then became apparent that the prosecution's strategy was to convince the jury that I was a notorious gang member. Strangely, many of their witnesses seemed to make things better for me, like a comedy of errors. One by one, the prosecution called on police officers from all over the county to identify me as a gang member, and they did. The problem was that they all identified a different gang that I was in, Rigsby Court Gangsters, Juvenile Blood Mafia, Sa Town Bloods, Vice Lords. Their identifications were technically true, though there was one other random Crip gang named that was completely false. You could tell by the jurors' faces that it was becoming a bit difficult to believe and that the prosecution was trying too hard on this gang member thing. The DA was getting frustrated. I guess they forgot to verify which gang the officers were going to say I was in, but they emphasized the point that at least all the officers had identified me as a *gang member*.

The prosecution's use of the victim's family as witnesses also proved to be ill fated. G-Rocc's mother got on the stand and blamed me for her divorce. I found that hard to believe, and I suspect the jury did too. Both G-Rocc and Zilla were dressed in gangster regalia when they got on the stand. Their stories of the event were bewildering, nonsensical, and ultimately useless. Zilla's version of what happened was so outlandish that she seemed to be talking about some other incident entirely. The DA could not get her off the stand fast enough.

Everything really came down to my testimony, and I walked the jury through everything that had happened, from the attack on Daisy and me to

the drive-by shooting. I admitted my guilt for what I had done and understood that there would be consequences for it. I expressed my remorse and
my desire for another chance.

The defense asked that I be given probation. Even I thought that was
laughable. The prosecutor was ticked off that I had not accepted the plea
bargain, so she started from the top. "Twenty years is the maximum he can
be sentenced, but let's give him some credit. Take off one year because of
his age, one year because he admitted to his crime, and one year out of
benevolence. That leaves seventeen years. The state asks you, the jury, to
sentence him to seventeen years." The jury left to deliberate.

The morning I went to court for sentencing, DJ waited on the corner of
our street, Cascade Ridge, to wave to me. I could see the tears in his eyes as
we drove by. In the courthouse, all witnesses and families from both sides
were allowed in to observe the sentencing. "Have you reached a decision?"
"We have, Your Honor." "We the people, sentence Christian Lamont
Bolden to eight years in the Texas Department of Criminal Justice." Eight
years . . . one year for every time I pulled the trigger. The judge affirmed.
My head dropped to the table and tears rolled down my cheeks. My life was
over. All other thoughts drained from my mind. The bailiff walked me out.
I heard my dad using some sharp words toward G-Rocc and Zilla's family
as they cheered my sentencing. The other bailiffs were holding him back.
I walked out of their lives with my hands and feet shackled.

Part I Postscript

The violent gang members in San Antonio began to eliminate themselves through homicide and incarceration.[8] After 1993's peak carnage of
1,200 drive-bys and 230 homicides, violence began a steady and steep
decline, dropping to 339 drive-bys and 142 homicides in 1995.[9]

T-Note (3-5-7 crip): When they talk about '92, '93, it's a whole different
world. I mean these niggas like if they were in Compton, you know
they were really killing each other in motherfuckin' grammar school.

The city itself implemented innovative and drastic tactics to tackle its
gang problem. They kicked everyone out of the Rigsby Courts and gentri-
fied it, marketing it to wealthier people. They bulldozed some of the housing
projects that circled downtown, like the Victoria Courts (VC). Home to the
Fellas, a non-Crip blue-rag gang, the VC was the most crime-ridden neighborhood in the whole city. They demolished some of it and built fancy sports
arenas and entertainment venues in its place. The city went after the East
Terrace Gangster Crips with a vengeance, dismantling them through several
federal Racketeer Influenced and Corrupt Organizations Act (RICO) cases
and civil gang injunctions,[10] which prevented members from even speaking

JUDGMENT OF CO_ ICTION - PLEA OF GUILTY B_ JRE THE JURY
PUNISHMENT ASSESSED BY JURY
SENTENCED TO INSTITUTIONAL DIVISION

THE STATE OF TEXAS   NO.**95CR3843B**   IN THE **290**TH DISTRICT COURT

VS   OF

CHRISTIAN LAMONT BOLDEN   BEXAR COUNTY, TEXAS

JUDGE PRESIDING: JUDGE PAT PRIEST   DATE OF JUDGMENT: **DEC 20** 1995

APPEARANCES   APPEARANCES
FOR STATE: FOR DEFENDANT:
OFFENSE CONVICTED OF: AGGRAVATED ASSAULT W/DEADLY WEAPON
  22.02 (A) (2) PC   DATE OF CONVICTION: **12-04-95**

DEGREE OF OFFENSE: **2ND**   DATE OFFENSE COMMITTED: **05-23-95**

CHARGING INSTRUMENT: **INDICTMENT**

PLEA TO JURY: **GUILTY**
VERDICT OF JURY: (GUILT) (PUNISHMENT)   FOREPERSON: **MAX PENA**
WE, THE JURY, FIND THE DEFENDANT, CHRISTIAN BOLDEN, GUILTY OF
AGGRAVATED ASSAULT WITH A DEADLY WEAPON AND ASSESS THE PUNISHMENT OF THE
DEFENDANT, CHRISTIAN BOLDEN, AT CONFINEMENT IN THE TEXAS DEPARTMENT OF
CRIMINAL JUSTICE FOR 8 YEARS.

PLEA TO   FINDING ON
ENHANCEMENT: **N/A**   ENHANCEMENT: **N/A**

FINDING ON SPECIAL ISSUE(S): DEADLY WEAPON FINDING

DATE SENTENCE IMPOSED:**12-06-95**   DATE TO COMMENCE: **12-06-95**
SENTENCE OF IMPRISONMENT
(INSTITUTIONAL DIVISION):
8 YRS TDCJ-ID AND A FINE OF $ 0.00
CONCURRENT UNLESS OTHERWISE SPECIFIED:

TIME CREDITED: **13 DAYS**   COSTS: $ **119.50**

TOTAL AMOUNT OF   RESTITUTION TO BE PAID TO:
RESTITUTION/REPARATION: $ **0.00**   NAME:
     ADDRESS:

     On   __DECEMBER 4, 1995__   the above numbered and entitled
cause was reached and called for trial, and the State appeared by the attorney stated
above, and the Defendant and the Defendant's attorney were also present. Thereupon, both
sides announced ready for trial, and a jury having been empaneled and sworn, said
Defendant, having been duly arraigned, entered a plea of __GUILTY__ to
__AGGRAVATED ASSAULT W/DEADLY WEAPON__
The Court, outside the presence of the jury, admonished the Defendant of the consequences
of said plea and that if the defendant persisted in pleading __GUILTY__ the judge
would instruct the jury to find the defendant guilty and assess punishment within the
range provided by law. It appearing to the Court that the Defendant was competent to stand
trial and that the defendant was not influenced in making said plea by any consideration
of fear or by any persuasion prompting a confession of guilt, the free and voluntary plea
of __GUILTY__ was received by the court and is now entered of record in the minutes
of the Court as the plea of the Defendant. The defendant, in accordance with the law
requested that the Jury assess punishment. Evidence was submitted, the Jury was charged
by the Court and rendered a verdict as shown above.

(JSD32M)

6-1. Sentence. (Bolden personal file / Bexar County 290th District Court.)

to each other under threat of arrest. Gang members that continued on shifted away from the violence and conflict toward monetary pursuits. Over time, the gangs would become a mere fraction of what they were.

But I would not see any of that. I was entering a whole new world, and the trajectory of my life would change in ways that I could not even imagine.

Prison

CHAPTER 7

Texas Hold'em

THOUGH A MYRIAD of social forces served as drivers toward gang involvement, I accept responsibility for my actions and recognize that the consequences were due to my own decisions. Would another diversionary tactic work? Possibly. Was it an appropriate deterrent? Rigorous study has shown that being taken out of the community and having longer stays of incarceration have no effect on rearrest probabilities for youth offenders.[1] Do I think I deserved punishment? Absolutely. Do I think my punishment was just? Well, that is harder to answer. In prison, control was lost and decision making was minimal. The idea that someone could come out the other side a better person was a long shot. I was 17 years old, and I was being sent to the Texas prison system, which was in the midst of the largest prison expansion the world had ever seen. It was a place where prison gangs reigned, and rehabilitation seemed to be the lowest priority. Though the streets were intermittently deadly, prison was consistently a violent nightmare. To survive it and change my life for the better, I would have to contend with the prison gangs and the relentless pitfalls of prison. The following narrative is from my journey through the Texas Prison system. The vast majority of the narrative was reconstructed from the letters I sent and received during that time. I kept all of the correspondence sent to me, and my mother, brother, and cousin kept all the letters I sent to them. In all, 1,009 letters were used to reconstruct the events that follow.

December 1995—Bexar County Jail

With thirteen days' credit from previous incarceration, I began my sentence at the Bexar County Adult Detention Center on December 6. This time around I was put in a wing reserved for inmates that would be shipped off to the Texas Department of Criminal Justice (TDCJ). The population was sparse in this area, and most people had their own cell. The inmates were generally laid back, and if people got out of line, the ninja turtles (deputies in riot gear with batons) would come to get them. I briefly had a cellmate named Panda, who had accidentally crashed into a police car and fled the scene instead of rendering aid. Panda would give me daily pep talks about surviving prison. He was transferred quickly but promised to write me. Much to my surprise, he kept his promise.

My chamber was on a higher floor, and I had a window overlooking the city, a sight that was both beautiful and melancholic. I rarely came out except for meals and to watch the occasional movie. I preferred to spend the time reading, writing, or doing push-ups and crunches. There were very few people to interact with anyhow.

By the end of December, I had a visit from a TDCJ representative who gave me some brief information and had me sign papers. She told me that I would be shipped off in two weeks, which did not happen. Three weeks later, as my 18th birthday passed, I was still in the county jail and glad for it, despite the boredom and the temperature always being arctic. Every weeknight was filled with a sense of dread, as each person wondered if this time would be his turn. When it was your time, you would be called for "chain" between 2 A.M. and 4 A.M. and brought to the TDCJ representatives downstairs, who were waiting like grim reapers to collect their due. If you made it to the weekend without being called, you breathed a brief sigh of relief, knowing that you had escaped the reaper at least for a couple of days. A person could potentially serve a year of their sentence in the county jail, though I'm not sure how often that happened.

My time came in early February; two months after my sentence began. They called people to go downstairs to join about forty others coming from different wings. They confiscated our belongings and stripped us naked to give us cavity searches. We were given brief instructions, but I was too frightened to pay much attention. The couple of guys who had been to the penitentiary before were trying to give the rest of us advice. It sounded like buzzing in my ears, as the witching-hour doldrums and the surrealness of standing naked with all of these men made it impossible to function. They gave us our white pajama-like uniforms to put on and then shackled us hand and foot to the person we were adjacent to. The uniform was thin, so the chill of winter and iciness of trepidation were simultaneously causing me to freeze. We loaded up onto the Blue Bird bus. The vehicle had caged wiring on all sides, and correctional officers roamed the aisle while their armed counterparts watched from one end or the other. I hoped that I wouldn't need to relieve myself, as I would have to drag the person I was shackled with to the toilet in the back of the bus. We drove with steady purpose out of the city and into the darkness. I was off to a Texas penitentiary less than one month after turning 18.

The early to mid-1990s saw a wave of "tough on crime" legislation fueled by the myth of the juvenile super predator, a creature believed to be prone to violence without motive or remorse. Though political scientist

Texas Prisons

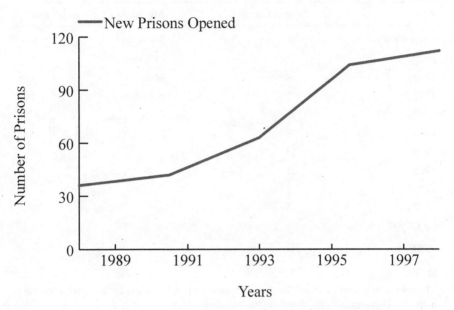

7-1. Texas prison boom, public data. (Graphic by LukePruettArt.)

John Dilulio, who initially put forth the idea, would later debunk the super predator characterization of youth, the immediate effect of the belief had serious consequences. Texas was at the forefront of the tough on crime movement with the fastest-growing mass incarceration experiment, adding 100,000 more prison beds in the early 1990s. In a move unparalleled anywhere on Earth, Texas built 80 prisons between 1989 and 1997, 28 of which were in a single year, 1995. Now having 111 correctional facilities, Texas received one out of every five inmates in the country for incarceration. The budget of the TDCJ jumped from $700 million to $2.2 billion in a few short years. In an effort to remedy the financial downturn from the oil industry going bust and agricultural decline, the prisons were used as fiscal solutions for economically depressed rural areas.

The state legislature also passed laws to restrict the release of prisoners. Previously, inmates with good behavior could expect to be incarcerated for about 15 percent of their sentence. After the new laws were passed, an individual who was sentenced to nonviolent "state jail" time (a different sentencing structure with penalties of five years or less) was required to complete their whole sentence, and a person convicted of a violent offense under the normal sentencing structure had a requirement of serving half of

TABLE 7-1
Texas Prisons[1]

Year	Prisons Opened	Attributes	Prisons
Before 1989	30^2	State	94
1989	6	Private	17
1990	4	Male	94
1991	2^3	Female	14
1992	13	Co-ed	3
1993	8		
1994	13		
1995	28		
1996	3		
1997	5		
Post-1997	1 (2004)		
Total	*111*		

NOTES:
[1] Information compiled from the Texas Department of Criminal Justice Unit Directory. http://tdcj.state.tx.us/unit_directory/index.html.
[2] The Central Unit was closed in 2011 and not replaced.
[3] The North Texas Intermediate Sanction Facility opened in 1991 and was closed in 2011.

their sentence before being considered for parole. With an eight-year "aggravated" sentence, I was facing a mandatory minimum of four years. I was about to learn on a very personal level what it meant to be one of these statistics.

February 1996—Garza West, Time Served: Two Months

It was a short bus ride before we were offloaded at our destination. Though I was wracked with anxiety, I also could not believe how fortunate I was. We had arrived at the Garza West Unit in Beeville, Texas, which was only an hour and a half outside of San Antonio and also the place where Daisy and her mother now lived. Though Garza West, a 2,278-man unit, was only an intake and transfer facility, I took a tiny bit of solace in knowing that I was still relatively close to home.

Unlike the cell blocks usually depicted in movies, Garza West was one of the new, rapidly built prisons that contained rows of blue-gray tin warehouses surrounded by barbed wire fences. Inside the warehouses were panopticons,[2] with an elevated electronic guard tower, called the picket, in the center, encircled by three or four acrylic-glass-covered dormitories (also called tanks). Within each of these housing units were fifty to one hundred bunk beds separated by just enough space for one person to walk through, tables bolted to the floor in the center of the room, and a large open bathroom with several toilets and showers clearly visible to the guards.

Terrified, I did not sleep for the first thirty-six hours as I was processed through diagnostics. Upon entry, I was strip searched again, they cut off all of my hair, then put me against a wall and sprayed my whole body for lice. I was given an identification number, which I would be known and tracked by during my entire time incarcerated. These degradation ceremonies let me know that I was being stripped of whatever status I had in society. I had now become just a number, and I was at the mercy of the overseers conducting my status-shaming rituals. Cut off from the rest of society, in a highly controlled environment, with an insurmountable social distance between the keepers and the kept, I was now in a total institution.[3]

The correctional staff immediately let me know that they had no mercy. I told both the chief of security and the female psychiatrist who evaluated me about what had happened in county jail. Both of their responses were that I was just going to have to fight to defend myself. The woman who conducted my personal history review also encouraged me to fight. "It is better to get your jaw broken than to be considered a punk [someone used for sexual purposes]," she said.

The rest of processing included a medical examination, tuberculosis and tetanus shots, a blood sample, and an immigration interview. I was also given an IQ test during that time. The people around me were not taking the test seriously, and I was too delirious from lack of sleep and freaked out about everything that was occurring to even care about taking a test. Though I was never told what I scored, I would have a hard time trusting the validity of those scores for anyone who was tested under those conditions.

In a later processing experience, I was called out to visit "Sociology." I walked into a large room where several inmates were sitting across desks from social scientists and talking to them. I was directed to a man with rust-colored hair and a comical mustache. The chair I was to sit in seemed to be ten feet away from the desk, so I picked it up to move it closer. "DID I FUCKING TELL YOU TO MOVE THAT CHAIR?!" the man screamed at me, spit flying out of his mouth. I set the chair back down where it was and sat in it. The man began asking me questions in an extremely aggressive, sarcastic, and disparaging manner that I would realize later was designed to test my temperament, but, at the time, just felt like I was in the twilight zone. I answered his questions politely, despite his constant yelling and cussing, but as his inquiries got more personal, I told him that I did not feel comfortable answering from across the room. He seemed to be taken aback by my lack of volatile response to his incessant belligerence, and he finally allowed me to approach his desk to finish the conversation. Though he still attempted to give me a hard stare, the interview's dynamic change was not what he had expected and seemed disconcerting to him. He began reading over my personal history and in the end promised me that I would never encounter Blacky or Ghoul in the prison system, before sending me on my way.

Classification of incarcerated individuals has been a focus of prison administration for decades. Reportedly there are several sophisticated algorithms and programs that can be used to determine the most appropriate placement of prisoners, albeit there has been very little evaluation of their actual effectiveness. Errors in classification are likely to occur as false positives, or overclassification, which results in people being placed in environments far harsher than needed, and the taxpayer footing the bill for more costly security measures than necessary.[4] I do not know what Texas was gambling with at the time, but I either did not fit their assessment models or the system was intentionally designed to make inmates fold. It could also be that they were overwhelmed by the sheer number of new inmates to process. Whatever the reason, they would bounce me like a pinball between penitentiaries for years to come. I had no idea about the hazards that awaited me.

Like everyone else, my mind became obsessed with thoughts on what I would encounter. Conversation was rife with rumors and advice from old-timers on how to survive. "Trust no one," and "limit yourself to a few people you can converse with so as not to go crazy," seemed to be the laws of the land. People told you not to make friends, because they would constantly be taken away from you. One of the main topics of conversation was what prisons people hoped to go to and which ones they hoped they could avoid. The criminal veterans could give info on the older prisons, but there were so many new prisons that everyone was in the dark about what they would likely be facing (Garza had only been open since 1994). Inmates colloquially called the prisons farms, since most of them forced inmates to do agricultural work. Places that you did not want to end up at were the Coffield Unit, which generated the Partido Revolucionario Mexicano (PRM) and Barrio Azteca prison gangs, or "gladiator farms," like the Ferguson and Clemens Units, where younger, violent offenders were constantly at war with each other. You also did not want to end up across the field at the twin prison Garza East, which was considered one of the most violent prisons; it was a longer-term transfer facility where the inmates seemed to riot constantly. There were several occasions when we would be put on lockdown (confined to our bunk with severely restricted movement) because the guards at Garza West were rushing over to help quell the riots at Garza East. We heard that a guard was stabbed more than thirteen times during one of the riots.

Prior to the 1980s, Texas prisons operated under a "building tender" system, in which the biggest, baddest inmate was given complete authority to keep the prisoners on the cellblock in line. The system was unconstitutional, brutal, and racially charged, with White inmates serving as the bulk of building tenders. Beginning in the late 1960s, the Texas prison system would meet its match in an incarcerated San Antonio native and Mirasoles pachuco named Fred Cruz. This old-school, Mexican American zoot suit gangster became what is known as a writ writer in prison. Cruz filed important and successful court briefs,[5] despite serious opposition from the prison administration, which tried to stack his record with constant violations and attempted to prevent his access to reading and writing materials.[6] Cruz, his lawyer, Frances Jalet, and other writ writers, known as the 8-Hoe squad, would win a series of court cases, starting with *Cruz v. Beto* (1972), which upheld the freedom of prisoners to practice their religious preference, and culminated in the class action suit *Ruiz v. Estelle* (1980), which brought the Texas Prison System, as it existed at the time, to an end. The *Ruiz v. Estelle* decision was that Texas prisons and all they entailed—building tenders, overcrowding, unsafe working environments, insufficient health care, and arbitrary and severe sanctions—equated to cruel and unusual punishment. Massive and sweeping reforms of the prison system were ordered. Things did change, but the new ways of operating were not all good.

The dissolution of the building tender system needed to be addressed by the hiring of adequate correctional staff; however, with a prisoner/officer ratio of ten to one, the staffing problem would not be resolved quickly. The inability to provide safety and security in a timely manner led to a new element filling the void—prison gangs.

The Texas Syndicate (TS) had originally formed as a self-defense group by Texas prisoners incarcerated at Folsom State Prison in California. Upon returning to their home state, the gang reformed in the Texas prison system in 1975 and was the only known gang to exist inside during the 1970s. With the prison administration almost completely unaware, the TS organized a clandestine resistance against the building tenders.[7] Though the original Hispanic members largely hailed from El Paso, they soon had a presence representing every major locale in Texas. After the *Ruiz* decision, the prison administration lost their inmate snitches and sentinels, and TS was poised for predatory dominance in the prison system. However, their aggression and predation caused other groups to form and respond in kind, and gangs began popping up at a steady pace in the new power vacuum. White allies of the Texas Syndicate created Texas Mafia in 1982. This was followed by the Aryan Brotherhood of Texas in 1983, Texas Mexican Mafia in 1984, both Mandingo Warriors and Hermandad de Pistoleros Latinos in 1985,[8] Barrio Azteca in 1986, Partido Revolucionario Mexicano in 1987, Texas

Chicano Brotherhood in 1989, and both the White Knights and Raza Unida in 1991. In the previous decade before the gangs, Texas had one of the lowest prison homicide rates in the country. The years of 1984 and 1985 would see all-out wars, with Texas Syndicate against Mexican Mafia and Aryan Brotherhood against Mandingo Warriors. In two years, these conflicts would rack up 641 nonfatal stabbings and 52 homicides, more prison murders than the state had experienced in the previous twenty years.[9] The prison authorities lost control. They regained stability by placing known gang members in administrative segregation, which dramatically reduced the violence, but with a prison expansion juggernaut on the horizon, the return of gang warfare was inevitable.

Beginning with Bill Clements in 1987, each subsequent Texas governor would spend considerable effort expanding the prison system and making criminal laws more punitive. Even though Democratic governor Ann Richards wanted to focus on drug rehabilitation centers, she would also be caught up in the mass incarceration era, reducing parole approvals by 50 percent and expanding the penal system more significantly than had her predecessors. Governor George W. Bush brought *Ruiz v. Estelle* back to trial in an effort to rid the prison system of judicial and federal oversight. Judge William Wayne Justice, who had presided over the original case, agreed that the prison system had become a professional agency but strongly rebuked the state for its relegation of the mentally ill to administrative segregation and for failing to protect inmates from the predation of prison gangs and from "sadistic and malicious" correctional officers. Governor Bush generally ignored the ruling and instead focused on expanding the incarceration empire by converting Ann Richards's rehabilitation centers to prisons, allowing for 14-year-olds to be charged as adults, rapidly growing the juvenile inmate population, and expediting executions.[10] Tough on crime played well with the electorate, but on a personal level, being one 18-year-old among 200,000 people in the volatile and deadly Texas system meant facing a whole lot of uncertainty and chaos.

Though I existed in a constant state of dread, problems of violence were not readily apparent. Instead, prisoners struggled through things that most free people take for granted. The inmates did not cause many problems, as the majority were still dealing with the shock of incarceration and trying to figure out how they were going to survive. The main problems were eating and sanitation. The toilets were in a perpetual state of nonfunctionality. To get rid of bodily waste, one inmate would have to hold the flush button while other inmates poured buckets of water down the toilet so that the water pressure would force a flush.

We went to the cafeteria three times a day for meals. Lunch was around 11 A.M., and dinner started around 3:30 P.M. Breakfast was served at 3:00 A.M.

If you did not have the presence of mind to be awake at that time, you would miss it. I tried to go as much as possible because it was the only decent meal, even though it was always eggs or pancakes. During mealtimes you were given three to five minutes to eat, depending on the mood of the guards. You had to quickly learn to scarf your food like a dog, or starve. I chose to starve. The taste and texture of the food were unbearable. In 1995 the executive director of TDCJ awarded a $33.7 million contract to Vita Pro to provide food for inmates. Vita Pro was a soybean-based meat substitute used in dog, cat, and horse food; it wasn't intended for human consumption. Inmates would complain of digestive problems for years to come. I refused to eat it. When the TDCJ executive director was forced to resign in 1995, he immediately went to work for Vita Pro. A jury would convict both him and the president of Vita Pro on charges of bribery, fraud, money laundering, and conspiracy. Even though they faced seventy years and $2 million in fines, they were allowed to remain free on bond. A federal appeals judge overturned their convictions, without a jury, and they walked away from the scandal with no penalty.[11] In 1998, the Texas Supreme Court would rule the Vita Pro contract invalid, and they would stop serving it to inmates. In the meantime, though, we were given thousands of meals fit for farm animals.

I survived in the interim by buying food through the commissary. Texas inmates did not earn any money, no matter the type of work or amount of work they were required to do. Loved ones sending in a check was the only way to put money on one's financial books, and the biweekly spending limit was $60.00. The commissary had a decent variety of food and hygiene items available. My mom tried her hardest to make sure that I had money in my account. Most people were not so lucky. If you had no money, you were considered indigent, and the state would provide you with a toothbrush, toothpaste powder, deodorant, some paper, and a few envelopes. Indigent prisoners needed to run with a gang or develop some type of hustle, such as artistic drawing, for envelopes and handkerchiefs, or tattooing, if they wanted to have toothpaste or sustain themselves on something other than Vita Pro. Belongings were kept in slots underneath the bunk beds. It cost $10.50 to buy a lock to protect what you owned. Twenty-five-cent Ramen noodle soups, $3.00 coffee, $0.75 sodas, and $1.50 pints of ice cream were the major items used for trade between inmates. The underground market was not allowed, but unless you were blatant about it, the guards didn't care.

Inmates could receive one visit per weekend between 8 A.M. and 5 P.M., provided the inmate was not under any disciplinary consequences. Two adult visitors and an unrestricted number of children under age 13 could see their loved one for two hours. One contact visit per month was allowed with immediate family only, and all other persons and visits were conducted through reinforced double glass windows with phones to communicate. Phone calls were nonexistent.

We also had to work. Inmates did all the physical work in the prison, despite not receiving any pay. Part of the justification for this was rehabilitation through a work ethic. But when considering the social and educational deficits of most inmates, combined with all of the negative aspects of prison, forcing people to work for no pay did nothing for rehabilitation or lowering recidivism.[12] Correctional officers (COs) were supposed to keep order, and there were specific specialty jobs to oversee things like maintenance, but inmates did all of the work. "Boss" is what prisoners called the guards, a clear reference to slave plantation overseers. Some of the correctional officers reveled in the term, though a few despised it. My first job assignment was Utility Squad third shift, which usually began at midnight. The Utility Squad was called out for any miscellaneous tasks the administration deemed necessary, which ranged from scrubbing showers to sweeping up thousands of raisins that were inexplicably scattered everywhere.

On March 26, 1996, as I was lying down to sleep, an officer came over the intercom, "Bolden, fall out for chain." "Chain" meant you were going to be shackled and transported to a new location. I was nervous, angry, and completely caught off guard, as I had not even been at Garza West for two months. I packed my things and went outside to be shackled with the fellow inmates being transported. We stood in the cold weather for over an hour, waiting in silence and anticipation for our fate. We were sifted into two groups; the one I wasn't in took a Blue Bird to the Darrington Unit. My group had a bus ride that lasted less than ten minutes. Fuck. They had taken me to Garza East.

CHAPTER 8

Fellowship

I'VE ALWAYS HEARD it said that gangsters only end up dead or in jail. It is a well-intentioned message, but far from the truth, which is perhaps why the message isn't very effective. It is a mistake to believe in the folk-devil myth that gang members operate as malevolent predators, seeking to destroy and devour everything they encounter. The impetus for gangs comes from the more basic need of survival. If society is functioning the way it should, then people grow up having their needs fulfilled and learning the appropriate ways to interact, feats accomplished through the social institutions of family, school, the government, the economy, religion, and the media. But what happens when most of the institutions fail to provide for the needs of segments of the population? What happens when absent or abusive fathers eliminate the refuge or safety of home, or when the working-class kids cannot live up to the standards of the middle-class measuring rod and are relegated to slow-learner classes, or worse yet, are kicked out of school? What happens when the government, the media, and sometimes even religion see you as the problem and demonize your existence? What happens when you are constantly faced with the bleakness of poverty and an economy that provides no paths for escape? What happens is you find an alternate institution that provides you with the things that are missing—a family, street knowledge, informal rules and modes of communication, an underground economy, and something to believe in—a gang.

While the gang as an institution is highly dysfunctional, it still has functions, as it brings a semblance of order to chaos. Within these groups, there are core members, like I was, whose identity is entrenched in the gang and who engage in most of the serious delinquent activities. The core members are often consumed by gang life, and they do end up dead or in jail. But the majority of gang members exist on the fringe, or the periphery, seeking passage through the volatile adolescent years, and avoiding the riskier adventures.[1] Most of these individuals will eventually walk away from the gang or simply fade out of the scene. In fact, two-thirds of all gang members will leave the gang and go on to live conventional lives.[2]

The homies that sent me letters told me that I had been the glue that kept many of them together, and after I was gone, they began to drift away. I kept in contact with as many as I could through written correspondence and learned about the others through any gossip medium that could reach me. I was amazed by the various life paths of my friends, and I followed their trajectories with interest, sadness, and hope. Some people, particularly P-Ma and Devil, tried to keep the gangs together, but attrition and the inevitable personal problems they faced took their toll. It wasn't long before the Sa Town Bloods, Vice Lords, and Lady Watts would all disintegrate.

DJ (STB): The gang ended up pretty much breaking up. That core ended up in jail, that core ended up shot, that core ended up getting girlfriends, you know that core ended up doing the music thing, that core ended up doing this and that, you know what I'm saying, and waking up to the fact that we can't do this forever.

There are many paths out of the gang, though they are not always straightforward.[3] It might be a combination of circumstances that provide the final push. Some people drift out of the scene as a gang dissolves. Some mature out of it as they realize it is not what they want in life and just walk away. For a few, it might be having a child that results in gang desistance. For others still, their path out might come through incarceration, religious conversion, or military service. For the STBs, it was just about all of the above.

Though Ricky and I were the only ones to get serious prison time, incarceration still played its part in removing others from the gang. Chaps, the STB who drove the truck during my crime and wrote an affidavit against me, got busted on unrelated activity and was sentenced to a year in county jail. When Chaps got out of jail, he moved up North and wasn't heard from again. Ace had been in and out of county jail on minor charges and was getting really tired of the gang life.

ACE (STB): I just left it, I moved along and lived my life. [I was] put in jail a lot of times and I just got tired of it, so I figured I just got to build a life and I moved on.

There was plenty of growing up going around. After B-Loco was shot, Bret began to distance himself from gangs, and by this time, he had faded completely out of it. He set about getting his life together working two jobs, delivering pizza and teaching swimming classes at the YMCA. At first, DJ stayed wrapped in his cocoon of marijuana and music. As this increased his isolation from the others, he eventually decided to back all of the way out of the gang life. With both Chaps and myself, his closest allies gone, and constant pressure from the police, who would randomly handcuff and question him, he decided that it was not worth continuing. Once that decision was made, DJ was quick to land on his feet. He went to Belgium to train for his new job painting airplanes. Ace and Stick also found success in the field of aviation, going to technical school and landing jobs fixing airplanes. P-Ma moved on with her life, becoming a nursing assistant and getting a job at a school for kids with special needs. She also got married and had kids of her own.

The military was a source of escape for several of the homies, though their experiences with it would be vastly different. Devil joined the Air Force and became a military police officer; I was highly amused by the irony in that. K-Dog joined the army and post 9/11, saw combat in the Middle East. The experience of war caused more psychological scarring than the streets ever did, and the trauma prevented his successful adjustment to civilian life. After that, he had constant run-ins with the law as well as domestic disputes and dissolutions. Many years would pass before he could achieve stability and success with a family and a business of his own. Caleb took the long route and had been going full force in the gang life.

CALEB (STB): Well actually, my cousin he went to jail for about five years for a drive-by, I mean it hurt because when he left I had nobody to look up to and I thought I was left alone. I was just put out in like an island and left. But after I learned to cope with it, I learned to deal with, um I went ahead and figured that I could learn to do what he did but even better, so I started stealing guns, selling them, started selling more weed and putting in more work that I needed to do.

He began to slow down a little when he had a baby on the way. But it took eight bullet holes in his car and a shotgun blast taking out the back window for him to finally decide that he was through with gangs. His ticket out was the U.S. Navy.

Kids contributed to the many reasons for the desistance of P-Ma and Caleb, but for others, having children was the primary factor for leaving gang life. Stick had begun to fall out with some of his former friends and developed a long-standing beef with Ace over women, further separating the core of STB. Ultimately though, it was the birth of his baby boy that took him completely out of the gang scene. For Daisy, it was a much longer road. She had a hard time handling my incarceration and immediately began heavy drinking. It didn't take long for her to break up with me, though she still maintained contact. I was pissed and devastated, but everyone had been psychologically preparing me for this inevitable occurrence. It would eventually happen to almost everybody on the inside. Daisy moved to the South Side of San Antonio and began running wild in the streets for a while before she ended up dating an East Side Player Crip. He became severely abusive to her and her family. The normative violence of gangs increased the likelihood that female gang members in San Antonio would be victims of intimate partner violence. Issues of jealousy, disrespect, and control could lead to severe instances of domestic violence. Ironically, the social networks of female gang members made it more likely that third parties would intervene and help them escape before the domestic abuse became chronic.[4] After some very violent episodes, Daisy was able to escape the abuser and afterward began dating an Ambro. This caused a significant rift with P-Ma, as the Ambrose were the ones who killed her brother. Once Daisy had her first child, the days of running with gangs came to an end.

As the core disbanded, it provided an easy path for some of the more peripheral members, like Remington, to just walk away.

REMINGTON (STB): It was like nobody was around anymore, like I don't know, people were like all in, like we all met up at school basically, and then people like got kicked out of school, or went to alternative school, or went to this place or that place, or jail or whatever, so there wasn't anybody else around, so there I was, only one person, so I got lucky that I could leave it.

Others were not so lucky. Some people get stuck in a pattern of ambivalence, wanting to leave the gang but also feeling that it is their only refuge when the challenges of life become overwhelming. Coop would also begin to fade from the gang with the birth of his daughter, but a series of stints in county jails for petty crimes, the subsequent difficulty of maintaining steady work, and his family situation falling apart, would find him embracing the life he knew as a Blood once again.

COOP (STB): My first child, she is 10 now, so, when I had her is when I started slipping away some. Then me and her mother had problems and we split up and then they left and went a separate way and I just went back to it, started getting in crazy stuff again.

I tried to keep track of everyone I could, but in the world of gangs, people had a habit of dropping off of the radar. KO had moved to Rigsby to shack up with a girl, but was otherwise missing in action. I lost track of him early on and never heard from him again. And though I inquired with everybody, no one could get a bead on the whereabouts of Chuckles.

Like street life, prison society was made up of people trying to create order out of chaos. Correctional officers did very little to keep prisoners safe, so informal prison societies were necessary for survival. Though my friends in the free world were exiting the gang through a myriad of turning points in their lives, gangs were not yet done with me. Garza West had provided me with a brief respite from underworld brutality, but I was now entering the ultraviolent world of Garza East, and I knew that my gang affiliation might be my only protection.

Late March 1996—Garza East, Time Served: Three and a Half Months

My intake to Garza East was surprisingly brief. The 1,978-man unit was considered a longer-term transfer facility, and the administration seemed to take the "longer-term" part to heart, as processing was minimal. The officer in charge of classification wanted to assign me to a Hoe Squad, which was the most common and worst job to get. If you had no skills or were not liked, you were given this assignment. On the Hoe Squad you were given a garden hoe and sent out to do agricultural work for eight hours a day, regardless of the weather or if there was any actual work to do. If there was nothing to collect, you would till the ground for eight hours. The white uniforms of the prisoners were always brown or some other earthy color by the time they returned from work. I think the idea was to tire people out as much as possible, or maybe it was yet another throwback to slave plantations. My medical history of having asthma and severe allergies saved me from this fate, at least for the moment. The officer assigned me to the Broom Squad second shift (afternoon). My job was to constantly sweep the walkways and to be called out during rainstorms to push water off the walkways with giant squeegees.

The best part of receiving the Broom Squad job assignment was that it fit into the upper echelon of work placements and landed me in "A1" dorm, which was the best place to be, given the circumstances. "A" dorm consisted of inmates that had the more privileged jobs, so they were better behaved since they wanted to keep those positions. As you went down the alphabet, things got progressively worse. The last and worst general population housing was "E" dorm, filled with Hoe Squad. A tough-looking guy that came on the bus with me was assigned to "E" dorm. He threw a fit and refused to go. I'll never forget the look of terror in his face as they dragged him to "E" dorm by force. The only thing worse was the last level of housing severity, which was "F" dorm, also known as administrative segregation (Ad-Seg), where the most violent and problematic inmates were placed.

Upon entering A1 dorm, I was relieved that no one seemed to pay any attention to me. Once I determined that there was no clear or present threat, I collapsed into a deep sleep that could only come from escaping the suffocating anxiety of facing the unknown. I stayed in my bunk in a state of sleep recovery for a few days. When I woke, I decided that I wasn't going to be complacent about my own defense, and I quickly set about making acquaintances. At Garza West, I had allied myself with Gip, a Hispanic guy from a red-circle San Antonio gang called North Side Rollers (NSR), who had been given "shock probation" (where a person spends a short time in prison with the remainder of the sentence served on probation). Thankfully we didn't find ourselves in any conflict. A few days after entering this boiling-pot prison, I lucked into a ready-made alliance. I learned that there were only eleven known Bloods on Garza East, but over seventy Crips. Including myself, there were now three of those Bloods in A1 dorm, and serendipitously, T-Bolt, one of the others, was a Rigsby Court Gangster. T-Bolt and I hit it off instantly. He had heard of me as the "Rigsby who wasn't from Rigsby," and we had a good laugh at that. The other Blood, Hightower, was from Dallas. Between us, and a Mexican guy named Franky, who never revealed his affiliation but chose to roll with us anyway, we had a solid crew. I spent most of my time in that clique, hanging out, exercising, and eating with them.

My inclination toward San Antonio gangsters also resulted in me becoming best friends with my Hispanic bunk neighbor, Billy. He was a South Side Ambro from San Antonio, and we constantly teased each other about gangs in a nonthreatening way. We would stay up late at night telling each other our war stories and talking about our celebrity crushes. Billy was also on the road to Christianity, but because he was Hispanic, the Mexican Mafia was constantly trying to recruit him. It wouldn't be long before he'd be shipped off to the Segovia Unit, but he would continue to write me and encourage me to take a spiritual path.

Gangs weren't the only groups in the prison society. There was also a complex strata of ganglike hometown cliques called Tangos. Although talk about them was common, I did not really understand them at the time. Religions were also recognized as social groupings. There were the Black Muslims, which operated in a militant fashion. They were not mutually exclusive, and people could still hold on to their gang affiliation as long as they were working toward self-improvement. The Christians were a different story. They were much larger and more diverse. There was a general understanding in prison that if you chose to legitimately pursue Christianity, most people would respect that decision and leave you to it. The caveat was that if you were caught behaving in a thuggish or otherwise impious manner, then you would be considered a fake, and it would be open season on you.[5]

HOOPS (SKYLINE PARK): In prison, I used to see that a lot. . . . It was like, the policy in there was you had dudes that might be into religion, Christians or Muslims and stuff like that and they respected it if you were, just, you gotta be so devout, you gotta be so pious, but if any sign that you backsliding and you not for real about Christianity or Islam, then they going to go ahead and regulate on you.

Most people enter the system with plans to avoid prisonization, which is adhering to the subcultural norms and values of prison.[6] The chances of successfully sticking to that plan were slim to none. Except for the people who followed the religious path, most ended up in a clique that provided a sense of belonging. Depending on the circumstance, these cliques might evolve into protection groups that would come together for defense. If leadership emerged or general sentiment toward criminal activities prevailed, then the cliques would further evolve into predator groups.[7]

T-NOTE (3-5-7 CRIP): Some of them stay institutionalized once they get in. They find more comfort there. And I guess that is even more so for the cats infatuated with violence. Cause in jail, you got a violent habitat to where you can't escape that shit. You trapped by it. You know what I mean, and all your free time is almost dedicated to plotting out a violent act. Cause you have the opportunity to hit 'em up every day, you know, you don't take a week off. Cause well shit, every move counts. Cause for every move there is a countermove and shit. So, you always gotta watch out, and see every which way you are going to get hit from.

Most of these groups would eventually disband or be absorbed into something else, but occasionally they would evolve into an official prison gang.

Wanting to be left in peace to do your time alone was only allowed under certain demographic stipulations. For Whites, going it alone was extremely dangerous. Most Whites I encountered ran with Aryan Circle. Even though many of the individuals were not actually racist, the racial divisions in prison and the numerical minority of Whites left them no choice but to run with a gang. Other Whites chose to pay protection to the Black or Mexican gangs.

For Hispanics, it was just as bad. The Mexican prison gangs were constantly battling throughout the prison system and were always looking for new recruits. People could resist with all of their willpower, but the gangs would never stop trying, knowing that danger and manipulation had a way of making people do things that they didn't want to do. Blacks had the easiest time, at least socially. Their numerical majority provided for a general protection of individuals. A person could choose to ride alone, and if interracial conflict occurred, Blacks in the dorm would unite for defense. Any intraracial conflict would have to be handled without help though. Although there were Black gangs, they did not care about controlling the penitentiaries like the Mexican prison gangs did. People would often enter prison hollering out their free-world neighborhoods like 3rd Ward, 5th Ward, or Alief out of Houston, or Oak Cliff out of Dallas, but that would die down pretty fast. If you were not on a gladiator farm or in a bedlam brewery like Garza East, then Bloods and Crips actually got along. Asians were few and far between, and they could choose to ride with Blacks or Mexicans without being relieved of their commissary. Most of those who rode alone were in an older age range (over 40), though older Whites were still vulnerable to the more unscrupulous of predators.

The Christians would often hold Bible studies near my bunk. I would listen with interest to what they had to say, and sometimes they would chat with me. One of them, Preacher, an older African American man, took it upon himself to mentor me whenever he could. Between Preacher and Billy's entreaties, a religious curiosity began worming its way into my brain. I had always believed in God, and I had gone to a series of Southern Baptist churches in my childhood. I never really understood God or religion in any mature way though, despite being baptized. Since I had a lot of time on my hands, I decided to learn, and began going to church and studying both the Bible and the Quran. My Blood clique didn't approve, but they also did not feel threatened by it.

Inside of A1, I began to feel the illusion of safety. But I was antsy anytime I walked out of the dorm, and for good reason. I would have a few months of relative peace before anything happened, but the slide toward negativity would be abrupt. It started when I was called out to be interrogated by gang intelligence officers because Caleb had sent me a gang-related picture. I played dumb and thought it would be done at that, but the seemingly arbitrary harassment from the guards began to ramp up. I had hoped to avoid getting caught in the crosshairs of the correctional officers, but found myself subject to being written up on minor violations and becoming the choice of harassment for "random" searches.

My next encounter would heighten my sense of imminent danger. I was accosted unexpectedly in the cafeteria line as I was getting my food. "I heard you is a Slob" (disrespectful name for a Blood). The words came from one of the serving inmates on the other side of the food counter. He was an Altadena Blocc Crip from San Antonio, though we didn't know each other. "Nah, I'm a Blood, you got beef (a grudge)?" I responded. We mad dogged each other with the serving bar of corn and Vita Pro slop between us. I felt certain that my days of things being uneventful were over. T-Bolt who was behind me in line tapped me and said not to worry about it and keep moving. I spent the next few days in turmoil as I thought about what the intentions of that Crip were, and whether or not I should attack first when I ran across him again. Fortuitously I got the news that he caught chain, and the threat passed.

As spring turned to summer, the extremely oppressive South Texas heat began its reign over the tin warehouses we were living in. There was no air conditioning in the buildings, and the agonizing days started to bring out the worst in people. Tensions between Blacks and Mexicans were rising, and arguments over what to watch on the television in the dorm were becoming more frequent. Inmates loved to watch soap operas (*The Young and the Restless* seemed to be the favorite), but if other daytime dramas were on at the same time or there was a sporting event in the same time slot, conflict was likely to ensue. We got locked down for a while over an attempted escape of four inmates working the Hoe Squad. It turned out that they were not actually trying to escape but ran across a rattlesnake while working and ran away from it. Starting in mid-July, I would finally see what Garza East's violent reputation was all about.

On Friday, July 12, someone got jumped on the recreation yard. I felt thankful that I stayed in that night as I preferred to avoid trouble, but it wouldn't matter, because violence was about to explode everywhere. The weekend turned deadly on Saturday morning when a 19-year-old Hispanic kid was being called for a visit. One of the prison gangs attacked and killed him while his family waited in visitation. I thought about the horror of that family being given that news, and it weighed heavily on my heart. It inspired me to go to church the following day, which I had been erratically and tentatively attending. This particular Sunday, my thoughts and prayers would have me in the wrong place at the wrong time. Things at church seemed good. They were videotaping the singing for a gospel music video, and the crowd was lively. I let myself get lost in the spirit of things and started to have a good time, closing my eyes and clapping my hands. I was either naive or too much of a fool to not realize that the laws of the streets were the same as those of prison gangs. The events of the previous days would not go unanswered.

Church was held in an extremely large tin warehouse, and the majority of inmates showed up for it on Sunday, whether they were Christian or not. Gangs often took the opportunity to conduct their business at these large gatherings, so their presence seemed normal. During the videotaping, while everyone was clapping and singing praises to the Lord, the Mexican gangs erupted into fighting throughout the crowd. The guards rushed in with batons and gas guns, but flanked by hundreds of confused bystanders dressed exactly the same, the gangs had extra time to handle their business. One of the officers pointed his gun directly at my head, I'm assuming because I looked Mexican. I don't know if the firearm was loaded with gas, rubber bullets, or something more final, but having a barrel pointed between your eyes has a very sobering effect in that moment and forever after. I slowly put my hands behind my head and laid on the ground. The correctional officers tried to get everyone down, but people kept popping back up and going at it. The assaults seemed to have a life or death desperation to them, and the officers struggled to pull people apart, even as the fighters trampled and tripped over the other inmates beneath them. Once the guards had finally gotten us all on the ground, they sent everyone back to their dorms. The scene must have been too chaotic for them to sort out any of the culprits that were not bleeding. Strangely, the rest of the day continued with normal operation.

The pattern of my Blood clique was to go on the rec yard and exercise. I did not want to go that evening, as the tension in the air was palpable, but T-Bolt insisted that we stay together. Despite my reservations, I knew that my best option was to stay with my clique. We weren't on the rec yard long before Blacks started fighting over basketball, and a few minutes later, Blacks on the other side of the fence from us were also fighting. I don't know if these were real feuds, a result of the tension, or simply planned distractions, but in rapid succession, the Mexican gangs in C, D, and E dorms went after each other in a full-scale riot. The guards were scrambling and forcing everyone on the ground as they tried to regain control. Everyone was coughing and their eyes began to water as the smell of tear gas was carried by the wind. The next morning, we were locked down and the U.S. Marshals were at the prison to assist.

Lockdowns were abysmal anytime, but especially during the horrendous heat. We were confined to our bunks and could only get up to use the bathroom one at a time. For meals we received "johnnies," which were small brown paper sacks that contained two slices of bread and a piece of bologna or a small dab of peanut butter. We were only allowed to shower once during the whole week of lockdown. When we were finally back to normal operations, the violence was reduced but certainly not gone. Before the month was through someone else would get stabbed and another person would get his head smashed with a hard-plastic drink pitcher in the cafeteria. They took away the drink pitchers after that.

Over the summer, the violence began to take its toll on my psyche, causing me to question my gang identity and participation in a violent subculture.[8] Learning about my gang dissolving in the free world, transitioning from adolescence to adulthood, and witnessing the violence of Garza East caused a great deal of consternation. I became more introspective and began mentally wrestling between my life as a gangster and knowing what the eventual outcome of that would be or trying something different and turning my life onto a spiritual path. I started to really think about the people around me, and not just as an assessment of whether or not they were a threat. I began to think about their lives, their families, and what it meant that we were all here. There was a vast array of people incarcerated, but through observation I discerned that two types constituted the bulk of the inmate population. Most of the incoming prisoners were very young, 17- to 19-year-old violent offenders with extremely long sentences. Many of these kids, who were just like me, would never be free again. Even if their sentence was short enough for them to have some hope of getting out, it seemed just as likely that they wouldn't make it, as prison gangs would swallow them up. The other primary category of inmates was middle-aged drug addicts (crack or heroin) who were on their third, fourth, fifth, or sixth trip to the penitentiary. I became more and more determined that I was not going to spend my life in prison. I had come to a crossroads. I decided to become a Christian. From this turning point, my view of life began to change.

There are negative stereotypes about "jailhouse conversions," suggesting that prisoners fraudulently adopt religion, hoping that the authorities will fall for their con game and let them out. If those types of things ever occurred, their days had long since passed. The mere notion that a religious awakening would help someone get out of the Texas prison system was laughable. It might however, help people survive their experience on the inside.

While there were certainly the types who turned to religion for the sodas and cookies brought to church services, or for the possibility of gaining access to volunteers from the outside, those types were rare. Under the constant scrutiny of inmates checking the validity of one's religiosity, those who were faking would rapidly fall to the wolves. On the social side, the religions provided safety and a chance for genuine friendships. But those were not the only ways in which the religious course helped people survive.

Religion helped us deal with the experience of being social outcasts of society. For some, it excused or alleviated the guilt of their actions through the seeking of forgiveness or by attributing causation to extraworldly beings like demons or the devil. For others, it provides a new lifestyle with doctrinal prescriptions for routines and behavior or through ceding control of one's life to God. For others still, it is a coping mechanism for dealing with the loss of freedom and a way to find peace in an environment that is anything but peaceful.[9]

Coping and peace allowed for a more successful path of gang and crime desistance. Religious conversions and gang recovery helped people reinterpret their lives of involvement in gangs, crime, and drugs, as comparative to spiritual parables.[10] This reconstruction of personal narrative served to give one's life meaning and mitigate shame by providing a new identity, a spiritual purpose for imprisonment, a method of empowerment, a path to forgiveness, and hope for a better future.[11] Those who were able to reorient their life narratives toward a goal of helping others tended to be more successful in positive life transitions.[12]

For me, religion sated my growing intellectual and spiritual curiosity about the world, about my experience, and the experience of others. I wanted to understand why terrible things happened, and what, if anything, I could do about them. Despite each group's claim of owning the "truth," I did not presuppose the validity of any one religion over another, and I continued to study various religions even after selecting one to follow. I was most comfortable and familiar with Christianity, so my choice in pursuing that route felt appropriate.

Coming to the decision to take the spiritual path was hard enough, but it took every ounce of courage I had to bring my decision to T-Bolt and Hightower. I was ready for whatever consequences would come my way. Their reaction surprised me. "You're on your own. Do not come to us for anything. We won't help you," T-Bolt said, and then he turned his back on me. I officially dropped my rag, quitting the Bloods.

There is pervasive mythology about the process of leaving a gang, in which people believe that it is not possible without violent consequences from the gang. This myth is even more pronounced regarding gangs in prison, with pervasive "blood in, blood out" rhetoric. Reality is far from the myth, however. The most comprehensive study on gang members in prison, specifically ones in Texas, found that it was more common to leave gangs in prison than to leave gangs in the street.[13] Very few of those who left gangs in prison were attacked by their former gang and even fewer were attacked by other gangs. Except for a few gangs with strict policies and severe consequences for leaving, the majority of gangs were understanding of those who wished to leave and often allowed it, albeit with certain stipulations. On the streets, people could leave gangs passively by just fading out of the scene. In prison, it was required that a person give official notice to the gang.[14] Religious conversion was seen as one of the most legitimate reasons for leaving a gang. I had given notice and my reason was accepted. It was time to move on.

I began immersing myself in religious activities. I looked forward to going to church. One of the best things about the church services was the music. A Black inmate named Candle, who had a beautiful voice and contagious spiritual charisma, was the primary praise and worship leader. At a smaller religious gathering, Preacher introduced me to Candle, who was extremely impressed when he heard me rap. Chaplains have a certain amount of power in prisons, and a popular worship leader like Candle had enough clout with the chaplain to get me called out of the dorm for choir practice. Just like that, we began making music together. During one of the Sunday services, Candle put me on the spot, calling me up out of the crowd to rap. More than half of the prison was there. There was no time to think about it, I just did it. I was on a spiritual high, flowing gospel rap in front of over a thousand inmates. It was amazing and life changing. This public, emotional, and embodied experience served to legitimize my religious conversion among the inmates.[15]

Around the end of August, someone in administration decided that Broom Squad did not qualify as a prestigious job. My relative safety in A1 was upended, and I was booted all the way down the social ladder to the outer ring of hell—D dorm. There was no need to fret over whether or not the reputation of the housing unit was real. D dorm was all it was cracked up to be. As soon as I entered D-4, the Mexicans rushed me, encircling me, demanding to know who I ran with. "I'm Black, I'm Black, Soy Negro," I said it wrong, but they eventually got the gist, leaving me alone to accost the next person who arrived. I hopped up on my bunk, which laid lengthwise against the wall, and checked out the dayroom scene. On my first night I saw Mexican gang members signaling through the acrylic glass to their counterparts in one of the other dorms. The response from the higher ranked individual on the other side caused them to take one of their members into a corner and beat him up (a violation), while someone held up a sheet to obscure the vision of the guards. When they were done, they took him to the glass for their ranking member to see the damage. He signaled back—not enough, do it again—and they did it again. The next day, a Crip from Corpus Christi and a Crip from Dallas were playing dominoes. Every time they scored they would shout out their gang sets, which annoyed the other person. This pattern started escalating until they were fighting with domino-filled fists. Even though it was during the daytime, in plain sight of the guard tower, either no one saw or no one cared to intervene. Everything went back to normal when the fight was over. I decided instantly that I was going to stay on my bunk as much as possible and only ventured into the dayroom to join the prayer circles before lights out or when the dispatching of Hoe Squads left the dorm all but empty. I still had some social interaction in the dorm as two Christians, Matty and Cowboy, were assigned to bunks on both sides of mine. The three of us would converse and encourage each other to stay strong.

I immersed myself in the Bible and Christian correspondence courses. Every Sunday, I was pulled up from the crowd at church to rap. I began writing solo gospel raps with choruses that required audience participation, and the entire crowd would be involved with my songs. The most popular was "Join Up with the Lord's Gang." The song co-opted gangster lingo for religious purposes, and the crowd loved it, no matter if they were Christian or not. It connected with them through the language of the street, which they understood and appreciated.

JOIN UP WITH THE LORD'S GANG   7/30/96

Written by: Christian Bolden

Chorus: Join up with the Lord's gang, join up with the Lord's gang,
    somebody sang
Join up with the Lord's gang, join up with the Lord's gang, if you
    wanna change
Join up with the Lord's gang, join up with the Lord's gang,
    everybody sang
Join up with the Lord's gang, join up with the Lord's gang

Verse 1

Let me tell you 'bout my mission, everybody listen
Lord Jesus Christ told me I should go fishin'
And catch him a sinner, turn him into a beginner
A baby in Christ, who'll grow up to be a winner
He told me to look for someone walkin' round tough
Cause in his heart, he's really got a lotta love
He told me to find him, hanging round with the cliques
He'll be down with the Mafias, Bloods, and Crips
And when you see him, his heart will be full of pain
Tell him that the Lord says "Son you need a change"
And if he asks what clique am I down with
I'll be bold and I'll tell him like this
I'm down with the Blood that Jesus gave for my life
I'm down with the C that represents Jesus Christ
I'm down with the D for Disciples of the Lord
When it comes to battle, I use a two-edged sword
In other words, I'm down with the Lord's gang
And showing love to my brothers is how we bang
So if you are tired of the sin and pain
I'll tell you what, join up, somebody sang

(Chorus)

Verse 2   7/30/96

So you wanna be a gangsta, well be a gangsta for the Lord
Believe in him and your life will not be void
You wanna know, so I'll tell you how it be
No need to worry, Jesus Christ is our O.G.
The only homie that will always be around
When in need, he will never let you down
Plant the seed of love within your soul
Feed it truth and watch until it grows
I won't lie, you gonna go through a lot of things
But let me tell you how the Lord's crew gang bangs
Others carry weapons, we carry Bibles
They go to meetings, we go to revivals
They're about lust, and we're about love
And we're protected by our Father above
You see, your enemies will be at peace with you
If you please the Lord in what you do
He sent me to give you an invitation

Choose salvation or eternal damnation
The Book of Life is waiting for your name
Why wait, join up with the Lord's gang (sang)

(Chorus)

Verse 3   8/12/96
Join up with the best,
You don't believe, then put the Lord to the test
And you will see, that he gets respect
Christianity is the name of his set
The only choice that you'll never regret
Get right with Christ, it's time to quit half-steppin'
Only neighborhood that I love is heaven
Your righteous prayers will avail you much
The Lord's gang gonna kick up dust
Put trust in the Lord, gird up your sword
Cause it's time to do battle with the devil's hordes
You ask me, if I'm down with L-O-C
Yeah, love of Christ is what it means to me
Can't be no colors in my life
Only color on my mind is a robe of white
Christ gave me the cue, now it's time to set trip
We gang bang when we sang in a fellowship
You must choose what you gonna do
Christ Almighty's looking for some new recruits
So join up and be upon one accord
Now you found salvation cause you down with the Lord

I quickly became a celebrity among the inmates at Garza East. And just as quickly, Candle caught chain to the Jester II Unit (renamed the Carol Vance Unit in 1999), the first explicitly Christian-faith-based prison in Texas. Due to Candle's absence, the praise and worship team began to rely on me more heavily during services.

My localized celebrity status went a long way in gaining me clout and peace, things that were necessary in the volatile environment of D dorm. The brutality there was regular. With the transitional nature of the inmate population at an extended transfer facility, new people were constantly coming and going, and the threat of interpersonal and large-scale violence always loomed.

Almost half of the state prison population was incarcerated for violent offenses.[16] Combine that with the restriction of all freedoms and subjection to dehumanizing treatment, and bloodshed seemed inevitable. Fights were an almost constant occurrence, and on rare occasions guards would openly assault inmates. I grew weary of seeing people battered and bloodied, which was ironic given my former experience as a gangster. We were regularly on lockdown. Sometimes it was the whole prison. More often it was just D and E dorms. It seemed like we ate johnnies just as often as we went to the cafeteria. Between the fights, the riots, the lockdowns, and the extreme temperatures, it was pure misery.

I was able to stay sane through it all by a tremendous amount of social support. The lifting up I received from the outside world went a long way toward reducing hostility and mediating the psychological trauma of the environment.[17] I regularly received visits and steady correspondence that came from family and occasionally from friends. The most important of all though was my mom, who vowed to never stop supporting me and made sure to send a letter every couple of days. Her zealous reinforcement of my spirit coincided with her own transformative journey. She divorced my father and later married Brian. This union gave me a stepsister, Delilah, and a stepbrother, Shawn. My new brother and I had gone to Judson High School at about the same time, and he knew of me by reputation, but I did not know him. My mom joined support groups for relatives of incarcerated individuals, starting with Families Who Care and then moving on to the Texas Inmate Families Association (TIFA).

At some point, the president of the San Antonio chapter of TIFA decided to step down, and my mom was elected as the new president. She went at it with gusto, trying to get the word out that the organization existed, because she constantly found people with incarcerated loved ones who had no idea that there was any support to be found. She had really come into her own, becoming bolder in her public speaking. She also began approaching government representatives and legislators with ease and confidence, and she earned the respect of TDCJ personnel who would come to speak at her meetings. I was extremely proud of her.

I also received letters from the friends I made while incarcerated, especially Billy and Baron. Continuous spiritual encouragement came from Billy, while Baron provided advice on how to survive in prison. Baron was a White, 57-year-old former army sergeant major that I met at Garza West. He was a heroin addict, armed robber, and penitentiary veteran. He was perverted, hilarious, and crazy as hell. He ended up in the Dalhart Unit. Both of them would continue to write me and track my journey through the system.

The other prisoners gave me passive-aggressive flack about getting the lion's share of the mail. Some of the people around me had poor literary skills and would ask me to write letters for them. It was always awkward, as they rarely knew what they wanted me to write. But I would do it anyway, as any goodwill I could endear improved my chances of maintaining a peaceful existence.

The peace I was able to attain was tenuous, as the dorm was always chaotic and transitional. In mid-November, I heard the call "Bolden, fall out for chain." I was relieved to finally escape the dismal dungeon of D dorm at Garza East, but I also knew that it meant I would be starting all over. This time it was at the Dominguez Unit in my hometown, San Antonio.

CHAPTER 9

Between the Lines

THERE IS A cliché that the worst parts of prison are the boredom and monotony. I strongly disagree with that. The worst parts of prison were the lack of safety and the ever-present state of uncertainty. In the late 1950s, sociologist Gresham Sykes's study on a maximum security prison in New Jersey was published in his seminal treatise on incarceration.[1] In it, he describes the pains of imprisonment, including the deprivation of liberty, which is the loss of freedom and being cut off from friends and family in the outside world; deprivation of goods and services; deprivation of sexual relations; deprivation of autonomy, which meant the stripping away of individual choice from all things, down to what you could eat, how you could wear your hair, when you could use the bathroom, and when you could sleep; and deprivation of security, as the prison habitat virtually eliminated the possibility of ever being safe. The cumulative effect of these deprivations was a psychological brutality that crushed the minds and spirits of prisoners. To resist the mental torture and mitigate the pains of imprisonment, some people would lash out in a war against everyone, and others would form an alliance with fellow prisoners to resist authority.

Either by purposeful intent or by haphazard design flaw, the mode of operation in the 1990s Texas prison system was chaos. This was achieved by the constant shuffling around of inmates within and between the 110 prisons. I had been incarcerated for less than a year and was now being transferred to a third penitentiary. It would be here at the Dominguez Unit that I would begin to climb a Mt. Everest of self-improvement, against an avalanche of shit that life and the system were rolling downhill toward me. Just as bad, I was about to find myself once again embroiled in gang conflict, but this time I would be tangled up in the web of affairs of something even more dangerous—prison gangs.

Originating in jails and penitentiaries, prison gangs exist on an interstitial level between organized crime and street gangs. They share some characteristics of organized crime such as organizational capacity and profit motivations.[2] They also differ from street gangs in that they are more likely to engage in instrumental violence, are stricter in racial and ethnic membership requirements, are covert and collective in their illegal behavior, and have more serious repercussions for disloyalty.[3] Researchers conducting an extensive study on gang members in Texas prisons concluded that official designations of prison gangs versus street gangs are of little practical value, as gang members do not actually differentiate the two. The culture of the street and prison were significantly intertwined.[4] To my chagrin, this interweaving of gang culture was about to teach me that prison gangs are not to be trifled with.

To exacerbate the chaos, one of the side effects of Texas's 1990s venture into mass incarceration was the rapid expansion of prison gangs. Besides the influx of street gang members that were being newly incarcerated, Texas had also retrieved the excess inmates that were being housed in California, which had previously had the largest prison system. These returning inmates brought back with them a sophisticated array of gang culture. Although Los Angeles and Chicago had long been known as the street gang capitals of the United States, California and Texas became the major sources of prison gangs, generating 70 percent of the known security threat groups (STGs— the official term for prison gang) in the country.[5] Gangs were delineated by race, and the Hispanic prison gangs formed along geographic lines. There were constant riots as gangs battled for control of the prisons.

Late November 1996—Dominguez, Time Served: 11 Months

It seems odd to think of a prison destination as lucky, but with over a hundred penitentiaries that I could possibly end up in, landing in my hometown was fortuitous. This meant that visitation for me would be fairly steady, and even though there was the dread of having to adapt to a new prison, I was elated that my family would not be far away. The Dominguez Unit had the same general transfer unit layout as Garza East and West. I was put in E dorm, which worried me at first, but I was relieved to find out that it did not have the same violent reputation as its counterpart at Garza East.

Upon entering the tank, the Mexican gangs who wanted to see which group I ran with rushed me, but they were disappointed when I announced that I was Black. The Black inmates with clout in the dorm welcomed me. This included Big Ringer, who was the spokesperson for the Blacks in the dorm, Little Ringer (no relation to Big Ringer), who was a former Crip and who now led the Christians in the dorm, and Wolf, an OG Blood, who didn't give me flack about leaving the Bloods and chose to mentor me anyway. I would spend much of my initial free time in Little Ringer's prayer circle and Bible study. Though most of the Christians were Black, it was nondiscriminatory, and everyone was welcome. Without any trouble, I had

TABLE 9-1

Texas Black and White Prison Gangs (Late 1990s)[1]

Group	Enemies	Allies	Notes
W-Aryan Brotherhood of Texas (ABT)	All Black, AC, BA, HPL, TS		Attempted to reorganize as a religion[2] to circumvent TDCJ anti-gang measures
W-Aryan Circle (AC)	ABT, All Black, MM, WK	TM, DWB	Spreads racism through written materials
B- Bloods	Crips		
B- Crips	Bloods		
W-Dirty White Boys (DWB)	All Black	TM, WK	Transplanted from federal prisons
B- Mandingo Warriors	All White	Bloods	
W-Texas Mafia (TM)		DWB, TS, WK	Created by White allies of Texas Syndicate (TS)
W-White Knights (WK)	All Black, AC	TM, DWB	

NOTES:

W = White; B = Black

BA = Barrio Azteca; HPL = Hermandad de Pistoleros Latinos; MM = Mexican Mafia; TDCJ = Texas Department of Criminal Justice

[1] See Fong, "The Organizational Structure"; Santana and Morales, *Don't Mess with Texas.*
[2] Texas Aryan Brotherhood–Church of Aryan Christian Heritage (TAB-COACH).

secured a place in the subculture of E dorm, and it wasn't long before I had an unintended climb up the Christian social ladder.

Each night, before lights out, we would hold a prayer circle, and anyone was invited. Our prayer circle continuously grew larger, and people began to recognize me as Little Ringer's protégé. I led the Bible studies on Wednesday nights, and I was asked to rap in church on many occasions. Though I did not enjoy the same celebrity status I had attained in Garza East, I became a recognizable face and voice among the Christians. Once Little Ringer caught chain to Bartlett State Jail, everyone expected me to lead the prayer circles and Bible studies, so I became the de facto head of the Christians in the dorm. My place in the prison social system was set, but I still had a multitude of other problems to overcome.

My history of asthma and allergies did not save me at Dominguez. The classification officer had no patience for my health problems, and I was assigned to Hoe Squad. Some people take issue with referencing the work done by inmates as slavery, but if it is not slavery, it is the closest thing to it. The Thirteenth Amendment to the U.S. Constitution abolishes slavery

TABLE 9-2

Texas Latino Prison Gangs (Late 1990s)[1]

Group	Region	Enemies	Allies	Notes
Barrio Azteca (BA)	El Paso/West Texas	ABT, MM, PRM, TXCB, TS, RU	West Texas Street Gangs	Enforcement arm of the Juarez Cartel
Hermandad de Pistoleros Latinos (HPL)	Laredo, Corpus Christi, Galveston	ABT, BA, TXCB, RU, TS	MM, Los Zetas	Factions—the .45s and 16/12s
Mexican Mafia (MM or Mexicanemi)	San Antonio, South Texas	TS, RU, BA	HPL, Bandidos, Latin Kings, Cartels	Separate from CA Mexican Mafia
Partido Revolucionario Mexicano (PRM)	Mexican Nationals	BA, TS	Sinaloa Cartel, Border Brothers	AKA Borrachos, Mexicles
Raza Unida (RU)	Rio Grande Valley, Corpus Christi, Dallas	BA, HPL, Latin Kings, MM, TS	Corpus Christi Street Gangs	Raza Unida Surenos— south Texas faction
Texas Chicano Brotherhood (TXCB)	Rio Grande Valley	TS, TCB		Split from Tri-City Bombers street gang
Texas Syndicate (TS or Ese Te)	Houston, Austin, Dallas, Ft. Worth	MM, ABT, BA, HPL, PRM, RU	TM	Created and imported from California

NOTES:

ABT = Aryan Brotherhood of Texas; TM = Texas Mafia

[1] See Fong, "The Organizational Structure"; See Santana and Morales, *Don't Mess with Texas.*

except in the case of punishment for a crime. Texas is one of only three states that does not pay prisoners for their work, the other two being Arkansas and Georgia. Being forced into exhaustive labor without pay and having restricted freedom certainly fit the definition of slavery, and Texas had a history of working inmates almost to death.[6]

My first time out in the fields was abysmal. It was bitingly cold, and my ultrathin white clothes and slim green jacket were all I had for warmth. The inmates were lined up in small rows of four or five, and we hit the dry, cold dirt endlessly in synchronized step chanting, "one-two-three-four-step." The bosses who rode horses and carried shotguns yelled at us if we fell out of pattern. Snot was constantly running down my nose and crusting over my face, but I could only wipe it at brief intervals, so as not to fall out of line. The repeated chant was maddening, so I began to think of rhymes in my head; then I sang them out loud to keep our cadence. "Our fingers are cramped and our arms are sore. One-two-three-four-step. We do this crap cause we want to make parole. One-two-three-four-step." I was timid at first, but the other inmates either appreciated it or didn't mind, so I kept going. It was the only distraction from the misery. I endured through sheer willpower as my body had never been conditioned for a full day of agricultural work. The next day, I was so sick and sore that I could not get out of bed. Mercifully, my Hoe Squad was not called out that day. I lay in bed thinking about the suffering of my ancestors on slave plantations and realizing the clever insidiousness of keeping a population too exhausted to revolt. It was not lost on me that the Hoe Squads were lined with black and brown people. Subsequent days would find me back in the fields, continuously hitting the dirt with the garden hoe and coming back exhausted and sick, while the Texas Department of Criminal Justice and private farmland owners reaped the benefits of our unpaid labor.

Winter brought both harshness and blessings in disguise. My 19th birthday passed without fanfare, and I felt like I had already lived three lifetimes. The days got unusually cold by San Antonio standards. The prison walkways iced over and needed to be sanded. The weather gave me a brief reprieve from the Hoe Squad, as even the bosses didn't want to deal with the cold. I was promoted to trustee status and that meant that I was eligible for better work assignments. But prison was just like anywhere else; it was all about whom you know. So I set about networking, trying to find a way out of the hellish Hoe Squad. It wouldn't be easy, as no one was going to give up a coveted job of their own accord, but I had nothing but time on my hands.

As the temperature began to warm, creatures started to appear. Scorpions were one of the main problems at Dominguez. Inmates learned very early on to bang their shoes and flip them upside down before putting them on, in case any creepy crawlies had decided to take up residence. That tactic once saved me from stepping into a scorpion that was squatting in my boot. Snakes were a concern on the Hoe Squad, though most of those we encountered were not harmful. We would occasionally have to deal with rattlesnakes, which the inmates would hack to death with garden hoes. As the heat increased, I renewed my efforts to get out of the fields.

In early April, after five months in the Hoe Squad, the good name I had made for myself and my persistent job change requests finally paid off in a big way. I was assigned to the Commissary. In a unit of 2,276 people, only 8 inmates were assigned there. Though it was considered a prestigious job assignment, having air conditioning was really the only perk.

Even though most of my time was consumed with work and spiritual endeavors in prison, I was still determined to make something of myself, and I was not idle about my education. My problem was that the system was working against me. During processing, I butted heads with Individual Training Program (ITP) interviewers, who lambasted me for not being able to verify my GED. The copy I had in my possession did not satisfy them, and they said that my inability to verify was the same thing as refusing to take GED classes, which would look bad for me when I came up for parole. I was flabbergasted at their refusal to accept my GED, and taking more GED classes would feel both fraudulent and wasteful on my part. In prison, I usually acquiesced to whatever the authorities required of me, but being accused of lying about having a GED was too much like the injustices that used to cause me to lash out. I felt the old familiar anger from the strain of being treated unfairly. I was telling the truth, and I refused to back down. In retrospect, I suspect that they had some incentive to get butts in seats for the GED classes, an inmate's academic record be damned!

After months of an impasse, my GED was finally verified, which allowed me to take non-GED courses from Windham School District, which provided all of TDCJ's noncollege education. I took a life skills class, which I found very useful, and I dove into the assignments with gusto. We had to learn public speaking, which I took to, but most people dreaded. One of our first projects was to design a gang-awareness campaign to discourage youth from joining gangs and educate parents on warning signs. This was right up my alley, and I shined. One of the visitors to the class was my old history teacher from Judson, Ms. Mary Wynn. She was now working as the director of public education for the rape crisis center. We began occasional correspondence, through which she offered positive encouragement.

There was a tradition in some of the Texas prisons in which the warden would walk around outside, and inmates could approach to discuss issues they were having. It had mostly been a ruse,[7] as the warden would reassure the inmates that the problem would be taken care of. It would boost prisoner morale, but the issue was often never addressed. The warden at Dominguez was different. A middle-aged African American man, Warden Roy Washington was highly respected by the inmates. Many of the situations brought to him saw some form of redress. I requested a word with the warden as I passed by him. I was surprised because he remembered me regarding the GED verification problems. I requested to join his new Inside Look program, which brought in juveniles who had been in trouble with the law to spend the day with inmates. It was a little different than Scared Straight, because the goal was realistic communication with the kids about what the future held, rather than scare tactics. By the middle of May, I was added to the ten-man Inside Look team.

A couple of Saturdays a month, a group of ten to twenty kids would be brought in. They would sit in a semicircle, and four or five of the inmates would take turns speaking to them about life choices. They would then ask us questions, which we would answer truthfully, but we would shut them down if they attempted to glorify us. They would eat johnnies, and we would show them various aspects of prison life, such as the Hoe Squad. At some point, I encountered a kid who started trembling when I was speaking. It turns out that he had been at the Crip/Ambrose party where I fired the warning shot. He thought I was going to hurt him. I went out of my way to be kind to him and to provide as much wisdom as I had to offer in hopes that it would inspire him to change directions in his life. On some occasions, the media would show up to report on the program. My family saw me on the evening news two nights in a row and went wild over it. Some of the inmates were playfully asking for my autograph. I recall watching a news program later where they checked up on the kids who had gone through Inside Look. There was one boy who had saved the johnnie sack lunch and kept it in his refrigerator. He looked at it every day to remind himself of what he had seen.

In Texas prisons, we walked single file on a path we called the yellow brick road, because it was delineated by a yellow line. Crossing the yellow line was grounds for serious trouble and disciplinary action. On the surface, it would seem like staying on a positive path should be as clear cut as following the yellow brick road. Having attained a higher-status work assignment and a rewarding spiritual social life, along with an eager pursuit of both religious and secular education, I was on a positive trajectory, and things were looking up. But it is not that easy in prison. Staying in your lane felt just short of impossible as the system was set up for constant upheavals. Just when you thought you had your footing, TDCJ would sweep your feet right out from underneath you.

With the heat constantly rising, and both Little Ringer and Wolf having been transferred, I found myself being tested by inmates on all sides. Heading up the Christians in the dorm was becoming taxing, because there were people who were trying it as a con game. This put me in a difficult position, because once the gangs became aware of the behavior, they would approach me concerning any individual in question. I would then have to choose to defend a person or not, which felt like throwing someone to wolves. Beyond this, I would face internal challenges from Christian factions arguing that they were the only ones with the "truth." The most defeating obstacle, though, was feeling inadequate when someone came to me with problems that were beyond my realm of experience. With all of my new responsibilities, I was no longer able to conduct Bible studies very often and was relieved to finally let it go. I passed the torch to Bedrock, a former heroin addict and old Hispanic dinosaur that I got along with well. But my issues with other prisoners were not limited to my religious role. I would also have to navigate conflicts with another commissary worker who was trying to get away with stealing, and with a member of Aryan Circle trying to bait me into a fight so that I would lose my privileges. I should have learned my lesson that all of these foreshocks were indicators that a massive earthquake was coming, but I was overly distracted with things coming at me from all sides and was unprepared for everything that happened after.

In the early 1970s, the rise of Fred Carrasco and his organization Los Dons would change the San Antonio underworld landscape, leaving a gangland legacy that influences the modern groups of today. Characterized as a charismatic genius and a folk hero, Carrasco, it was believed, could have been a great leader in legitimate society had circumstances been different.[8] Raised in the Victoria Courts gang, he was familiar with barrio networks and street-level gang warfare. He later became a soldier for the Melchor de Los Santos quasi-rueda (drug entrepreneur) distribution network in the 1960s.[9] After a few minor offenses, he picked up a murder charge at the age of 18, and his trajectory was set. Upon returning, he recruited from San Antonio's barrio gang networks and built a drug distribution empire.[10] Refusing to tolerate competition, he taxed, converted, or eliminated other dealers, ultimately expanding his empire beyond San Antonio, throughout South Texas, into other states, and across the border into Mexico. He was ruthless. Changing up the tactics of the drug game, he required a blood oath from people he worked with, usually extracted during critical junctures in gang operations—and he meant it.[11] By the end of it all, he would allegedly rack up a body count of forty-eight people, many of whom had been members of his own organization.[12]

No stranger to prison, Carrasco refused to be caged. After being caught by Mexican authorities in a roundup of his operations, he successfully escaped from the Guadalajara military prison in 1972.[13] A year later, he was recaptured during a motel shootout with police in San Antonio. In 1974, Fred Carrasco managed to have a cache of firearms smuggled into the Huntsville Unit where he was incarcerated. Fred and two associates captured twelve hostages, including inmates and staff, and staged an eleven-day standoff. The culmination of that event was a shoot-out ending with the death of one associate, two hostages, and Carrasco himself.[14] Though it seemed as though the violence surrounding Fred Carrasco was finally over with, the captains of his organization, Los Dons, would show up again a decade later, this time as high-ranking members of the newly founded Texas Mexican Mafia.[15]

Initially a defensive unit against the Aryan Brotherhood of Texas, the Mandingo Warriors, and the Texas Syndicate (TS), the Mexicanemi (Texas Mexican Mafia) claimed San Antonio as its Capital de Aztlan and proceeded to push TS out of its turf. The legacy of Carrasco showed up in the group through ruthless violence, blood oaths, strong marriage connections to drug organizations in Mexico, and taxation of independent drug dealers.[16] Having solid connections with the Gulf Cartel and Los Zetas, and later establishing relationships with the Sinaloa and Juarez drug trade organizations, the Texas Mexican Mafia consolidated a large portion of the heroin trade.[17] As members were released from prison and found no viable economic occupations outside of the drug trade and related criminal enterprise, they began recruiting from the barrio gang networks in San Antonio. Heroin use and lower-level drug dealing increased among San Antonio gang members, as did the ambition of gangsters to eventually graduate into a prison gang.[18] As mass incarceration brought more and more street soldiers into prison, gang members with established street reputations became prime recruits for the Texas Mexican Mafia, eventually making it the largest prison gang in Texas.

True to penitentiary patterns, as the heat increased in the beginning of May, violence began to increase as well. The Mexican Mafia had been at war with Aryan Circle for the past year, with intermittent flare-ups. A lockdown resulted from Mexicanemi cracking open the skulls of some of the White gang members. Though shanks were plentiful, they weren't actually used that often. They were clearly contraband, so getting caught with one spelled major trouble. It made little sense to take that risk, when one could instantly create a tool of destruction from what we were allowed to possess. The most common prison weapon was the "jack mack," which consisted of placing a canned good bought at commissary in a sock and swinging it at someone's head. The largest, heaviest weapon to use was a can of jack mackerel fish. The amount of people who got their heads split open seemed to far surpass the number of people who were stabbed.

The prison gangs were continuously becoming more sophisticated and, through a variety of methods, were able to communicate between prisons. One method was to have people in the free world call up radio shows and give shout-outs that had encoded messages in them. Gang members at different locations would hear them. When gang wars and riots occurred at one prison, they would simultaneously occur at several other facilities. TDCJ responded with preemptive lockdowns of penitentiaries whenever a riot contagion started. On occasion we would find ourselves confined to our bunks, eating johnnies, even though nothing had occurred at our prison. To disrupt power bases, TDCJ would ship some of the people involved in riots off to other institutions and move the remaining inmates around within the prison. After the Latino versus White incident, there was a major inmate shuffle, and our dorm landed a large contingent of Mexican Mafia.

Two of the Mexican Mafia additions were assigned to bunks in my corner area. Broc was a short Hispanic and Blanco was a very tall, blond, White guy, who seemed to have no Latino heritage but had still cast his lot in with MM. Two of the other Mexicanemi newcomers were important for me. One was Milo, who was very short, bespectacled, and gentle in character. Milo wanted to genuinely learn about Christianity and was struggling between that desire and his obligations as a gangster. I spent a great deal of time in one-on-one Bible study with Milo. The other important newcomer was William, a skinny guy who was a bit taller than me. William and I knew a little of each other from the free world. He used to run with one of the Hispanic gangs at Judson. We hit it off and spent a lot of time chatting about girls and reminiscing. I was naive and thought nothing of it, but what I did not realize was that William was the highest-ranking Mexican Mafia in the tank. The Mexicanemi would "spread" (pool commissary items together to make a big meal) almost every night, and they would invite me to eat with them. I always made sure to contribute my own portion of commissary, but I still thought nothing of it, other than that I was enjoying the company of people from San Antonio.

I wasn't the only person invited to meals that was not a part of MM, but the guests were mostly Tango Orejon (Tawn-go Or-e-hone). The Tangos were Hispanic hometown cliques that used to serve as backup and recruitment pools for the prison gangs.[19] Dissatisfied with their role in prison gang politics, they had now arisen as an alternative to the traditional prison gangs. When they began to rise in numerical membership, TDCJ classified them as loosely affiliated STGs. They united for defensive purposes, and it naturally connected individuals who decided to pursue criminal activity together. However, they had no hierarchy or structure. Inmates who wanted to leave could do so, and most went back to their original street gangs or to nonaffiliation when they left prison. Their popularity would send them to war with the major prison gangs on occasion.

ROYAL (BIG TIME KING): The Texas Mexican Mafia, they recruit notoriously, so it is a different kind of gang situation, once you go to jail you have to decide like in San Antonio, if you are Mexican, it is either Orejon or like La Eme, you know what I'm saying, you better choose real quick or you get out real quick or whatever the case might be you know.

Table 9-3

Tango Blast: Hispanic Hometown Cliques (Late 1990s)[1]

Name	Hometown	Enemies	Alliance
Capirucha /ATX	Austin	Texas Syndicate	Four Horseman/ Tango Blast
Corpitos/Charco	Corpus Christi		
D-Town	Dallas	Texas Syndicate	Four Horseman/ Tango Blast
EPT (El Paso Tangos)-915/ Chucos	El Paso		Barrio Azteca
Foritos/Foros	Ft. Worth	Texas Syndicate	Four Horseman/ Tango Blast
Houstone/H-Town	Houston	Texas Syndicate	Four Horseman/ Tango Blast
Orejones/ San Anto	San Antonio		Mexican Mafia
Valluco	Rio Grande Valley	Texas Chicano Brotherhood	Puro Tango Blast
West Texas Tango/ Wesos/Puro West	Lubbock, Amarillo, Abilene, West Texas	Barrio Azteca	Puro Tango Blast

NOTES:

[1] See Mike Tapia, "Texas Latino Gangs and Large Urban Jails: Intergenerational Conflicts and Issues in Management," *Journal of Crime and Justice* 37, no. 2 (February 2013): 256–274.

The alliance of Tangos from the cities of Austin, Houston, Dallas, and Ft. Worth was known as the Four Horseman. The Tangos from West Texas and the Rio Grande Valley would later join that coalition, and they would be known overall as Puro Tango Blast. Most of the other Tangos were not on good terms with the organized prison gangs, but Tango Orejon were considered the eyes and ears of the Mexicanemi at the time. I did not realize that other people were watching my association with the Mexican Mafia very closely.

While there were specific ranks in Hispanic prison gangs, William was very secretive about them. He did explain a basic classification system for me though. He referred to the Tango Orejon and the lowest levels of association as Esquina, which means corner or backup.[20] The line was blurred as to whether or not they were actually a part of Mexicanemi. Esquina were viewed as helpers, but from an outsider's perspective, they largely seemed to be cannon fodder as they took the brunt of violence being dished out. The next level, Prospecto, comprised Mexican Mafia soldiers. William was a Prospecto.

The final stage would be a full-fledged member, called a Carnal (brother). Interestingly, unless there was war, or if someone had express permission or orders to do so, it was taboo to disrespect or harm anyone that was a higher level than you, even if they were in another gang. Doing so would result in a severe punishment from your own gang (known as a "violation").

I also interacted with the Mexicanemi's primary enemy, Texas Syndicate (TS). On the other side of the cement half-partition from me was Stumpy, who was the highest-ranking member of the TS in the dorm. He was short and chubby, and I loathed him. He and his right-hand sidekick, Culebra, a skinny, pale-skinned guy who barely spoke English, always seemed to be plotting some con hustle. Stumpy and Culebra tried to rope me into a scheme to steal from the commissary for the Texas Syndicate. They were very displeased with my flat refusals. Stumpy was also extremely annoying, as he was incessantly whistling and making unnecessary noise, which would keep me from sleeping. He knew that I didn't dare call him out on his obnoxious behavior. I did not care for the pair of them, but I did not have any issue with the Texas Syndicate per se. In fact, there was one of the TS, named Big Tex, on the other side of the dorm, who I got along well with. Big Tex was extremely tall. At six-foot-something, he easily towered over most Mexicans. He was also impossibly ripped and looked like he belonged on a cover of a muscle magazine. He had a kind heart, and I enjoyed conversing with him. I went to him once, when I desperately wanted to look at a *Penthouse* magazine. He politely turned me down, saying I was a respected Christian in the dorm, and he was not going to contribute to corrupting me.

On an evening in early July, I noticed tensions were getting high. One of the occupants of my corner area was Bullet, a short, ripped, Black guy with a shiny bald head. Bullet told someone that while he was masturbating he caught Blanco watching him. The rumor spread, and it was an insult that the Mexican Mafia could not let stand. One of the clear cues that something is going to happen is when inmates keep their boots on as they lie down for the night. The MM kept their shoes on that night. Nervous, I stayed awake as long as I could before finally drifting off to sleep, but the shuffling woke me up. Blanco spun a jack mack sling and slammed it into Bullet's head. Bullet fell off his bunk but, amazingly, popped back up. He broke out of the corner and got to the open space of the dayroom where he boxed with Blanco and Broc. Even though Blanco had the jack mack sling, he had lost the element of surprise, and his weapon was no longer effective. Bullet seemed to be easily handling both Blanco and Broc in the open space. The guards finally rushed in and took them away.

The bosses knew it wasn't over, though. They waited outside with a video camera and their gear. The Blacks and the Mexican Mafia lined up in

V shapes facing each other. Big Ringer and William were at the tip of each spear. I cared about both of these groups of people and did not want this to go down. I got off my bunk and began to approach them, seeing the mass of guards outside the dorm and the video camera out of the corner of my eye. Both Big Ringer and William yelled at me to stay out of it, and I reluctantly got back in my bunk, praying to God to not allow this to happen. Miraculously, it did not. They talked it out and agreed that the wrong had been addressed, and there was no more beef. Everyone went back to their assigned bunks. The bosses did not let it go with that, though. They kept us up all night, taking us out one by one to be interrogated. Bullet, Broc, Blanco, and five other Mexican Mafia/Tango Orejon were moved from the dorm.

I had a conversation with Big Ringer the next day, and he lectured me on my associations. I found out that the Texas Syndicate had targeted me because they disliked that I was hanging out with the Mexican Mafia, and they were really pissed that I refused to steal for them. Big Ringer had caught wind of it and told them that if they harmed me they would face off against the Blacks in the dorm. The TS decided that it wasn't worth it. An attack on me had been averted with me being none the wiser. I decided to take Big Ringer's advice, and I stopped eating with the Mexican Mafia.

The violence was just getting started both inside and outside of prison. On an afternoon in late August, I was watching the local news in the day-room when the bottom dropped out from under me. On the top story, they showed a drive-by shooting from the previous night. My stepbrother, Shawn, and my homegirl, Blondie, were two of the victims. They had been at a club that night and were just leaving a Taco Cabana when a black low-rider full of Crips pulled alongside them and unloaded an Uzi and a 9-millimeter. Blondie was shot in the back, and her lung collapsed. She was in critical condition. Another girl who was with them was also shot in her lower back and through her hand. Parts of her intestines were removed, and she needed to have major reconstructive surgery on her hand, as the bullet had shattered all of the bones in it. Shawn was shot through both of his legs, and a bullet was still lodged in him.

I lost my mind and almost lost all my progress in that moment. A few weeks before, a Crip had accosted Shawn, outside of an Albertsons grocery store. The guy threatened to kill him for being related to me. My first thought was that he had tried to follow through on that threat. Tears streaming down my face, I was in a rage. I called out for any Crip to come and fight me. There were either no Crips in the dorm at the time or no one cared to take me up on my challenge. A guard came in to see what the commotion was about, and someone said that my brother had gotten shot. They took me out and brought me to an administrative office where they allowed me to call home. My stepsister, Delilah, was the one who answered and gave me all the details. I went back to my dorm and bunk and stayed in it the whole night, mentally wrestling with how I should deal with the situation. I finally came to my senses before falling asleep. Thankfully, no one seemed to hold my outburst against me, given the situation. The Crips who did it got caught, and it turned out to be a case of mistaken identity. Shawn just happened to be driving the same type of car as someone that they were after.

Soon after that incident, William came back from a visit with his mom, in which he gave her cryptic warnings about calling to check on his status before attempting to visit again. He looked very worried and pulled me to the side. I asked him what was wrong, and he told me that it would be best if I stayed inside that night and avoided the recreation yard. I asked him not to do anything stupid and normally would have pressed the issue, but I was still mentally tapped over Shawn and Blondie being shot. I stayed inside but regretted not taking more time with him.

During rec time I was sitting on my bed writing a letter, when one of the other inmates said "Everybody is fighting," in a nonchalant voice. There were windows at the top of the dorm that didn't open but let in the sunlight. You could see out of them if you stood up on the top bunks. As I stood up on the bed, I could see the barbed-wire fences shaking and clouds of dust swirling. He was right, it looked like everyone on the rec yard was fighting. A war had kicked off, and the Mexican Mafia, who had greater numbers and the hometown advantage, was tearing the Texas Syndicate to pieces.

All of a sudden it felt like someone had shot fire into my eye, and I fell face first into my pillow. I could hear the sounds of people choking and gasping all around me. The guards had shot pepper gas into the rec yards, and it was leaking into the dorms through the vents. The officers turned on a giant fan in the roof, and all the coughing, gasping, and red-eyed people in the tank rushed to get under it. Mercifully, the gas began to dissipate and only faintly lingered. Everyone was called back from their work assignments, and the prison was locked down. We heard that the war had kicked off in the C and E dorm rec yards and that there were a lot of people who were badly hurt. My stomach was turning flips as I worried about my friends.

A few hours passed, and then the guards brought all the people from the rec yard back inside and told them to go to their assigned bunks. The Mexican Mafia came in first. I asked William if he was all right, and he was. The MM had clearly been the victors on the rec yard. The Texas Syndicate came in next, and they were in bad shape. The bosses made sure that everyone got in their bunks and took their shoes off. I had a nauseating feeling as I tried to lie down, but immediately the dorm started to shake. They were already going at it in one of the other tanks. The MM and TS were on their feet. The Mexican Mafia may have had the upper hand on the rec yard, but due to their loss of people after the Bullet incident, they were outnumbered seven to four by Texas Syndicate in the tank. They went at each other. I felt sick.

Milo was fighting somebody and was backed up into Stumpy, Culebra, and another person. The four TS beat him so badly that he crawled under a table spitting up blood and snot while they continuously kicked him. William was holding his own against the person he was fighting, and he kept moving around so as not to get cornered. Big Tex was beating up Guppy, an MM that was half his size. William came to Guppy's rescue. He picked up the steel trash can and slammed it on his head. Big Tex's skull split open, and he crashed to the ground. William kept smashing the trash can into his head over and over. Seeing Milo and Big Tex lying motionless on the ground with people still beating them broke my heart. I never abhorred violence as much as I did in that moment.

The remaining people on both sides regrouped. William held the trash can in front of him. He was speaking in either Spanish or Nahuatl, the Aztec language that the Mexican Mafia used for code, but since his mouth was full of blood, it just sounded like a snake spitting venom. The intense violence seemed to last an eternity, and the guards just videotaped and watched the whole time. Then the gas finally came. Three grenades. The door was on the other side of the dorm, so I wasn't going to get the worst of it, but I knew that it was going to be bad. Culebra grabbed my sheets to wipe off Milo's blood, which he was covered in. I was more concerned with the gas than I was with responding to the symbolic threat. I put a dry towel on my face as I had learned from previous times that water only makes it worse. I then rammed my face into my pillow. The sounds were nightmarish as people were coughing from the gas and from blood and snot. The bosses were yelling over the intercom for everyone to get on the ground. Injured people and others who were panicking from the gas were banging on the acrylic glass, leaving bloody handprints and begging for help. I wondered how the correctional officers felt, watching all of this happen.

I tried to breathe through my nose and it instantly felt like it had been set on fire. Breathing through my mouth was still painful but much better. I prayed for the Lord to keep me calm through it all. The guards told us to get off of our bunks and get on the floor. As I got down, avoiding the bloody sheets, I slipped on the snot-covered floor. I never imagined that people could produce enough mucus to make a floor slick, but I had to quickly and carefully hold on to the bunks to find a spot on the floor that was a safe enough distance from the Texas Syndicate. There was someone who would not get down from his bunk and kept crying for his mother. The bosses were done waiting, and they shot a bouncy gas grenade. I hated the whizzing sound it made as it bounced around the room releasing gas. As it bounced over me, I felt like fire was creeping down my neck, shoulders, and back. Someone jumped in the shower. The guards rushed in with gas masks and pulled him out. His screams were blood curdling, as he did not know that water makes it worse.

The officers bound everyone's hands behind their back with zip ties that were extremely tight. My circulation was cut off, and my hands almost immediately began to feel numb. The guards then took us to the rec yard and laid us on our stomachs. I thought the worst was over, but I was wrong. Whatever gas concoction we were doused in was an intense attractant for insects. Within minutes, I had ants all over me, and my inability to do anything about it was maddening. Other people were being bitten by mosquitos and a few were stung by scorpions. Beetles and gnats began swarming all over us. Some of the inmates were overcome with panic from the deluge of insects. It was all we could do to use our feet to knock the bugs off of each other.

The bosses were airing out the dorms and taking people to the hospital. After about an hour, they finally cut the zip ties off and strip-searched everyone before sending us to the infirmary. My hands were purple, and my wrists were bruised and throbbing with pain. They gave us each one-minute to shower and then a cursory dry off before issuing us a pair of boxer shorts. In nothing but our underwear, they locked us in a freezing cold room for hours. As we sat there shivering, the guards' walkie-talkies began blaring "Code Red!" The war had broken out in other dorms. I remember looking at my watch. It was 3:17 A.M. I didn't think the night was ever going to end.

After awhile they said our dorm was clear, and they gave us clean sheets and mattresses as they sent us back. I was nervous because they were putting everyone, including all of the remaining combatants, back in the dorm again. They seemed to quickly realize their mistake and they rushed in to grab William and Guppy. They left all of the Texas Syndicate and one Mexican Mafia member. I didn't know him at all but I was terrified for him. He slept with his boots on. My sleep was restless, as I worried that it was not over. By noon the next day, we heard about war jumping off in more places. My bruises and wrist pain would last for days. They punished us further by putting us on lockdown for a whole month, and the johnnies we were given were extra shitty. All visitation was stopped, and we were going to have to earn our privileges back. We settled in for our bunk confinement under the hellish heat of late summer.

Chapter 10

Transitions

THE MASSIVE PRISON construction effort in Texas would grind to a halt after 1997, but the number of people that were regularly being incarcerated did not decrease until the later years of the postmillennium decade. At that time, the private prisons began to sue the State of Texas for not fulfilling their contracts, which required that 80 percent of prison beds stay occupied. Prisons didn't start closing until 2011, at which time the Central Unit and the North Texas Intermediate Sanction Facility shut down. Even still, in 2010, the cost of the Texas prison system to the taxpayer was $3.3 billion.[1]

Texas maintains the largest prison system in the United States, which has the largest prison population in the world. The United States has over two million people incarcerated and another six million under the purview of the criminal justice system. Within that system there are more Black men currently incarcerated than there were slaves in the United States. Law professor Michelle Alexander[2] explains how mass incarceration has reversed civil rights by taking all of those rights away under the guise of a "colorblind" system that in actuality incarcerates Black men at twenty to fifty times (depending on the state) the rates of White men for nonviolent drug offenses. While Alexander places the responsibility on the harsher laws and sentencing from the drug war, economist and law professor John Pfaff disagrees, pointing out that the drug war argument is only applicable to the federal system, but state prisons have a larger proportion of violent offenders. Pfaff goes on to argue that mass incarceration can be traced back to a change in prosecutorial behavior, as the powers of district attorneys became unrestricted and they began to relentlessly pursue convictions at rates heretofore unheard of.[3] I do not see Pfaff's and Alexander's positions as mutually exclusive, as much of the power given to prosecutors came from drug laws. Either way, the end result is the same—the largest prison system in the world, and one that is mostly filled with Black and Brown people.

Not only are people subjected to callous barbarity within prisons but they may lose the right to vote, the right to government assistance, and the right not to be discriminated against in housing and employment after they've been incarcerated. With one in three Black men being incarcerated within their lifetime, the resulting loss of rights and destruction of family cause widespread devastation and ensure a cultural and economic system that will keep feeding the prison complex. Mass incarceration has instituted another racial caste system just as severe as those that have come before it.

Gangs have caused uncounted amounts of family destruction, but the collateral damage of mass incarceration all but ensures that families won't recover. On my road to redemption, I tried to build bridges across oceans, but the seemingly insurmountable tidal waves of gangs and prison would just knock them down.

September 1997—Dominguez Unit, Time Served: 1 Year, 9 Months

A strange transition began to occur in that a peaceful relationship between G-Rocc's family and my own emerged. My cousin Cheryl began dating G-Rocc, and though all sides were wary of the situation at first, no one had hard feelings about our conflict. I had Cheryl relay a message to G-Rocc's mom, Sandra, apologizing for the pain I had caused her family. She said that she knew and that everything was all right. Things were not all right for them though. Soon after, G-Rocc got caught for an armed robbery of a restaurant and was on his way to prison.

Sandra called Texas Inmate Families Association (TIFA) looking for support, not knowing that my mom was now the president of the San Antonio chapter. It was not a problem. They immediately bonded, spending hours on the phone together. G-Rocc had a rough road through the prison system, battling it out at gladiator farms, dealing with multiple assaults and theft of his personal property. He finally got to the point where he was doing well, educating himself and getting into ministry.

In the spirit of healing, I also tried to bridge the gulf with my father. The previous year, my dad was supposed to come visit me for the Christmas weekend. I got up at seven in the morning and prepared myself for the visit. Most inmates tried to keep a fresh white uniform, pressed by keeping it under the mattress, for visiting occasions. He never showed. Despite the major Christmas letdown, my dad began to visit frequently as well as write a lot more, and our relationship improved significantly. But the system was prone to creating difficult obstacles. On December 3, I heard the words that I had grown to dread, "Bolden, fall out for chain!" There would be no more visits from my dad from this point forward, and the flow of his letters would also dry up. I had experienced several waves of friends come and go and seen terrible things at Dominguez, but I had still been near my family in San Antonio. That time was now ending for me. I had been digested enough by the system to finally reach the belly of the beast, the Diagnostic Unit in Huntsville, Texas.

December 1997—Diagnostic Unit (Byrd Unit) and Goree Unit,
Huntsville, Texas, Time Served: 2 Years

The Blue Bird bus seemed to take the scenic route out of San Antonio. We passed through downtown, and Christmas lights were up everywhere. The city had never looked so beautiful to me as it did then. We passed through streets like Rittiman and Walzem, which were my old stomping grounds, and I was flooded with emotions. I felt melancholy because I missed everyone, and now I was being taken even farther away. I felt anxiety and grief over the things that would happen. I also felt worried that anything could happen to me and that I might not see these sights again. After that, the five-hour bus ride in a cramped vehicle, shackled to someone else, was very uncomfortable. Having to be cuffed to someone while they defecated was a nauseating and impractical ordeal. I also experienced motion sickness as it had been so long since I had been in a motor vehicle.

Huntsville was the heart, brain, fist, and anus of the Texas Department of Criminal Justice. The small town boasted Sam Houston State University and seven penitentiaries. The Byrd Unit, which was more commonly known as the Diagnostic Unit, was where determinations were made about the placement of prisoners in the system. The Huntsville Unit, which was known colloquially as the Walls Unit, is where executions take place. It was also the location where 90 percent of inmates were excreted out into the world after being consumed by the Texas prison system. The town housed the Ellis, Estelle, Goree, Holliday, and Wynne Units as well. It was also home to the prison cemetery, where inmates were buried. Those who were unclaimed or whose families were too poor to provide funeral accommodations were laid to rest under wooden crosses with only their inmate numbers inscribed, forever stripped of even the dignity of a name. Huntsville was four hours away from San Antonio. Although I knew this would not be my final destination, the impending distance weighed heavily on me.

Every aspect of the Diagnostic Unit was misery, from the impractical shower practices of shoving forty-five inmates into a room to share twenty water spouts, to the food that I could not stomach. However, the most difficult thing to mentally overcome was the boredom. We spent nearly all of our time confined in the cell. There were no tests or interviews, so the "diagnostic" part was lost on me. We just sat in our cells all day, every day. The only new reading material I received was the inmate orientation handbook; I thought about the irony of receiving it two years into my incarceration.

I only witnessed one fight, but seeing as how we spent all of our time behind closed doors, there was no telling what was going on. The cells at Diagnostic looked like they did in the prison movies, with barred doors that slid open. There were two persons to a cell, and we were paired by age and race. The people the system had swallowed up flowed through the unit in rapid succession. Every two or three days I would get a new celly (cellmate), all of them age 17 to 20, African American, and current or former gang members. I was again reminded of the generation of kids being thrown away. Each newcomer, when first entering the cell, would square up against me in preparation for a fight. I would have to talk him down, assuring him that I was not a threat. Sometimes we got along and sometimes the tension remained. It was exhausting. There were multiple 17-year-olds occupying a monstrously tragic developmental state between immaturity and being forced to grow up too fast. Their punishments ranged from two years, which felt gracious given the circumstances, to sentences that ensured that they would be well into middle age before they could even dream of freedom.

Outside of the Texas Department of Criminal Justice (TDCJ) existed a completely separate juvenile prison system called the Texas Youth Commission (TYC), which had fourteen correctional facilities, nine halfway houses, and numerous residential arrangements with private contractors.[4] The system incarcerated kids between the ages of 10 and 19, and its history of civil rights abuses rivaled that of its adult counterpart.

In the early 1970s, parents' complaints about the illegal incarceration of their children without a hearing led to attorneys Stephen Bercu and William P. Hoffman Jr. filing the class action lawsuit *Morales v. Turman*. The purpose of this landmark case was to stop the commitment of minors without due process. Judge William Wayne Justice surveyed the TYC residents and found that 280 had been committed without seeing a judge and another 863 had not been given legal representation during their hearings. The follow-up investigations conducted by the media, lawyers, law students, clinicians, psychiatrists, academics, and the FBI discovered that the conditions of confinement were brutal. Girls were confined to tiny dark cell blocks rather than the private rooms that TYC had claimed. Boys lived in isolation cells, were forced into utter silence and punitive Hoe Squad labor, and were subjected to random and severe physical assaults from the correctional staff, who also permitted and orchestrated beatings by other youth.[5]

Judge Justice ruled against the State, finding that the conditions of confinement constituted cruel and unusual punishment. The use of physical force was to cease immediately, and the entire system needed to be overhauled with a focus on the right to treatment for juveniles in custody. The ruling would cause the closing of the Mountain View State School in 1975 and the Gatesville State School in 1979, because their punitive environments had moved far beyond the capacity of any possibility of rehabilitative restructuring. Though the State would resist the other changes from *Morales v. Turman*, miring the case down in appeals for the next decade, the scandals uncovered created significant administrative turnover in TYC. The new regime of authorities favored and implemented the mandated reforms, turning the system into a model example of humane juvenile justice. The case was finally settled to the satisfaction of all sides.[6] However, the era of mass incarceration was fast approaching, and it would shift criminal justice philosophy to focusing on kids as the enemy.

Driven by the panic surrounding fears of juvenile violent crime, the Texas mass incarceration binge included a widened net for locking up young offenders. In 1987, Texas adopted a determinate sentencing law that allowed for blended sentencing. Juveniles could now start their sentence in the TYC and then be transferred to the adult system for the remainder of their time. The incarcerated juvenile population began to rise simultaneously with the explosion of street warfare in Texas. This made TYC ground zero for gang proliferation. Administrators recognized the contribution of gangs to the TYC population. The 1991 attorney general's report on gangs in Texas described one-third of TYC referrals as members of named gangs, and another third as members of smaller groups that behaved like or thought of themselves as a gang.[7]

What the authorities did not recognize, was that TYC itself was a gang-generating milieu. On the streets, everyone knew about TYC; its violence, abusiveness, and inescapable gang warfare were legendary. Unaffiliated people who entered the system could no longer remain neutral and often returned fully committed to a street gang.

HOOPS (SKYLINE PARK): A lot of dudes started getting locked up, going to TYC. So, in TYC, it was all about are you a Crip? Are you a Blood? Are you Disciple or People Nation? You know, what category do you fall under? You better pick something, you know what I'm sayin' unless you gonna fade everything. So it was almost like they were either forced to fight everybody, or to pick a gang you know what I'm saying. So, a lot of my homeboys you know became Crips in TYC.

As the panic over juvenile crime reached a fever pitch, blended sentencing was no longer a sufficiently harsh punishment for those wielding the criminal justice hammer. The election of George W. Bush as governor in 1994, and the subsequent passing of the Juvenile Justice Reform Act, greatly expanded the five juvenile offenses subject to determinate sentencing to thirty crimes, lowered the age of adult adjudication in court to 14, and provided $55 million to increase TYC's inmate capacity.[8] In 1995, TYC's average daily juvenile population was 2,263. Four years later, the population of

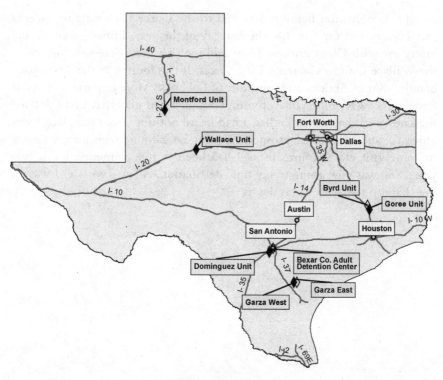

10-1. Texas prisons where time was served. (Graphic by Melissa Tetzlaff-Bemiller.)

youth under its jurisdiction had more than doubled to 5,476.[9] TYC still had room for more and would continue to increase those numbers for the next few years, but the extra space was no longer as pertinent. The new laws meant that some kids would now bypass TYC and be dumped directly into the adult prison system. Many years later, a study found that between 2005 and 2010, the number of juveniles certified as adults in Texas was 49 percent larger than those given a determinate sentence.[10]

As each one of my cellies was transferred out, my heart would feel heavy for him. I was only 19 and had seen plenty of the horror of Texas prisons. I feared what awaited them, as most were sent to the Youth Offender Program at the Clemens Unit, a place with a notorious reputation for violence. Their prognosis for rehabilitation was not good. Juvenile offenders in the Texas adult system were involved in more disciplinary infractions and violence than older individuals.[11] This often landed them in administrative segregation, in more restrictive custody levels, and with more time to serve on their sentence. It was all counterproductive, as it also meant that they were more likely to reoffend quickly upon release,[12] unless of course that was the intention all along.

It was only after being transferred to the Goree Unit for a few weeks that I learned of my fate. On the last day of the year, I finally went to my interview with Classification. They told me that they were sending me to the Wallace Unit in Colorado City, Texas. It was located in the Texas panhandle, west of Abilene and southeast of Lubbock. More importantly, it was four hours away from San Antonio. Though I was glad that I had dodged the known gladiator farm bullet, I had heard nothing about the place I was going to, and I knew the prospect of eight-hour round trips for my family to come visit me was unrealistic. I had been to five penitentiaries in two years, and was now going to my final destination. A few days later I was on the chain to the West Texas desert.

CHAPTER 11

Wally World

AFTER A SIX-HOUR bus trip from Huntsville, we arrived at the Wallace Unit. Colorado City was only twenty-eight miles from Sweetwater, Texas, where the annual rattlesnake roundup occurs and four to five thousand pounds of snakes are captured, with the claim that it only makes up 1 percent of the serpent population in the area. Colorado City was also home to apocalyptic crimson sandstorms, large spiders, and extreme temperatures. I was in a new form of hell.

January 1998—Wallace Unit, Colorado City, Texas,
Time Served: 2 Years, 1 Month

As we got off the bus, the buzz among the inmates was that we had arrived at a gladiator farm after all. One of the buildings was completely locked down and full of prisoners who had just participated in a riot the previous month. It was three of the Four Horseman (Dallas, Ft. Worth, and Houston) against Mexican Mafia and Tango Orejon. It became immediately clear to me that people from San Antonio were not welcome in West Texas. Fucking great!

Survival in prison requires understanding and adapting to the convict code very early on, but it is not enough. Texas's constant shuffling of the inmate cards meant that you never knew where you would end up on the flop, and being prepared for what was hidden in the deck was near impossible. This place would take everything I knew about the prison social strata and flip it upside down.

I thought I would find my place in the social sphere through fellowship with Christian brothers, but instead got a shocking upset to my reality. I was the only person who openly acknowledged being a Christian in the entire K1 dorm. I was told that the church was weak at this prison and plagued with problems. Almost complete dominance was held by the Black Muslims, also known as the Nation of Islam (NOI).

The NOI immediately set about trying to recruit me. Any attempt I made at being social resulted in an NOI sales pitch. It was part of their *da'wa,* a call to proselytize their religious and political beliefs to others. They believed that Islam was the historical religion of Black people and that Christianity had been imposed by slavers and oppressors. Being a young Christian, I was prime fish for the catching. I was approached by NOI at every turn, and by dinnertime on the second day, the rumor had already gotten out that I was a Black Muslim. They had effected a social blockade inside of K dorm. I attempted to stay in my cell as much as possible to avoid the constant attempts at conversion, but to no avail.

My celly, Crescent, was a Black Muslim, and he was the most relentless of recruiters. Crescent and I debated Islam and Christianity every day and every night. Some of our arguments would get heated, and we would go to bed pissed off. I worried what I might wake up to, if I woke up at all. I generally could hold my own when it came to religious arguments, but when Crescent shifted the conversation to revolutionary politics, I became very uncomfortable. Religious texts were my forte, but I was out of my depth on other subjects. I knew very little about history, and certainly nothing substantial about Black history or Black Muslims.

There are a few factions that represent "Black Muslims," but none of them should be mistaken for traditional Islam, which is the second-largest religion in the world. Although they have adopted many of the tenets of Islam, they have taken a different direction, combining those tenets with racialized politics and ideology. The major groups developed independently of one another but are somehow lumped together under the term "Black Muslims." One group derived from the Moorish Science Temple, with beliefs that their ancestors were the Moors that conquered Spain and that their natural religion was Islam. This movement existed for decades, achieving moments of brief popularity in the cities of Detroit, Milwaukee, and Philadelphia. However, a full third of its members lived in Chicago, making a profound impact on gangs in the area. The most notable connection was the conversion of Jeff Fort, the founder and leader of the Black P Stone Nation. Whether or not Fort was accepted in the Temple is disputed, but either way, he changed the name of the upper echelon of the gang to the El Rukns, and the group adopted some of the symbols of Islam. The symbology also became prevalent among the Vice Lords.

The farther-reaching and more widely known segment of the Black Muslims is the Nation of Islam. The founder, Wallace Fard, and powerfully charismatic leaders, Elijah Muhammad and Malcolm X, all served penitentiary time. Since they witnessed firsthand the needs and tribulations of the incarcerated, prison ministry became a major component of the NOI. The ministry focused on self-sufficiency, self-improvement, self-defense, and creating the network necessary for people released from prison to find homes, food, and work. The movement inside of prison steadily grew, doing very little in regard to political agitation except when it came to the protection and expression of their religious rights. During the 1960s civil rights era, they were considered one of the most organized political entities, and though they still lost most of their legal cases, they did win a significant number, which advanced religious rights of prisoners.[1] Through the 1950s and '60s, the Black Muslims made up the only organized group in Texas prisons, and despite expectations to the contrary, they remained peaceful.[2] After protecting the guards and negotiating an end to the Attica prison uprising in 1971, their reputation as prison peacekeepers spread to more areas of the country.

Criminologist and former Arizona prison warden Mark S. Hamm points to a confluence of factors that shifted the Black Muslims away from their positive momentum and toward radicalized politics and prison-gang-like behavior.[3] These factors included Malcolm X's repudiation of the NOI with a stated realization that nonracial, nonsectarian Islam was the only true way forward; the political agitation of the Black Panther minister of information, Eldridge Cleaver, and his popular prison memoir *Soul on Ice*, which began to overtake religious teachings and the directions of Malcolm X, in prominence among incarcerated Black Muslims; the counterintelligence programs (COINTELPRO) of the FBI aimed at destroying Black Power organizations, sometimes through illegal means; the widespread retaliation of prison authorities against Blacks for the deaths of correctional officers during the fatal escape attempt of revolutionary Black Guerilla Family founder George Jackson; and the need to respond to the rise of white supremacist prison gangs, such as the Aryan Brotherhood.

All of these factors, combined with the increase of the African American population in prison and the rise of heroin in the urban ghettos of the 1970s, resulted in a mixture of incarcerated Black Muslims who operated in ways similar to prison gangs, or who were prone to radicalization. Though their reputation would be tarnished, they still remain a prominent force throughout the U.S. prison systems.

Other than my social embargo, the NOI did not wish me ill will. Their constant attempts at recruitment meant that they were always around me and provided me the unintentional benefit of protection. As fistfights were a regular occurrence, the protective shell may have been a barrier from other dangers in the dorm. Outside of K wing though, there were plenty of others who would have liked nothing more than to see me fall.

My first work assignment at Wallace Unit was in the laundry, making rolls of towels and clothes. This should have been an easy thing to do—a straightforward and laid-back, albeit monotonous, assignment. The problem was that I was surrounded by Aryan Circle and the occasional Aryan Brotherhood.

The aggregation of Aryan gangs at this prison was quite large, and consequently, the members were that much bolder. The previous Aryan Circle I had encountered ran with the gang out of necessity, not really buying into the ideology. I was now in the presence of true believers. It was hard enough for me to try to wrap my brain around the NOI's revolutionary ideology, but the belief system of the Aryan Circle was beyond comprehension.

There is a general misunderstanding about how members of White supremacist groups can also be Christians. The simple answer is that they are not. They follow a few different religions, but the confusion comes from their most popular one, which is called Christian Identity. This ideology is nothing like Christianity as most people know it, and it includes the beliefs that the British are God's chosen people and that God made "mud people," which were imperfect Black and Brown people, before his "perfect" White creation of Adam and Eve. They believe that Eve had congress with the Serpent, and Jews were born from that union. The Jews and "mud people" are aligned against Whites, and Armageddon will be a call for Whites to exterminate everyone else.[4]

In response to the prison social system shakeup caused by the end of the building tender system with *Ruiz v. Estelle* in 1980, and an end to the racial segregation of prisoners in Texas with *Lamar v. Coffield 1977*,[5] white inmates organized into the Aryan Brotherhood of Texas (ABT) by 1983. To combat the partially real and partially perceived threat of Black inmates and their assertive advancement in the prison milieu, the ABT established a reputation as being ultraviolent, committing more than a third of all prison gang homicides in its first few years of known existence.[6] The Texas Department of Criminal Justice (TDCJ) responded by placing known ABT members in administrative segregation. As the years went by and people became more adjusted to the new prison system, an internal conflict arose regarding whether the group should focus on continuing the mission of white supremacy or on profit generation as a crime syndicate. The latter option seemed to hold favor.

The Aryan Circle (AC) had once been a small gang in Texas, but crackdowns on ABT, and their relegation to administrative segregation, provided for a massive expansion in the void of White power gangs. Recruiting on a platform of White nationalist ideology, which also disparaged the Aryan Brotherhood as sellouts for letting criminal profit take precedence over racial identity, the AC rapidly expanded in two branches. One "leaf" includes Arizona, Arkansas, Colorado, Florida, Indiana, Kansas, Oklahoma, and Texas.[7] The other leaf includes Louisiana, Pennsylvania, South Carolina, and West Virginia. Rather than attempting to gain power in prisons, their goal is to return to the free world to spread their White nationalist message. For this goal to be successful, it would require staying out of the line of fire. Unlike the confrontationally violent ABT, the Aryan Circle preferred to use sub-terfuge and manipulation, to orchestrate feuds between Black and Brown gangs, or to arrange someone's downfall. This allowed them to fly under the radar, not earning status as a security threat group until 1999, when they declared war on the White Knights.

Though they hated Black people, the ACs' view of mixed-race indi-viduals like me was even more disdainful. I was an object of their disgust and, also, as the only non-Aryan around, I was the primary threat to their plans being overheard. They made blatantly racist remarks toward me and spouted off their Christian Identity rhetoric. I only responded to them with kindness. The harassment let up every once in a while, when their fear, dis-like, and paranoia about the Aryan Brotherhood moved to the forefront. The AC wanted me gone and subjected me to all sorts of mischief, such as contraband randomly appearing near my work station, or the rolls of clothes I made being knocked over and scattered when I wasn't looking. Their machinations finally worked, and I was demoted down to the folding table for my perceived incompetence.

An accidental misfortune brought me a reshuffling of the social cards at Wallace. While exercising with the NOI, I suffered a severe and bloody injury when my foot slipped off the leg press and the pedal came crashing back into my leg. That night I was put on chain to the Montford Unit, which was the medical prison in Lubbock. After a three-day interlude, I was back at the Wallace Unit.

My return back to K-1 dorm came with lots of changes. My social embargo had been removed, mostly because the NOI wanted to dispel the rumor that they had shanked me on the rec yard, and I was put in a different cell. My return to K-1 also came with a job reassignment to the garment factory, where inmates engaged in sweatshop labor making clothes. Most of the clothes were inmate uniforms, but there would be some occasions in which we made unfamiliar items for unknown destinations. I was given the position of janitor, working from 7:00 A.M. to 4:00 P.M. This assignment created a catch-22; since janitors were the only people in the factory with relative freedom of movement, the Mexican gangs were incessantly trying to get me to pass contraband back and forth. If I did it, I would be putting myself at risk for disciplinary action. If I didn't do it, I would be provoking the ire of the gangs. I chose not to participate, which earned me negative marks with them. Each workday was filled with discomfort, as I knew that my position as a Christian was providing me grace by only the thinnest of margins.

Violence, lockdowns, and riots were regular fare for the Texas prison system. Random punishments were also par for the course as prison admin-istration would try to reexert control. Due to a successful death row escape, numerous escapes from TYC, riots, and the sexual assault of a female guard, the year ended with a punitive lockdown.[8] We were shaken down, moved around, and fed peanut butter sandwiches every single meal for ten days— thirty peanut butter sandwiches! The effectiveness of such procedures was questionable, as just a few weeks later, the Barrio Azteca (BA) murdered a member of the Partido Revolucionario Mexicano (PRM) at the Terrell Unit, sparking a gang war systemwide. On Wallace Unit, due to their inability to ascertain gang affiliation, they would segregate and lock down all Hispanic inmates. It did not matter how well anyone was behaving; they would all be punished, and their rehabilitation efforts would be disrupted.

It was rare to get through summers without riots, and the next summer was no exception. The garment factory was on the far side of the prison from K building, so every day the workers would have to walk a long, serpentine path on the yellow brick road. There was a White guy named Poppi in my dorm who worked at the garment factory with me. Poppi was short and husky, with a bald bullet head, large glasses, and several rolls of fat that seemed to take the place of a neck, cushioning his head on his shoulders. He was a Bandido, which is one of the major outlaw motorcycle gangs in the United States and the most dominant one in Texas.[9] Like prison gangs, the outlaw motorcycle clubs (OMCs) occupy the interstitial level of criminal sophistication between street gangs and organized crime and are sometimes the graduation destination of street soldiers. Though the OMCs favor members with criminal records as a way to prevent law enforcement infiltration, their natural habitat was the open road, and while incarcerated, they maintained an existence in the background. The lack of younger members preserved them from most of the conflict, but in the chaos of Texas prisons, anything could happen.

Poppi was walking three people ahead of me in our single-file trek to the garment factory. The bosses stopped us, and we began waiting in the sun for a considerable amount of time. Finally, the word began to trickle down that there was fighting in the factory. The bosses were now frisking all the inmates in line. Someone ran up from behind me. He had a shank that was a toothbrush handle fitted with a razor blade. He ran up to the side of Poppi and stabbed him in the neck area. Blood sprayed out like a sprinkler. There was more screaming as attacks occurred all down the line. The screams and the guards yelling at us to hit the ground was all that could be heard. They corralled us back to our cell blocks, and we found ourselves on lockdown due to another systemwide gang war. That summer, a drug trafficking dispute in the free world resulted in the Mexican Mafia attacking Raza Unida (RU), killing one of their members at the Connally Unit, and bringing overwhelming force down on the few members at the Dominguez Unit. Now RU was fighting back. The Bandidos were allies of the Mexicanemi and were thus subject to RU's rage. After the initial lockdown, Wallace Unit once again segregated all the Hispanic inmates and selectively began releasing them, but for some it would be an extended period of time. When they were finally released, they would not be allowed to return to classes or programs that they were enrolled in due to being gone so long, and some would give up trying to do better.

Erratic gang warfare kept me on edge, but it was not the only source of instability. The guards at Wally World, the derogatory nickname for the Wallace Unit, were predictably awful. Wallace had only been opened since 1994 and seemed to be staffed by small-town good ol' boy correctional officers who had no other job prospects and who relished the opportunity to take frustrations with their personal problems out on the inmate populace. To be fair, a career in corrections is probably far from glamorous. Even at the least threatening, minimum-security prerelease prisons in Texas, correctional officers had low job satisfaction, viewing themselves as bored "prison watchdogs," with an emotional disconnect from the prisoners.[10] Even still, that was no excuse to pour extra torment on others. There were plenty of decent guards who just did their job, but they were not going to go out of their way to prevent any abuse dished out by other officers. Even though witnessing coworkers engaging in abuse may create moral tensions and job stress, the prison guard subculture held little tolerance for employee snitches.[11]

The guards seemed to enjoy harassing the inmates and would write people up for things like standing around in the dayroom. On my way to the chow line or commissary, I would often get pulled out of line, frisked, and accused of being involved in some type of criminal activity or mischief. When I would say that I was not doing whatever it was they suspected me of, an officer would scream in my face, tell me to shut the fuck up, call me a liar, and pile on the insults. I would feel the old, familiar strains of being treated unfairly, so it took great patience to endure this treatment. I knew that the bored guards were just trying to get a reaction so that they would have an excuse to play their punitive torture games. What I didn't know was why they so often picked me as a target.

Being arbitrarily harassed while going to the cafeteria was bad enough, but I also had to deal with it at work. I did not feel good about continuing in my janitorial job, partially because there were far too many sharp objects and volatile characters for me not to feel anxious, and partly because I felt like it was a complete waste of time and energy. I put in a request for a job change based on skill set and received a classification change to support service inmate clerk. My job was also changed to maintenance. In my new assignment, I spent the days locked behind one of three cages and issued out tools as maintenance crews came to get them. Due to an order mix-up early on, the civilian bosses took an immediate dislike of me, and referred to me as stupid and a retard from that point forward. Over time, their attempts at crushing my spirit started to wear on me. My thoughts turned morbid as I wondered if I would ever make it out.

Like the sudden violence of prison wars, you never know when death will come calling. I was unexpectedly summoned to an administrative office one evening. When I arrived, they put me on the phone with my mom. They were allowing her to talk to me to inform me that my grandmother, Rosie Beatrice Bolden, had passed away due to complications with diabetes. I had not seen my grandma since the Thanksgiving before my incarceration. I was never going to see her again. That thought weighed heavily on me. I also wondered if people on the outside were ever going to get the chance to see me, or if this place was going to swallow me up completely. With gang violence and pitfalls on all sides and the psychological warfare of the guards trying to tear me down, I knew that my survival up to this point had been miraculous; my number would come up sooner or later. There had to be a way to overcome this living hell. I didn't want to die or to live a life in prison. I had to climb out of this hole. But how?

CHAPTER 12

Starting from the Bottom

ALTHOUGH THE NATION of Islam (NOI) never stopped try-
ing to get me to turn my back on Christianity, it was my own unquenchable
thirst for knowledge and self-improvement that would cause the Christians
to turn their backs on me. Religious adherents in prison have a tendency
toward literal interpretations of scripture, fundamentalist teachings, and a
refusal to engage with complexities that go beyond basic faith.[1] My desire to
learn more was something that they could not tolerate.

January 1999—Wallace Unit, Colorado City, Texas,
Time Served: 3 Years, 1 Month

The perceived weakness of the Christians at Wallace was due to a couple
of factors. The bulk of the Christian inmates were old, almost elderly. They
were either stuck in their ways or too worn out and tired to put forth any
effort to make the church stronger. Between the gangs and the NOI, young
people were snatched up almost immediately, and the Christians had little
chance for recruitment. Inside the small body of those that were faithful to
biblical teachings, there was just as much strife as there was gang conflict,
and denominational turmoil splintered the Christians into even smaller
groups.

After the NOI's social embargo was lifted, I set about trying to immerse
myself in the church. There was some enthusiasm about me at the beginning, and I was asked to give the message for a Friday service. I started off
rapping in church, but it did not turn out as expected. Although it ignited
excitement among the few younger Christians, Wallace had larger contingents of older, stricter Christian groups, and they did not approve of me or
my gospel rap.

I received more acceptance from a prominent Christian leader named
Kinsey, who ran innovative religious study groups seeking to capture the
younger crowd. Kinsey and the unit chaplain were constantly in conflict
with each other. After Kinsey left, the chaplain loyalists made sure that all
of Kinsey's associates, including me, remained in disfavor.

Though my disapprobation with the older Christians was extensive, I still remained popular with the younger crowd. As time passed, and the population changed, the NOI's stranglehold on the dorm lessened, and I became the de facto leader of the Christians in my wing. I was already running Bible studies, so it was a natural progression.

It was through my role of heading up the Christians in the cellblock that I would commit the final transgression, earning almost complete ostracism from the Christian fellowship. There was another Christian in the dorm that was also shunned by the church. Malcolm was half Black, half Mexican, and mostly an unassuming loner. Curious as to why he did not join the Bible studies or prayer circles in the dorm, I approached him in peace. He was a Jehovah's Witness, which is the reason the other Christians shunned him. That meant nothing to me so I invited him to sit down to discuss our differing religious views. I was astounded to find out that we shared many of the same beliefs. Intrigued, I agreed to come study with the Jehovah's Witnesses. Word of my new activity traveled fast.

At church, I was called up and confronted by a prominent Christian elder. I had still been on probation from my alliance with Kinsey, and now I was being rebuked for my involvement with the Jehovah's Witnesses. My seditious behavior was not going to be tolerated. I was subjected to a public scolding in which the church elders called me a Pharisee and accused me of thinking that I was better than everybody else. I stood there and took this tirade, responding gently, but they kept on. It was clear that I was no longer welcome in the church.

My celly at the time was Skullcap, a young NOI that I got along with well and who never tried to recruit me. After returning from my church berating, I asked Skullcap for a bird's-eye view of everything. He said that people misinterpreted my level of confidence as meaning that I felt superior to them. Here I was, the head Christian in the cellblock, a gospel rapper, and a prominent Christian at the prison for a year, and I made the choice to study with the Jehovah's Witnesses, not caring that the rest of the Christians will be furious and shun me. That, he said, was confidence. It was one of the most important things anyone had said to me. It was a turning point for me as I realized that I could advance on my own without needing to belong to a group or get approval from one.

I had already seen and been through so much. My religious experience was instrumental in catalyzing my mental, behavioral, and existential transformation,[2] but I needed to move beyond a mummified stage of rehabilitation. I was becoming a butterfly, and the congregational cocoon was no longer functional. Religion had created a cognitive change, but its ability to help me overcome social deficits was minimal.[3] I was on my own journey now, and my time with the Christians had reached its conclusion.

. The door to studying with the Jehovah's Witnesses would also close soon after. I had reached the point in their curriculum where most people chose to convert. Though I liked studying with the Jehovah's Witnesses, I could never be one, partly because they disapproved of my nonreligious educational endeavors and partly because they suffered from the same issue as most of the other religions—extreme rigidness and conflict with other religious groups. It all came down to one thing for me: God is Love. All the bickering about ideology and rules and restrictions about things felt hollow to me. I would show love to people even if they had no goodwill toward me, which often seemed the case. I felt all alone in my spiritual journey, but that was okay, as I had already begun to travel a different path.

A major cognitive turning point came through a course I took called Basic Progress. This optional life-management program provided me with a life-changing perspective and a solution for climbing out of the destructive realm of crime and prison. The course was developed and run by James (Jay) Holland Jr., who was a hard-ass that didn't tolerate any whining. His tough love methods seemed callous and extreme, but I felt like he genuinely cared about the students. He taught us that because we had the criminal label we could never be "normal" again, as no one would let us be that way or view us as such. The stigma of our past would be so powerful that most people would not be inclined to give us a chance at anything. We only had two real choices: accept the criminal stigma and stay at the bottom of the social hierarchy, or be exceptional. To be exceptional, we had to do things that were so far above and beyond what people expected or thought possible that there could be no reproach. I made the decision in my heart and mind that I would be just that—exceptional. To become exceptional, I knew I needed to pursue all possible avenues of improvement.

Courses from Western Texas College were available on the unit, but I had to wait until I had been at Wallace long enough to prove that I wasn't a disciplinary concern. When I became eligible, I jumped at the chance. We were allowed to take one class that could be paid for after release. Every other course needed to be paid for up front. Each class cost seventy-five dollars.

After passing all sections of the Texas Academic Skills Program (TASP) test, I was preparing to load up on a full class schedule, when something unexpected, fortuitous, and wondrous happened. The system had always worked against me, but it was about to drop a big gift in my lap. I was called to a meeting with several other inmates, and we were informed that Texas had issued a Youth Offenders Grant for individuals age 18 to 25. If we had maintained good disciplinary records, we were eligible for this benefit. The grant would pay for up to three college courses or a vocational class per semester. It was on! I could take a full load of college classes for the foreseeable future.

I discovered that I loved learning. I craved the intellectual challenge and devoured every subject. Though I enjoyed all of my classes, it was sociology that I fell in love with. The class material was mind-blowing. I began to understand the social and environmental factors that had influenced my life, and I realized that there were so many more people like me. There were predictable patterns of group and individual behaviors in society. It went a long way in helping me understand the world. The class dynamic also intrigued me. The other students included Black Muslim militants and Aryan Circle White separatists. We were deep into discussion on the very first night, and we engaged each other in serious debate throughout the course. On some evenings, you could feel the cracks in everyone's macho armor as emotions got raw.

My immersion in educational experiences did not come with a complete absence of gangs, but my experiences with them were quite unusual. One day when I returned to the dorm, a new batch of inmates had just been arriving in the cellblocks. Sitting on the first table as I walked into K-1 were two inmates; a plump, dark-skinned guy with small dookie braids, and a tall, lithe, light-skinned one. They were clearly Bloods as indicated by their tattoos and by the red shoelaces. They sat there displaying themselves to see if anyone was going to challenge them. No one did. I debated going up to talk to them, but thought the better of it and left them alone. When the doors opened for rec, the heavyset one snuck back out of our wing, as he was not supposed to be there. I would run into the one with dookie braids later on in a class. He sat behind me and told me that he knew that I used to be a Blood. Prisons rivaled small towns in the way that gossip got around. He wanted to re-recruit me, as he said the Bloods needed someone with my intelligence. I politely declined.

Another inmate, named Omar, was taking both the public speaking and a horticulture class with me. He was dark skinned, his size and height were almost identical to mine, and he had small, tight, cornrows. Omar was a Crip out of Dallas, and, knowing I had formerly been a Blood, he always sat by me, talked my ear off, and talked halfhearted shit in order to harass me. He could be extremely annoying and would never let up. At some point, this led to an intense wrestling match between us in the horticulture class that bordered on becoming a full fight. We both stopped when we felt it getting to that point, though I was very angry with him. I thought that he was going to be a problem for me, but I was completely floored a week later in the public-speaking class. The topic we were to speak on was "someone whom we admired." The person he chose to speak about was me. He admired my courage and resolve to leave the gang and to improve myself, and my ability to lead and inspire.

It was these three things that fed my soul—the admiration speech of Omar, a Crip and potential rival; the confidence-boosting conversation with Skullcap, an NOI; and the insistence of Jay Holland Jr., a tough-love Christian life-skills coach, that I had no choice but to be exceptional. Those three moments in time let me know that I could accomplish anything that I set my mind to. Prison had not yet broken me, and I could overcome it. Even though I could see freedom in my mind, there were still more things in the present that needed my attention.

One day I noticed something surprising on the unit. I saw kids in the prison and was astounded that Wallace also had a program like Inside Look. This one was called Operation Outreach. After the sergeant in charge of the program learned about my previous experience with a similar program, I was allowed to join the team. During my first session, the administration told me that they liked my contribution, even though one of the probation officers complained that I was too hard on the kids. The other inmates told me that they had never heard anyone speak like me, and one said that, in all seriousness, I scared him, even though he was already in the penitentiary.

Operation Outreach continued going strong, and I always left the session feeling good. There was one program where I was talking to a gang member and he asked me one of the best questions I had ever heard: "How do you pick friends?" I told him that you don't pick friends; friendship is a phenomenon. It is something that happens, friends find each other. A real friend will like you for whom you are, and anything that is conditional is false. If you have to do something to be someone's friend, then that is not true friendship. He seemed to take the response to heart. But the conversation left my heart heavy as I realized that at this point, I had very few friends left.

Meanwhile, I had been rescued from the abusive derision in maintenance by taking part in the horticulture trade program, which counted as elective credit for my college curriculum. The completion of vocational school found me back in the garment factory, but this time I was sewing clothes. I never felt safe or comfortable there because of the potential for volatility among all of the sharp objects. After the transformative journey I had undergone, this was something that I just could not abide. I had to get a job change, and fast. The garment factory was a far too dangerous place to be, but the kitchen and laundry were little better. Hoe Squad was out of the question. The maintenance bosses thought I was an idiot, and my time there had been hell, so that was also not an option. My job requests for the commissary were always rebuffed. It seemed like all of the potential work assignments were filled with a variety of psychological, social, and gang-related traps, and I was at a loss about what to do to survive any one of

Operation Outreach on the Wallace Unit

BY TONY CULPEPPER

As the boy walked through the back gate, his eyes widened at the sight of the offenders in the holding pen waiting for a chain bus.

The building sergeant yelled at the youngster's group to catch a pair on the yellow line. There he stood, 12 years old or so, among 15 bad actors, with his back straight.

Positive things are happening at the Wallace Unit through a program designed to reach out to boys who are headed for TDCJ if they don't change their ways. This is not a "scared straight" program. It is, however, a real eye-opener for these boys.

Upon arrival at the unit gym, the boys are turned over to nine volunteer offenders who spend about six hours sharing information with the kids.

The main thing the volunteers try to accomplish is to reach at least one of these boys.

Volunteers for this program include: K. Wallace, R. Ferguson, A. Merrick, A. Harrelson, C. Bolden, K. Henderson, M. Chairez, V. Lee and K. Richardson.

Said Ferguson, "I don't speak to these kids for personal gain, I speak to them because I am concerned about the way things are going. Change, true change, is in the youth, so if we don't teach them the right way to go, these kids will be doomed to repeat the past."

12-1. Operation Outreach. (Article written by Tony Culpepper.)

them. I had gained so much and did not want to lose it through the unpredictable chaos. Then something miraculous happened. After an interview with the sweet elderly librarian, I amazingly got the position! This prison had 1,384 prisoners, and I was now one of only four to be assigned to the library. The change of my work assignment to special clerk came with a living unit transfer from K building to the trustee dorm. With no Christian brothers and no friends, I had to face the last leg of my prison journey alone.

CHAPTER 13

Letters

THROUGH EVERYTHING, my mother was a solid anchor. She knew just how important outside support was and was determined to not let me down. But just as the system throws everything it has at those incarcerated on the inside, it also makes things difficult for families trying to help their loved ones through. The collateral damage of system policies would serve to vex her efforts, but she would fight through each time.

December 1999—Wallace Unit, Colorado City, Texas, Time Served: 4 Years

My first weekend at Wallace unit, my mom and stepdad Brian made the trek to come visit me. The drive was a long, dull four hours each way and necessitated an overnight hotel stay. This distance and the logistics of that trip were a burden too great for most families to overcome. Still, my mother attempted the trip at least once a month. Visits were the highlight of my existence and were necessary for consistent renewal of my spirit,[1] but the system worked against their occurrence. My mom carpooled with family members of other inmates from San Antonio, which would otherwise have precluded the visits from happening. All of her travel companions were Hispanic, so during Wallace's ethnic lockdowns, my mom would have no one to come with her, and I would lose my visits.

There were many other random obstacles, such as the Texas Department of Criminal Justice (TDCJ) falsely claiming I owed them a thousand dollars—something that they would later admit was a mistake—and my mom fought through every obstruction. When the date of my parole eligibility approached, we both went into full warrior mode. We began requesting support letters and mapping out a plan for when I got out. The list of people who wrote letters of support for me filled me with warmth and hope. I got letters supporting my parole from Ms. Wynn, who was now working at an alternative school; Mr. Alfred, my former principal at Judson; Mr. Griffin from TDCJ's Windham school district, who taught the Life Skills class at Dominguez; Ms. Scarborough, the substance-abuse counselor at Wallace; Jay Holland; and, finally, from Warden Washington at Dominguez.

13-1. Family picture at Wallace. (Bolden personal photos.)

My mother didn't stop there. She requested interviews with members of the parole board that would be voting on me. She ran into one at a Texas Inmate Families Association (TIFA) convention, and they had a very positive conversation about my prospects. The board member was impressed that a warden had written a letter for me, as that was a rarity.

Our hopes were high. We had done all we could. I waited anxiously for my parole hearing in November 1999. It didn't come. I tried not to panic, rationalizing things in my head. I waited patiently. But then December passed. In January depression set in, as time continued to tick away into my fifth year incarcerated. Something was very wrong. My review should have started six months prior to my November eligibility date, and I had not even received an interview. My mom's inquiries received more runarounds and no answers. Was the system toying with me? Had the light at the end of the tunnel been a pipe dream? A lie? The parole approval rate in 1999 was a dismal 18 percent.[2] Most people were getting parole rejections, called set-offs, and few were getting out. I knew my chances were slim, especially with a violent, gang-related offense, but I still had hope. Not even getting

TABLE 13-1

Free-World Correspondence

	Letters From	Letters To
Mom	217	202
Ian	12	13
Dad	8	
Cheryl and Caleb	103	13
Ace	2	
Bret	1	
DJ	6	
Stick	2	
K-Dog and family	27	
Devil	9	
P-Ma	78	
Daisy and family	104	
Blondie	5	
Other	69	
Total	*643*	*228*

TABLE 13-2

Penitentiary Letters

	Letters From
Panda	12
Gip	5
Billy	30
Baron	30
Preacher	12
Candle	4
Matty	5
Cowboy	9
Little Ringer	7
Wolf	2
Kinsey	1
Bedrock	6
Other Prisoners [11]	15
Total	*138*

an interview meant that I had no chance at all. By February, the complete radio silence surrounding my parole hearing managed to do something all of the other horrors of prison had not—it caused a mental breakdown.

The prospect of parole had given me something to look forward to, and it had not materialized. Most of the Christians had turned their back on me, and now I was in a dorm away from the friends that I did have. I had been locked up when I was 17, and I was now 22. For many people, these are the most exciting years of their life. But not for me; I had come of age in prison. I had been incarcerated so long that remembering what it was like before prison was difficult. I was numb. TDCJ had stabbed me with one last feces-laced psychological shank, and I felt paralyzed.

It took me awhile to climb out of the mental black hole. Thankfully, a person could function in prison in a zombie-like state without drawing too much attention. Having another statewide lockdown inadvertently helped camouflage my despondency. The official reason for the lockdown was to stop a gang war resulting from Hermandad Pistoleros Latinos killing a member of Texas Syndicate. Being forced to stay in bed was just as well. I knew that I needed to do something. My rational self had helped me survive thus far, but my emotional self was decimated. After the lockdown, I finally decided to have a chat with Jay Holland about everything, and he had just the advice and encouragement that I needed. I started regimenting myself with prayer and exercise and made sure that when I needed to talk, there would be someone I could speak to. I began coming out of my funk and making friends.

Most of the people around me were either Black Muslims or Aryan Circle. Everybody was cordial, and like the people I had met before Wallace Unit, most were not actually racist. They just did the bare minimum of what their groups required of them. Everyone was a trustee or had privileged work assignments, and all were focused on going home or self-improvement. If I wasn't going home, then this dorm was the best place at the Wallace Unit to do my time. I got back to work on my own self-actualization.

I spent my workdays trying to put the extremely disorganized library back into order using the Dewey decimal system. The organizational challenge somehow served to keep me grounded. I then set to reading everything that I could, from important classics like *Alice in Wonderland* and *The Odyssey*, to everything in the canon of my favorite author, Stephen King. As my mind was freed through these literary worlds, the sorrow over my predicament began to ease.

After I had readjusted to my perceived fate, I was finally surprised with a parole hearing in April. I was given no warning, just a pass to the parole interview. I tried to rehearse things in my head while I walked to the meeting, feeling the gravity of what was about to happen. I never got the chance to say anything. Instead of an interview, it was a brief session in which I was informed that I had made parole. In itself, the news was wonderful, but I left the meeting with mixed emotions. The decision came with stipulations. I wasn't going home just yet. They wanted me to complete five years, and, when I was released, I would be put on an electronic monitor. I was already close to halfway through my fifth year, so there was nothing I could do but press forward.

The summer of 2000 was filled with accomplishments. I received an on-the-job training certification as a library assistant. I passed the required test and received a Private Pesticide Applicator License from the State of Texas Department of Agriculture. Most importantly, I finished my college curriculum, graduating summa cum laude with an associate of arts degree from Western Texas College.

Earning my degree made me feel as if I was soaring above the clouds. In the larger scheme of things though, it would be bittersweet. They canceled our graduation ceremony for unknown reasons, which may have been an omen. Even though prisoner education reduces the chance of recidivism (going back to prison) and increases the possibility of postincarceration employment,[3] those programs are often on the front end of budget cuts. The Youth Offender Grant disappeared soon after I graduated, removing the opportunity for a multitude of young offenders to reform and better themselves through college education. Not all was lost though. While the Texas prison boom grew the system expansively, it let the "goal" of rehabilitation fall by the wayside. After extensive study, it was determined that Texas had only enough resources to educate prisoners for two to three years, and most inmates were getting only one year of schooling. Instead of a reinvestment in education, policy makers chose to reallocate resources toward developing literacy among the youngest prisoners with the least education,[4] as almost a third of Texas prisoners were considered functionally illiterate.[5] This would slightly improve their chances of not returning to prison once they made it out. A higher education meant that I had an even lower likelihood of recidivating. Still, a third of the people released in Texas in 2000 would be back in prison within three years.[6] My chance to buck the odds and stay out of prison was fast approaching, but it would be far from easy.

I was released on November 6, 2000, from the Walls Unit in Huntsville. I didn't have to use the bus voucher that TDCJ had given me; my mom and Brian were there to pick me up. After five years served, I was finally going home.

Part II Postscript

During my time as a gangster and part of my time as a prisoner, I, like so many of the people around me, bought in to this notion that I was a

State of Texas

DPS NO: 05458072

TEXAS DEPARTMENT of CRIMINAL JUSTICE
PARDONS and PAROLES DIVISION

Certificate of Parole

KNOW ALL MEN BY THESE PRESENTS:

The Texas Department of Criminal Justice Pardons and Paroles Division of the State of Texas has been furnished information by the Texas Department of Criminal Justice Institutional Division that

BOLDEN,CHRISTIAN LAMONT	00739405	WL
Name	TDCJ No.	

now confined in the Texas Department of Criminal Justice Institutional Division is eligible for PAROLE under the provision of Art. 42.18 C.C.P. A satisfactory release plan has been submitted; THEREFORE, the Board of Pardons and Paroles hereby orders that the said inmate be released under Parole to the confines of the state and that he shall be deemed on parole and that he shall immediately report as indicated below for supervision under the officer to whom he shall be assigned:

SAN ANTONIO RESOURCE CNTR
414 S. MAIN
SAN ANTONIO, TX 78205

Go directly to your approved residential plan. Report to your Parole Officer by 9 A.M. the first working day after release date. Failure to do so will cancel further gate money & result in the issuance of arrest warrant.

and that he be permitted to be at liberty in the legal custody of the Texas Department of Criminal Justice Institutional Division but amenable to the orders of the Board of Pardons and Paroles and the Pardons and Paroles Division, and under the rules and conditions of parole. The period of parole shall be for a period equivalent to the maximum term for which the prisoner was sentenced less calendar time actually served on the sentence. The time to be served under parole is also calculated as calendar time. This permit to be at liberty on parole is granted upon condition that the said inmate shall observe and perform all the rules and conditions shown on the reverse of this certificate and any Special Conditions listed which are imposed shall be indicated below by listing their corresponding letter(s) or specifying the context in writing below or in an attachment hereto. This certificate shall become effective when eligibility requirements for parole under Art. 42.18 C.C.P. have been attained by said inmate and when all rules and conditions both general and special are agreed to by said inmate. **BE IT FURTHER KNOWN THAT ANY VIOLATION OF SUCH RULES OR CONDITIONS SHALL BE SUFFICIENT CAUSE FOR REVOCATION OF THIS PAROLE, AND THAT ALL TIME SERVED ON PAROLE SHALL BE FORFEITED.**

SPECIAL CONDITIONS

(1) S   (2) T   (3) L   (4) V   (5) O
T -- ELECTRONIC MONITORING

Legal County of Residence : BEXAR
Approved County of Release: BEXAR
                    Due To:

ISSUED BY ORDER OF THE BOARD OF PARDONS AND PAROLES, AND UNDER THE SEAL, OF THE TEXAS DEPARTMENT OF CRIMINAL JUSTICE AT AUSTIN, TEXAS ON THIS THE _____6TH_____ DAY OF __NOVEMBER__, __2000__

BOARD OF PARDONS AND PAROLES

If Parole is satisfactorily completed, Discharge Date will be __11-03-03__

13-2. Parole. (Bolden personal file / State of Texas–Texas Department of Criminal Justice.)

defective individual. This belief, reinforced by negative experiences, worms itself into the mind, creating a fatalistic outlook on life. I did not believe I would live past age 18, and with that type of mindset, dangerous, reckless, and destructive behavior does not have the same meaning as it does for the conventional person. What does it matter, if you have no hope for the future? Another outcome of this fatalism is just as insidious. The negative feedback reinforcement loop keeps people believing that they will always be defective and, therefore, will always need "assistance" and management by correctional services,[7] forever trapping them in the criminal justice system.

ESOTERIC (EAST TERRACE GANGSTER CRIP/ETG): They will never make it. They can't dodge raindrops like we did. Some of us got shit. YOU got hit with a few raindrops. They can't come back through that maze. That maze is closed, and if you don't find your way out, there is a lot of people that are in the ground.

The penitentiary experience further diminishes self-esteem and self-worth, reinforcing the idea that an individual is worthless. One of the ways of mitigating the internalized stigma of being a convicted felon and reclaiming a sense of empowerment is achievement in higher education.[8] It was partially the study of sociology and criminology that freed my mind from the ideological trap of mental defectiveness. Without taking away individual responsibility, I began to understand the social forces and social constraints that had shaped my development. And though I was now more severely constrained, my mind was not. I understood my agency in making decisions and the interactions with people that created major turning points in my life. Key moments in time and the assistance of people who believed in me created opportunities for me to do things that were completely against the odds. I no longer thought of myself as defective. I knew that I could find ways to be exceptional. But it wouldn't be easy.

The majority of people incarcerated will eventually return to their communities. They bring home physical and mental scars that have not been addressed and are not easily healed. To make things worse, they face a society that is unforgiving, unwilling to provide opportunities, and insistent on reinforcing the notions that they are worthless or defective. The success of the returned often relies on the support of others and on the condition of being given a chance. Many people are afforded neither, and they eventually return to prison in a repeat of the cycle. If we want to reduce crime in our communities, it behooves us to help returned citizens to succeed. One of the ways this can be accomplished is by providing those who have come home the opportunities and confidence to contribute to society.

Of course, I wasn't the only one to make it out of the Texas prison steamroller. As further evidence of San Antonio's unique gangland experience, 62 percent of prisoners released to Bexar County in 2001 were violent offenders. This was an astonishing statistical fact when comparing it to the statewide portion of violent offender releases, which was 17 percent, and that of the other major metropolitan counties housing Dallas (1%), Ft. Worth (17%), Austin (15%), and Houston (15%).[9]

TABLE 13-3

Texas Fusion Center Gang Security Threats[1]

Gang	Type	2012 Threat Level	2018 Threat Level	Estimated Membership[2]
Aryan Brotherhood of Texas	Prison	Tier 2	Tier 2	2,000+
Aryan Circle	Prison	Tier 3	Tier 2	1,400–1,500
Bandidos	OMC	Tier 2	Tier 2	2,000–2,500 international
Barrio Azteca	Prison	Tier 1	Tier 1	1,000–2,500
Bloods	Street	Tier 2	Tier 2	—
Crips	Street	Tier 2	Tier 2	—
18th Street	Street	Tier 3	Tier 3	—
Gangster Disciples	Street	Tier 3	Tier 2	—
Hermandad de Pistoleros Latinos	Prison	Tier 2	Tier 3	1,000
Kinfolk MG[3]	OMC	NA	Tier 3	170
Latin Kings	Street	Tier 3	Tier 2	2,100
Mara Salvatrucha MS-13	Street	Tier 2	Tier 1	600–1,000
Paisas/ Mexicles[4]	Street/ Prison	Tier 3	Tier 3	See PRM
Partido Revolucionario Mexicano	Prison	Tier 2	Tier 3	14,000 international
Raza Unida	Prison	Tier 3	Tier 3	700
Sureños	Street	Tier 2	Tier 2	—
Tango Blast	Prison	Tier 1	Tier 1	22,000–25,000
Texas Chicano Brotherhood	Prison	Tier 3	Tier 2	400
Texas Mafia[5]	Prison	Tier 3	NA	
Texas Mexican Mafia	Prison	Tier 1	Tier 1	4,000–6,000
Texas Syndicate	Prison	Tier 1	Tier 2	3,400
Tri-City Bombers[6]	Street	Tier 3	Tier 3	500

NOTES:

[1] Information compiled from Texas Fusion Center, *Texas Gang Threat Assessment: 2012/2018* (Austin: Texas Fusion Center, Intelligence and Counterterrorism Division, Texas Department of Public Safety, 2013/2018). https://www.dps.texas.gov/director_staff/media_and_communications/2018/txGangThreatAssessment201811.pdf.

[2] Estimated membership is prone to significant error.

[3] Was created in 2016, with a large composition of former Bandidos.

[4] Conflation of reports suggest confusion as to whether or not Paisas/Mexicles and PRM are the same group.

[5] Not included after 2011 threat assessment.

[6] The tri-cities are Pharr, San Juan, and Alamo.

As the millennium flipped, the Texas criminal justice system continued its momentum, surpassing California in having the largest number of prisoners in the United States, and encompassing a quarter of all people on probation and parole in the country.[10] Shortly after the turn of the century, Tango Orejon finally broke from its parent Mexican Mafia.[11] Conflict between the groups became the new major problem at the Bexar County Adult Detention Center. The lack of hierarchical structure and loose coupling of the Tangos rendered the administrative strategy of isolating gang members ineffective.[12] As the Tangos got stronger, they became more and more defiant against the traditional prison gangs. A new generation of wars had begun.

Over a decade later, Texas created an information fusion center to gather intelligence on security threats inside and outside of prison. Gangs were designated in three tiers based on how much of a problem they posed to society, with Tier 1 being the most significant threat. On the street and in prison, gangs in Texas have shown no signs of slowing down.

In the meantime, I was thankful that I did not have to witness the new prison wars, but I was not out of the woods yet. I still had to contend with TDCJ's Parole Division, and I would find that it could be just as volatile and disruptive as its counterpart.

Redemption

CHAPTER 14

Outcast

How does it feel to be free? This is the question that everyone asks upon returning. The clichéd answer is that it feels wonderful, and indeed it does, but the reality is so much more complex. It was overwhelming in the sense that I felt like I somehow had been kept alive without breathing for years, and was just now taking my first breath. There was also the astonishment that I had survived the hell of the Texas prison system. I just couldn't believe that I had made it out. There was also a terrible feeling of disorientation as nothing was the same, and nothing made sense.

Realizing how much the world and I had changed in five years was both amazing and alarming. One of the things that gets lost in the drive to punish is that the incarceration of youth may arrest their psychosocial maturity. Becoming an adult meant competently mastering participation in society, having the appropriate social skills to create and maintain healthy relationships, having a positive sense of self-worth, and having the competence to independently set and attain personal goals.[1] This was a tall order for someone who had reached the age of maturity in the Texas adult prison system. While people my same age bracket were being taught how to adapt to the world, I was being released from prison far behind the starting line. I had never been an adult in the free world, and I had no idea how to function as one. But just like it had been when I entered prison, I was not provided the time or resources to overcome the learning curve. I was expected to hit the ground running, even though I was starting with severe deficits, including a felony conviction, being on parole, having an electronic monitor, and having no work history that any place of employment would consider legitimate.

I paroled to my mom and Brian's house in Ventura, a neighborhood that bordered Converse. The main road, FM 78, was now filled with commercial industry where there had once been large swaths of unkempt fields. Although there was the vague sense of familiarity, nothing felt the same. I approached the world in a timid and uncertain fashion. I felt like a child in a man's body, having to relearn everything. On the one hand, life was so beautiful, and I treasured every breath of free air. On the other hand, the simplest things terrified me.

It would be the small things that gave me trouble. Having to make everyday decisions left me overcome with anxiety. No one really understood. For five years, I always wore the same thing. All of a sudden I had to select a wardrobe and choose what to wear every day. Looking at the endless rows in clothing stores would cause my vision to warp and narrow, and I would flee the place in a panic. Having been conditioned to eat in three to five minutes, I constantly scarfed my food like a dog, and I would lift my head to find everyone staring at me. This was not the only prison habit to stay with me. I always try to have my back to a wall when sitting in a restaurant, and I bang the heels of my shoes on the floor and flip them upside down before putting them on, still expecting a cockroach or spider to fall out.

My loved ones were very supportive and happy to have me returned. For people coming home from prison, there is often a low expectation of receiving any help. However, families tend to step up and provide an outpouring of support that exceeds expectations, at least in the initial stages after being released.[2] For Thanksgiving, my whole family, including my dad, showed up to my mom and Brian's house. My old friends DJ, Isla, Stick, and Devil were also there to welcome me home. I felt loved and welcomed by friends and family, but other things would create considerable consternation.

The process of returning to society from prison is called reentry. It sounds like a medical term, and indeed, the social surgery of trying to reintegrate someone back into the community has a high rate of failure due to rejection by the rest of society. I had an edge in successful reintegration from strong social support, but every other barrier to reentry would be a significant challenge to overcome. Mastering and understanding the rules of legitimate society meant dealing with the institution of parole, and it was a bear that offered almost no value toward successful reentry.

To say that I was "free" would be a misnomer. Parole meant that I was under constant threat of my "freedom" being snatched away from me. Although I suppose it makes sense from the perspective of trying to keep people from committing more crime, it does not make sense in that it makes life much more strenuous for persons trying to comply with the requirements. The concept of parole seemed simple and feasible. I thought I would just have to pay a monthly fee, do what was required, and it would be fine. But that was not at all the case.

The machinations of the parole office seemed to purposely set people up to fail. I was drug tested every time, which wasn't a problem for me since I never cared for drugs anyway and was not tempted. I was, however, paranoid about any food I ate causing a false positive. This same paranoia also lent itself to dealing with the annoying electronic monitor locked to my ankle. I had limited time that I was allowed to be out during the day. This also seemed like an easy enough restriction to comply with, until I would experience the helpless, anxious, terror of getting caught in a traffic jam or stuck at a railroad crossing with a slow-moving train, when my curfew time was fast approaching.

The worst part of parole was the officers and their astounding turnover rate. Due to longer sentences and a very low percentage of parole approvals, the caseloads of parole officers had actually been cut in half from what they had been twelve years prior.[3] That reduction seemed to be insufficient to create a stable parole system, however. I had to report to parole monthly, and the officer I was assigned to was constantly changing. Having a quality relationship and rapport with a parole officer was essential to preventing recidivism,[4] but for me, this goal was impossible to achieve. I had a new parole officer almost every visit, and I never kept the same one for more than three months. It was nerve-racking to introduce myself to a new person who controlled my freedom over and over and over again.

The officers I was assigned to ran the gamut. Some were completely laid-back and did not seem to care what I did. Others seemed to genuinely care about my success and completion of parole, offering help and advice. Most were just doing their job, completely indifferent to me or my predicament. Occasionally, I would get a grade-A asshole who had the sole intention of violating me. The worst parole officer by far was a White kicker with a grudge of unknown origin, who always wore a giant cowboy hat and impossibly tight pants. I ran afoul of him because I was talking on the phone with a girl I liked one night, which momentarily delayed the monitor signal. The phone rang early the next morning, and it was my parole officer screaming and cussing at me, saying that if I wasn't in his office in an hour, then I was going back to prison. My mother had to leave her work to take me downtown. He berated me and called me all sorts of names, even though it was verified that I did not leave home. He continued to threaten me and said that he would violate me any chance he got.

Very soon after that, I got another phone call from him telling me to report immediately, because I was being violated and I was going back to prison. My mother had to get off work to take me again. I had no idea what had gone wrong, trying to play back all my movements in mind. I was trembling the whole way there, and my mom was in a panic. It must have been terrible for her watching me walk through that parole office door, not knowing if I was going to come back out of it in handcuffs. Once inside, the parole officer let me have it with a tirade of fury and told me he was sending me back to prison. He claimed that I was caught selling cocaine. I was flabbergasted. I truly had no idea what he was talking about and told him as much. "Shut your lying fucking face!" He said, "I have the police report right here." He shoved the papers in my face. "Sir," I said gently, "that is not my name." He looked at the police report and sure enough it was not my name. The only thing that was the same was the initials, C.B. "Get the FUCK out of my office!" and he let me go. I was extremely grateful that the next time I reported, I had a new parole officer. Even still, I often woke up with my heart pounding, covered in sweat from night terrors wherein I was falsely accused and sent back to prison with no one knowing.

Employment for an ex-felon is one of the hardest things to achieve, yet crucial for reentry. Having no work history prior to incarceration makes attaining a job much more difficult.[5] Although I earned an associate's degree in prison, I lacked the social network to capitalize on it.[6] Without a previous work history at a job, most employers were uninterested in giving an ex-convict an opportunity, believing that it would only lead to disappointment and more crimes being committed. Ironically, education and gainful employment are an ex-offender's best chance to be successful. Around the time I was released, postincarceration employment in Texas dropped the monthly likelihood of going back to prison by 60 percent.[7] Those returning from prison often need to rely on familial or social network ties to obtain a job,[8] and if that connection is available, it goes a long way toward keeping them out of prison. On the job front, my stepfather came through for me immediately. Brian helped me get a job as a bagger at H-E-B grocery on Harry Wurzbach and Austin Highway, where he was a manager. I did very well, had no problems, and was soon promoted to cashier. I always had a pleasant demeanor, even for rude customers. I no longer had an identity based on anger, so I was able to tolerate people cursing at me without lashing out.[9] My demeanor won me lots of regular customers who always chose to come through my line, even though there were usually ten other lanes open.

I was doing well at H-E-B, when six months into my employment, I was taken into the back of the store with managers and human resources personnel. "So, you wrote on your application that you had been convicted of a felony. We would like you to tell us more about that." I told them. After the inquiry, they said, "We are glad that you are doing well, but H-E-B has decided that we do not want you working for us. We're sorry." And just like that, I was fired. They had already made the decision, and they made me recount my story for them anyway. My current situation and how well I was doing did not matter. My past was going to haunt me, and now I was going to find out about the label and humiliating stigma of being an ex-convict.

Though Brian was generally supportive, he explicitly gave me three months to find another job. He taught me how to drive, and at age 22, I got my driver's license. I hit the streets, starting on FM 78, putting in applications everywhere. I got nothing. The demeaning feeling of getting rejected from minimum-wage jobs time after time became a mental hurdle that I dealt with daily. Every time I saw that box, "Have you ever been convicted of a felony?" I felt like I had a stamp on my head that labeled me as unworthy, and I knew my application would likely go directly into the trash. Even still, I would not lie, and I always checked the box. I turned in an application at Burger King; they looked it over and then stared at me like I was an axe-murderer. Needless to say, they never called. I felt my mom and Brian getting impatient with my lack of success.. They did not seem to understand what I knew all too clearly. I was an outcast, and no one wanted me.

Rejection is a hard thing, and dealing with it constantly takes a toll on one's confidence and mental well-being. Whether it was corporate decisions like that of H-E-B, or just general social bias, it did not matter. The result was always the same, never even getting the dignity of an interview. I did not have any lofty notion that if I just held on long enough I could find something, but I did not know what else to do. Parole was demanding it, and Brian was requiring it if I was going to be living under his roof. It would take the kindness of a stranger and a willingness to see the value in my personal history to give me the chance that I needed.

On a whim, I walked into Little Caesar's Pizza and applied, fully expecting a repeat of every other defeat. One of the managers sat down with me, asked me a couple of questions, and then hired me on the spot as a delivery driver. I was so in shock that I stupidly pointed out my felony conviction to him, just to make sure that he was aware of it. "Well," he said, "I guess that means you won't be afraid to go into certain neighborhoods." I had secured a job! Of course, I had to use my own vehicle, and I didn't have one. Continuing the extraordinary level of support by my family, my mom and Brian gave me their old car, a gold Ford Contour.

Working at Little Caesar's was great. I loved driving and relearning the area. I worked as many shifts as they would give me. I would often be the only driver working through extreme rainstorms and flooding. Lots of people are happy to put delivery drivers at risk for some comfort food. Very early on, I was confronted with having to use a manual credit card imprint machine, which I did not know how to use. I employed it improperly and broke the customer's credit card nearly in half. I fled to my car, while the customer chased after me. On the drive back to the store, I was filled with dread, knowing that I was going to lose my job and subsequently be in trouble with parole. When I got back to the store, the entire staff, including the two managers, were rolling with laughter like it was one of the funniest things that they had ever heard. The customer had been calling nonstop, and they compensated her with some free pizza. I learned then that they loved me at the store. I never got robbed, though a few people got over on me with fake checks. The store managers were always supportive, even through my bumbling and occasional newbie car accidents. It was such an adjustment to be forgiven for my errors, when previously, a mistake could have cost me everything.

Though I was making minimum wage, I was getting another $0.75 for gas mileage per delivery and could pick up an extra $200.00 in tips on the weekends. Starting from nothing, this was decent money for me, and I enjoyed the work. However, repairing the wear and tear on my vehicle would constantly deplete anything I had saved, and I knew that in the long run, it would not be sustainable.

Developing healthy relationships and achieving self-governance would be adulthood transitions that were intertwined but not easy to develop. The thought of returning to college was often on my mind, as I knew my job prospects beyond pizza delivery were dismal. I wanted to go to school full time, but most of my parole officers were dismissive of the idea. Some were outright hostile when I brought it up, forcefully iterating that my priority should be to remain gainfully employed. The clear message was that college is a pipe dream, and I should give up on the idea.[10] I was trapped between a rock and a hard place, and I hated my state of stagnation. I had to figure out a way to do both. The opportunity came unexpectedly when my mother's job transferred her to San Marcos. I applied to Southwest Texas State University (now known as Texas State University–San Marcos), which was the centerpiece of the town, and was stunned when I was accepted as a transfer student. Every weekday, my mother and I would take the forty-five-minute drive to San Marcos for work and school. I would work nights and weekends to maintain employment status. It was taxing, but worth it. I had made it into a legitimate university! The joy of learning and the potential to succeed were everything.

Being at a university with twenty-three thousand students meant being easily lost in the crowd. I knew how to navigate the social worlds of gangsters and prisoners, but I was unprepared for college life. With all of my social deficits, adapting to the college climate was difficult and alienating. I was majoring in sociology, and I loved the educational aspects of school, but my social life was almost nonexistent. Incarceration during developmental years stunted my ability to establish prosocial relationships with new people.[11] Attempts at making friends were extremely awkward or ended in abject failure. On the larger cultural level, the lack of diversity was palpable, and I felt uncomfortable as I walked through the sea of middle-class White people. It was even more ostracizing when the White students would rage against the concept of affirmative action. I did not know what all the animosity was about, considering Brown people were few and far between on campus.[12]

Most of the kids that I met through group work were doing drugs that I had never heard of. I got several offers to take a "bump" or "roll" with them, and I would politely decline. They were surprised but never gave me flack about it, although it clearly created enough distance to prevent friendships from developing. Anytime we ended up at someone's house I would have to leave because they wanted to do cocaine or ecstasy.

My past was a major obstacle preventing me from getting close to anyone. I did not feel comfortable disclosing my history to my peers. The one time that I did was to individuals in a Christian student life group. They reacted to me with fear after that, and I quickly learned that letting my guard down was foolish. There was a girl who always wanted to hang out with me and would invite me to her place. She got frustrated because I constantly turned her down. I did not tell her it was because of my electronic monitor. She finally became extremely upset with me because I was not going to vote in the midterm elections. She nagged and nagged me, but I wouldn't budge. I could not bring myself to tell her that I no longer had the right to vote. Our friendship ended after that.

I felt isolated due to my shame and inability to connect with the other students, but did not know how to overcome it. I was taking a criminology class in sociology, when one of the students responded to the material with, "It's not like any of these people we are talking about would ever be here with us." The comment bothered me, and I sat there simmering with it, until it sparked the idea of going to talk to the teacher. I met with the criminology professor after that and told her my story. Her response was not anything near what I had hoped for. She was uncomfortable with having the information and not in any way reassuring. Yet again, I had gambled with disclosure and failed. I felt defeated and lost.

The criminology professor broke my confidence and took the information to other members of the department. This was ultimately a positive turn of events for me, as their response was entirely different than hers. I was already a good student, but I noticed an increase in warmth from the faculty. They never asked me any questions, but they had an open-door policy. It could have entirely been my imagination, but anytime I wanted to talk, they always made me feel welcome. Under the nurturing and supportive wing of the sociology faculty, I began to thrive.

As my academic pursuits continued to be successful, I joined Alpha Kappa Delta, the Sociology Honor society, and eventually become the president of the school's chapter. I was also awarded the Clarence Shultz Scholarship for the Most Promising Sociology Student. The sociology professors were amazing. I could not get enough of their teaching, wisdom, and sage advice. Despite their busy schedules, they always had time for me to stop by. I was extremely thankful for their presence, availability, nonjudgment, and,

14-1. Graduation. (Bolden personal photos / Southwest Texas State University.)

most importantly, their confidence in me. They made me feel like I was a part of a community. They made me feel like I belonged.

To fulfill the final requirement of my undergraduate degree in applied sociology, I landed an internship as a youth mentor at Casa Esperanza, under Sonya Lopez. This house of hope provided holistic, wraparound services for young people in need. Youth who were assigned there by a judge received counseling and mentoring both on site and at home as well as at the local high school. The services seemed valuable and, although Sonya was an excellent grant writer, it was a constant struggle to keep the nonprofit running.

I loved the work, and making breakthroughs with young people was always uplifting. However, there were also a lot of failures. I started to understand why there was high burnout in the fields of social work.

Sonya also introduced me to Earl Moseley, who became my spiritual mentor. Earl took an immediate liking to me, and we developed a bond of friendship that I had been unable to establish with others. Since prison, I had very little communication with anyone about spirituality. I would attend church with my mother, but it always felt like it was just window dressing, barely scratching the surface. Earl and I would have long, soul-searching conversations, which helped keep me afloat in the face of adversity. He was well known in the community and pulled out all of his contacts to try to find me a job in the field of youth work. As hard as he tried, my background continuously eliminated me from being considered. Despite the constant defeat, Earl remained upbeat. He had been given a death sentence in the form of abdominal cancer, and he looked at every day as a wonderful gift. His enthusiasm was infectious and helped me continue to be optimistic, despite the constant rejections.

Between my family, the sociology faculty at Texas State, my mentors, Sonya Lopez and Earl Moseley, and a woman I began dating in my first long-term, postincarceration relationship, I was now attached to a solid social network of support. I was committed to my educational goals, my time was occupied by work and school, and I believed in all of it.[13] I had reached a successful turning point of having solid social bonds encasing me in conventional life.

In August 2003, I graduated magna cum laude with a bachelor of science in applied sociology. My family, DJ, Bret, and K-Dog's parents came to my graduation. Everyone was so proud of all I had accomplished. It was an amazing day! The dark blemish of my past still lingered, however, and I had no idea what would come next.

CHAPTER 15

Freedom

A LIBERAL ARTS education significantly reduces the chances of recidivism, but that may be rooted in the intrinsic motivations of an individual. It does not ensure postincarceration employment, and without sufficient social capital to network, job opportunities for an educated ex-felon were nonexistent.[1] I now had a bachelor's degree but still no job prospects. Family and friends were confused, believing that I should have no problem obtaining another job, but I was getting nothing. All the applications I submitted either resulted in outright rejections or no answer at all. I had worked for Little Caesar's for two years, but I finally had to give it up when my transmission gave out and my car fell apart. The cost of repairs was over two thousand dollars out of pocket. I knew that the job was no longer tenable.

I continued to apply everywhere that I could in San Antonio, New Braunfels, and San Marcos, but nothing came of it. There were no available paid positions at Casa Esperanza, and the financial situation there was tenuous. Sonya and Earl had exhausted all of their contacts trying to help me, but still my dreams of working in social services had not materialized. After graduation, I had no job and no prospects for one.

There is a societal tendency to treat people with criminal records as if criminality is part of their essence. The moment I left the gang in prison, I desisted from crime. Choosing to not engage in criminal behavior was easy. Being able to control my anger and not lash out against the perceived injustice in the world had been a bit harder, but I was able to overcome those impulses. The most difficult obstacle, however, was simply being allowed to improve myself and contribute to society. People who return from prison are the most successful when they are able to find meaningful work and reframe their life experiences as a pathway toward redemption and helping others.[2] I had hoped to use my experience in the field of social services to help youth travel a different path, but the stigma of my criminal record meant that people were not going to give me that opportunity. I needed to find a way to give my life meaning. I needed someone to give me a chance to flip the script.

I decided to take my plight to Dr. Susan Day, the chair of the sociology department at Texas State University. Though I regularly chatted with most of the other faculty, I held a reverence for Dr. Day, as she seemed to exude power and wisdom. If anyone could brainstorm a solution to my problem it would be her. I got over being timid and approached her with my situation. True to form, when I had finished speaking, she said with clear authority, "You are going to graduate school." I responded that I had not really thought about it. "No, I don't think you heard me. You ARE going to graduate school." I guess I was.

I already had the undergraduate credentials needed, so I quickly gathered all of my materials for my application and was accepted into the Texas State Masters in Sociology program with no problems. Though this had not been in my plans, I had a love of learning, and the sociological community at Texas State brought me pure joy. They made it feel like home there. I received one of the graduate assistantship positions, which was not substantial, but it paid enough for me to initially survive on, and it fulfilled my requirement of having a job. I spent all the time I could in the office, talking with the professors and conducting the research they assigned.

In November 2003, I showed up for my parole visit and, not surprisingly, had a new parole officer. He immediately took a stern approach with me, reading me the riot act, delineating a list of all the things he expected of me and wanted me to do. After he was done, I said "Sir, I earned a bachelor's degree in sociology over the summer, and I am now in graduate school. I am also employed at the university, and this is my final month of parole." I handed him the folder I had brought with me with evidence of everything I had said. He was stunned and stared at me in silence for a few moments. A big smile broke out over his face. "Wow! Well done! I guess you can forget about all the stuff I just said. Congratulations!" And he shook my hand. I successfully discharged parole, and my voting rights were restored. After five years in prison and three years on parole, much of which entailed the addition of an electronic monitor, I was finally free from the Texas criminal justice system.

The constant trek between San Antonio and San Marcos had taken its toll over the years, and now that I was free, I moved to the off-campus student apartment complex, Bobcat Village in San Marcos. I was living by myself for the first time. The community of sociology graduate students provided some of the most joyous times I could remember. I met Mike Whitehawk there. I am sure I was unapproachable at first, and I was dismissive of him always hanging around. He was persistent, as well as charming, funny, genuine, and down-to-earth. He finally won me over, and we became best friends. After all my years of being restricted and uptight, Mike taught me that it was okay to relax and enjoy the world again. He knew about my past, and it did not bother him one bit. One night when he was driving us up to Austin, we were pulled over by the police. Cops and sirens still immediately put me into terrified mode. After checking our IDs, they pulled him out of the car and asked him if he knew who he was in the car with. He responded that he knew exactly who I was. I was his friend.

Being a graduate assistant was intrinsically rewarding, but paying for an apartment and a car was difficult with that amount of money. I knew I would have to get another job to make ends meet. Despite all of Sonya Lopez's hard work, the grant money had finally dried up, and, sadly, Casa Esperanza closed its doors. Little Caesar's shifted business strategies, concentrating on having five-dollar readymade pizzas and eliminating delivery, so the prospect of returning to that had also gone away. Once again, I found myself with no employment options. I canvassed the outlet malls in San Marcos, literally submitting dozens of applications. I did not get a single callback.

I had never contemplated, considered, or planned on teaching, as I believed my criminal history put that profession beyond my reach. But a series of unfortunate events landed me in the classroom and shaped the rest of my trajectory. In rapid succession, two of the criminology professors in the sociology department died, having succumbed to breast cancer and brain cancer. The only people left to teach the subject matter were Dr. Day, who was the chair of the department and could not take on more classes, and me, the only graduate student studying criminology at the time. It was an awkward start to my teaching career, initially having to announce to the students that their professor had passed away. Once I got into it though, I took to it like a fish to water.

I absolutely loved teaching! I had not realized that my experiences in the penitentiary had prepared me for it. Rapping in front of a thousand inmates at Garza East, taking several public-speaking classes, and stepping up as the head Christian in several dorms were all things that reduced any fear of crowds. And now I was teaching my favorite subject to inquisitive minds who were eager to discuss and debate. What was not to love? The positive feedback I received from student reviews let me know that it wasn't just my imagination. Though I was awkward in interpersonal conversations, when I had the lectern, I was on fire!

In December 2005, I graduated with a master's degree in sociology. The department kept me on as a full-time instructor, teaching introduction to sociology and criminology classes. I now had a job with a decent salary and benefits. I had completely shifted to a prosocial identity, which kept me on a steady, positive trajectory.[3] I was happy, content, and amazed at how far I had come, and I did not think it could get any better.

CHAPTER 16

Pinnacles

I HAD DONE well for myself, all things considered. My occupation seemed stable, but I worked on contract, and at any time that could be upended. At some point, Dr. Day called me into her office. "Christian, we love having you here, and you are welcome to stay as long as you like. But I want you to get your Ph.D. Once you do that, all the doors that have been closed to you will then be opened. And we would love to have you back when you are done." This was, again, something that I had not considered. But her words drilled into me—"all the doors that have been closed to you will then be opened." It reminded me of Jay Holland's instructions that I had to be exceptional if society was to ever forgive my trespasses.

I would indeed find that despite how well I was doing, most doors were still locked for me, barring me from moving forward. I just needed some help in finding the right door and a person willing to grant me passage through it. There is a contention that the black mark of a criminal record is partially an ex-felon's self-stigma concerning anticipated negative reactions, rather than actual rejections.[1] While I always wrestled with what I believed people thought of me, I knew that the stigma was real. I had been rebuffed countless times in my job searches, and though I now viewed myself as successful, the blemish of a criminal past would constantly be an obstacle to moving any further. The prospect of going back into the unknown to assuredly face a great deal of rejection again, especially after finally having found a place in the world, was daunting. I did my research on schools and submitted applications. Some sent rejections and some did not respond at all. Dr. Day would check in with me regularly to see how my progress was going. It was going nowhere. The summer was getting closer, and the prospects of any funded acceptance had all but disappeared. She asked me what school I was really interested in from the remaining places that had not responded. I decided on the PhD program at the University of Central Florida. She called the chair of sociology at UCF, Dr. Jay Corzine, and asked about my application. He said that he had never heard of me. He

called admissions and found out that my criminal history had put my application in some sort of perpetual hold. Yet again, the criminal conviction
was blocking my progress. Had Jay not called, it is unlikely that the department would ever have seen it. He demanded that they finish whatever it was
they were doing so that he could see my application. I wondered about the
schools that I had never heard back from and if they had sent my application
to a similar limbo.

Very soon afterward, I got a call from UCF admissions. On speaker-
phone, I was required to recount the story of my life, my crime, and all
I had accomplished to a roomful of people whom I couldn't see and whom
I had never met. The anxiety of being judged by people I could not even see
made my stomach twist into knots. But it was progress, and that is all
I could hope for. It was successful, and I was accepted into the sociology
PhD program! I was in a state of disbelief. I had never dreamed of going this
far. Susan Day had guided me to the door and Jay Corzine had been the
gatekeeper who let me in. I don't know if the magic could have happened
without them. I had very little time to get my act together and quickly
found myself saying goodbye to Texas State and moving to Orlando, Florida, to start school again in August 2006.

Other doors were still closed to me though, and trying to get through
them would land me in a state of helplessness and panicked desperation.
I was well aware of job discrimination toward the formerly incarcerated, and
rejection in that realm felt routine, but I was unprepared for the next consequence of criminal stigma. I rented an apartment online in Casselberry,
Florida, a few miles from the university. When I arrived, the place turned
out to be a complete dump. There was a large hole in the front door, either
from a gun blast or from something having been punched through it, and
the surfaces were covered in hordes of roaches. The aura of the place felt
raw and dangerous. I knew I could not live there. The problem was that
I also could not live anywhere else. I did not know anyone in the city, nor did
I know where to go to seek help. I suddenly found myself homeless, living
in my car and motels. None of the apartment complexes would rent to me
because of my criminal history. It turns out that Florida was even harsher
on ex-felons than Texas had been. In Texas, applications asked if you had
been convicted of a felony in the last seven years. In Florida, the question
was had you *ever* been convicted of a felony. If so, you were shit out of luck.
No one was going to give you a job or a place to live. In the private rental
market, landlords could legally discriminate against people with felony
convictions and often did. For some residential corporations, the exclusion
of returned citizens was a mandatory restriction. My work history, ability
to pay, and references held no weight whatsoever. Housing insecurity was

yet another major roadblock for someone returning from prison and trying to stay afloat.[2]

After a week of desperation, someone suggested that I seek help from the Salvation Army. It was a good suggestion, as they did find me an apartment on South Semoran Boulevard. It was a busy, high-crime part of town, filled with the constant sound of sirens, but the apartment was decent and livable. I was sincerely grateful to have found a place that would allow me to rent.

I immediately went to apply for jobs, canvassing everything from retail to fast food. No one was interested in hiring me because of my background. School started, and the graduate assistantship they provided helped a little, but I had to take out large student loans to survive. Florida was also significantly more expensive than Texas.

After overcoming the housing crisis and finding a temporary income solution, I realized that Dr. Day's words had started to come true. In fact, the opportunities came so fast that it was hard to keep up with them. The sociology department and the university were amazing. UCF was like a small city in itself,[3] and I had no need to venture far from it. The sociology PhD program was new and I was in the second cohort. We had a strong cohort of nine, but they told us at orientation that statistically, only half of us would make it through the program. Sure enough, we lost one member in the first few weeks and would lose three more along the way. It was a rigorous program, and we learned from powerhouse researchers. Most important to me were my mentors, Dr. Jay Corzine and Dr. Lin Huff-Corzine. They pulled out all the stops in making sure that we had the best education possible, as they were determined that the new program succeed.

Through networking, I met professor Baboucar Jobe, who was the chair of sociology at Seminole Community College (now Seminole State College) and also an adjunct at Valencia Community College. He invited me for an interview and then hired me to teach at the Oviedo and Altamonte Springs campuses. Then, by extension, I was also hired to teach as an adjunct at Valencia's East Campus. I was paid per course, and I consistently had stellar reviews in my classes, so they brought me back each semester. Three professors also hired me to watch their dogs. I found myself going from being destitute and unemployed to teaching eight undergraduate classes a semester between UCF, Valencia, and Seminole, and dog walking three sets of canines, all while taking three doctoral courses each term. I was busy!

I knew that I wanted to study gangs, having significant admiration for the scholars I had been reading about for years, but I never dreamed about what could be possible with this course of study. My experience in the doctoral program provided extraordinary opportunities for me, and the subsequent networking would blow the doors to the world of gang research wide open. The sociology department at UCF continuously put forth effort to make sure we had all the tools necessary to be serious researchers. They also regularly brought in guest speakers from outside the school. One of those guest scholars was Jody Miller, one of the most notable gang researchers in the United States. I was a fan, spending every minute I could with her during the visit and asking if I could send my thesis to her to read. I waited in doubtful anticipation, sure that my fanboyish behavior had been off-putting. After she read it, she agreed to be the outside member on my dissertation committee. When I received the email, I screamed in elation and stunned disbelief.

I ran into Jody Miller again at the first large professional meeting I attended, which was the American Society of Criminology conference in Atlanta, Georgia. She introduced many of the prominent gang researchers. These were people that I had been reading about for years. It was like being introduced to every celebrity that I was a fan of. I was completely star-struck, and it was one of the best nights of my life.

Soon after, I was contacted by Jody and Malcolm (Mac) Klein with an exciting opportunity. Klein had been studying gangs for over fifty years and was at the top of the gang-research food chain. A decade earlier, during his travels in Europe, Mac had noticed that no one was discussing gang problems, even though there were clear signs that gangs existed. He discovered that European scholars understood gangs through their portrayal in American media, which was incorrect. He argued that there needed to be a standardized way of understanding what a gang is, as there previously had been hundreds of definitions of the concept.[4] With this, we could also comparatively study troublesome youth groups between geographic locations. From these arguments, a consortium of researchers, called Eurogang, was born. Mac and Jody informed me that instead of their typical meeting, they wanted to train a younger generation on the purpose and rationale of Eurogang and the methodologies used for gang research. Each of the primary researchers involved chose a young scholar for this, and I was Jody's choice. Offer accepted!

Eurogang IX was held at the University of Southern California in Los Angeles. Alongside other Eurogang young scholars, such as Robert J. Durán, Chris Melde, and Kristy Matsuda, I was trained by many of my academic heroes, including Klein, Miller, Cheryl Maxson, Finn-Aage Esbensen, Scott Decker, and G. David Curry. During that trip, I also got to meet Father Greg Boyle, a Jesuit priest. Since 1988, Father Boyle had been helping gang members and formerly incarcerated persons transition into conventional lifestyles with housing and job opportunities through a series of businesses called Homeboy Industries.[5] One of the most valuable things I learned from Father

Boyle was that through his work with thousands of former gang members, he had realized that they had not been bad people, they had just been people who had no hope. Loving people and providing them with hope for a better future were all that was needed.

Fired up on my return, I formulated a dissertation plan using Eurogang research methods and a comparative framework to study gangs in both Orlando and my hometown. To get my research started, I tracked down old friends and enemies in San Antonio, and their receptions of me were quite surprising. Most of the old homies were happy to see me, but a few responded with wariness and hostility, even to the extent of refusing to speak to me at all. Some of the former enemies I was able to track down greeted me warmly and ended up being the most extensive interviews in my studies.

Beyond old acquaintances, I had no problem finding other respondents. Even after all the years, my street history gave me easy access to gang members in San Antonio. Time and time again, the interviewees would tell me that they were only talking to me because "so-and-so" told them who I was. I rapidly amassed twenty-six interviews in three extended weekends, and only stopped there because I ran out of time and resources (see Appendix B for a list of interviews with San Antonio gang members).

Orlando would be a different story entirely. No one had ever researched gangs in Orlando, and I had only been involved in academic circles there. I knew nothing about Central Florida street life. The local social service agencies refused to help me make contact without a quid pro quo, and since I had no resources, those relationships were dead in the water. I was on my own, starting from nothing.

I began by advertising my study in the college classes I was teaching, hoping that there would be someone who knew someone that could help me. Eventually my strategy bore fruit, and several snowball sampling chains emerged in which gang members would introduce me to others. Of course, I had no street credibility in Orlando, so potential respondents would often change their minds and fail to show up for interviews. I did not disclose my past unless I felt it was absolutely necessary, and those occasions were rare. Unlike the rapid-fire pace of San Antonio data collection, it took me a full year to get twenty-two in-depth interviews with gang members in Orlando.

The dissertation process was grueling and filled with rewrites. Because my research was dealing with human subjects and not already-existing data, it took a full year longer than the studies of some of my cohort members. I watched them all graduate and take jobs elsewhere. The loss of my strong cohort support network made the process that much harder. As I drew closer to the finish line, I was hit with another major blow as Earl Moseley passed away in early 2010. The last stretch toward the goal was lonely and bittersweet.

16-1. PhD. (Bolden personal photos / University of Central Florida.)

I graduated with a PhD in sociology in August 2010. It seemed unbe-lievable. After all I had been through, I had attained the pinnacle in educa-tional achievement. I was now Dr. Christian L. Bolden. I worked extremely hard the whole way, but I also know that grace and the willingness of people to provide me with a chance were instrumental in allowing me to reach my goal. I took one swing at a job interview and knocked it out of the ballpark. I landed my first tenure-track job with the criminology department at Indiana

University of Pennsylvania, and then later earned tenure at Loyola University New Orleans. I had finally made it.

Part III Postscript

It was 2011, and I was sitting in my office at IUP when I received a phone call. It was from the FBI Behavioral Sciences Unit. I had encountered several of their social scientists at conferences and through relationships they had with other academics. They were aware of my research on gangs and wanted me to come to the FBI Academy in Quantico, Virginia, to present at a specialty conference. I was extremely flattered, but concerned that my background would be a problem. I told them flatly about my history. They said that they would get back to me, and a few days later they did. "Everything checks out. We know about your history and we know about your accomplishments since then. We still want you to come." So off I went to Quantico.

The conference was concerning gangs, terrorism, and weapons of mass destruction. My presentation on gangs seemed to make a profound impression on the practitioners there, and law enforcement lined up to talk to me afterward. Through that success, my relationship with the FBI Behavioral Sciences Unit continued to develop, and I was awarded a fellowship to do research with them on the future of crime, gangs, and terrorism.[6] I flew back and forth to Quantico for a year. Sitting in my dorm room at the FBI academy, I contemplated how I had been a young gang member thrown away in the Texas prison system, and through educational and occupational turning points, I was now sitting here. It felt like I had achieved the impossible.

In the world of research, I'm just an *n* of 1, meaning that I am just one case and thus could be considered an outlier. But each *n* of 1 is a person with a story, and every story can teach us something valuable. My story is intertwined with countless stories of those who have been lost and forgotten. My hope is to bring greater understanding and meaning for the lives of those lost in the streets and in prison, and that more will have the opportunity to become exceptions. That is my hope. This is my story.

Appendix A

LISTS OF SAN ANTONIO GANGS EARLY TO MID-1990S

San Antonio Blood Gangs Early to Mid-1990s

Blood Gangs [Red]
Bad Boyz, Inc. (BBI)
Blood Stone Villains (BSV)
Cartel Bloods
Dark Minded Kriminals (DMK)
Del Crest Gangsters (DCG)
Denver Heights Texas (DHT)[1]
Homestead Bloods
La Raza Bloods (LRB)
Lincoln Court Gangsters (LCG)
Olive Park East Bloods (OPE)
Rigsby Court Gangsters (RCG)
Sa Town Bloods (STB)
Skyline Park[2]
Third World Bloods
United New Light Village
   (UNLV/DOG)
Sutton Homes Gangster
Stixx Bloods
Wheatley Courts Texas (WCT)[3]

Blood Gangs [Other Colors]
Big Time Players (BTP) [Maroon]
Midnight Color Bloods (MCB)
   [Maroon]

San Antonio Crip Gangs Early to Mid-1990s

Crip Gangs [Blue]
Altadena Blocc Crips (ABC)
Bad Attitudes (BA)
Blue Crew Gangsters/True Blue
   Gangsters

Crip Gangs [Other Colors]
Acme Park DOG [Black]
Dope Overthrowing Gangster
   (DOG)[4] [Black]
Grape Street Watts [Purple]

Crockett Street Texas (CST)
Dignowity Lynch Mob (DLM)
East Side Latino Crip Gangster
    (LCG)
East Side Player (ESP)
East Terrace Gangsters (ETG)
Five-Deuce Hoover Crip (5-2)
Indian Creek Gangsters (ICG)
Jolly Time Gangsters (JTG)
Killing All Problems (KAP)
Lakeside Hustler Crip
Latin Crips (LC)
North Highland Crips (NHC)
Original Crip Gangsters (OCG)
Rollin' 30s/Rollin' 60s Crips
Southside Crips (SSC)
Southwest Crips (SWC)
Third World Gangster Crips
    (3WG)
Tray-Five-Seven Crip (3-5-7)

Lighter Shade of Brown Crip
(LSOB) [Brown]

San Antonio People Gangs Early to Mid-1990s

People Gangs [Black]
Almighty Latin Kings (ALK)
Bad Boyz/Bad Girls (BBZ)
Big Time Kings (BTK)
Kings of Perfection (KOP)
Lincoln Court Kings (LCK)
Los Primera Kings (LPK)
North Side Kings (NSK)
Parkside Kings (PK)
Puro Mexicano Kings (PMK)
Puro Ocho/8-Ball Posse (PO)
Puro Varrio Kenwood (PVK)
Queens
Rivas Street Kings
Rosedale Park Kings
Ruthless Kings (RK)
San Antonio Gangsters (SAG)
Southside Kings (SSK)
Southside Varrio Kings (SSV)

People Gangs [Other Colors]
Almighty Vice Lords (AVL)
    [Maroon]
Bishops [Orange]
Club Deu [Purple]
Dark Side Reds [Red]
Ghetto Boyz [Green]
Grand Theft Auto (GTA) [Red]
Kin [Green]
Klik [Red]
Latin Counts [Red]
Los Azteca Kings (LAK) [Gold]
Notre Dame Posse (NDP) [Green]
Puro Chicano Gangsters (PCG)
    [Brown]
Puro SA Browns [Brown]
Suicidal Locos [Red]
Valley Hi Mob [Green]

Timberhill High-life Crew
   Kings (THC)
Underground Kings (UGK)
West Side Gangsters (WSG)
West Side Varrio Kings (WSV)

San Antonio Folk Gangs Early to Mid-1990s [Gang Color]

Astor Street Necios Ambrose
   [Baby Blue]
Bad Boys Club (BBC) [Blue]
Bad Company (BC) [Blue]
Barrio Latino (BL) [Purple]
Bristol Boyz Ambrose
   [Baby Blue]
Carnales Por Vida (CPV)
   [White]
Crusaders of Converse (COC)
   [Gray]
Culebra Park Klan [White]
Cullerton Deuces [Green]
Damage, Inc. [Blue]
Imperial Gangsters (IG)
   [Dark Pink]
Insane Gangster Disciples
   (IGD) [Blue]
Klan [White]

LA Boyz (LAB) [Blue]
La Familia [White]
Latin Eagles (LE) [Gray]
Latin Syndicate (LS) [Green]
Legion of Doom (LOD)
   [Dark Pink]
Mexican Posse (MP)
   [Blue and Pink]
Murder, Inc (MIC) [Gray]
North Side Ambrose (NSA)
   [Baby Blue]
South Side Ambrose (SSA)
   [Baby Blue]
Spanish Gangsters (SG) [Blue]
Two-Six (2–6) [Beige]
Varrio Gray Eagles (VGE)
   [Gray]
West Side Klan [White]
Wrecking Crew (WC) [Blue]

San Antonio Sureño Gangs Early to Mid-1990s [Gang Color]

Chicano Azteca Mob 13
   [Brown]
Chicanos Taking Over X3
   [Brown]
Colorblind Artists 13 [Brown]
Esta Grande Varrio 13 [Red]
Florencia 13 [Blue]

Hispanic Assassins 13
   [Brown]
Lil Watts/Lady Watts X3
   [Black]
Poison 13 [Green]
Tepa 13 [Brown]
Sur 13 [Blue]

San Antonio 210/Independent Gangs Early to Mid-1990s[5] [Gang Color]

Another Born Gangster (ABG) [Blue]

Azteca Boyz [Brown]

B-52 Bombers [Red]

Bally Boyz [Baby Blue]

Brown and Proud [Brown]

Brown Pride Locos (BPL)

Brownleaf Posse [Brown]

Bud Smokers Only (BSO)

Cribbs [Blue and Red]

East LA Dukes [Purple]

Fearless Brown Soldiers [Brown]

Fellas/Victoria Courts Gangsters [Blue]

Golden Boyz [Red]

Hispanics Causing Panic (HPC) [Brown]

La Raza [Brown]

Latin Fag Crew[6] (LFC) [Pink]

Latino Mob [Green]

Latino Organization[7] (LO) [White]

Los Olmos Boys (LOB) [Blue]

Mirasol Thugs [Black]

Most Hated Boys [Camouflage]

New York Gangsters (NYG) [Blue]

North Side Rollers (NSR) [Red]

Polo Boyz/Polo Girlz [Green] [Brown]

Raiders [Gray]

Rebels [Red] [Blue]

Rifa Crew [Brown]

Rock Quarry Gang (RQ) [Blue and Red]

Spanish Homeboys [Blue]

Texas Tech [Red]

Tiny Rascal Gangsters [Gray]

Two-One Stone Nation (2-1) [Beige]

Varrio Chicano Gangsters [Black]

Varrio La Blanca (VLB) [Blue]

San Antonio Unknown-Affiliation Gangs Early to Mid-1990s[8]

Alazon Kapping Krew

Always Violent Unit

Authorized to Kill (A2K)

Deep West Vandals

Insane Chicano Gangsters.

Latin Crime Mob

Latino Party Crew

Latino Thugs

Locos Only

Lynch Mob

McKinley Thugs

One Big Familia

Presa St. Gangsters

Psycho Locos

Puro Violent Players

Rainbow Hill Rowdies

San Eduardo Thugs

Suicidal Force

Tommy Boy Players

West Side Posse

Appendix B

SAN ANTONIO GANG MEMBER INTERVIEWS

San Antonio Gang Member Interviews

Interviewee	Gang (s)
Ace	Big Time Players/Sa Town Bloods
Aztec	Alazon-Apache Courts (Alazones)
Balla	East Terrace Gangster/Denver Heights/SS Ambro
Boxer	414 Texas Cobras
Bret	Blood Stone Villians/Sa Town Bloods
Cajun	Dope Overthrowing Gangsters (DOG)/ Latin Kings
Caleb★	Sa Town Bloods
Cheryl (F)	Crip associate
Coop★	Blood Stone Villians/Sa Town Bloods
Daisy (F)★	Almighty Vicelord
Dama (F)	Bad Girlz
DJ★	Sa Town Bloods
Esoteric	East Terrace Gangster Crip
Hoops	Skyline Park
K-Dog★	Sa Town Bloods
Oso	Romos Klik
P-Ma (F)★	Lady Watts X3
Pranx	Wheatley Court Texas (WCT)
Prince	Latin Kings
Remington	Sa Town Bloods
Royal	Big Time Kings
Shorty (F)	Bad Girlz

(continued)

TABLE B-1 (CONTINUED)

Interviewee	Gang (s)
Shuga	23rd St. Hoover Crip
Sly	Blood Stone Villians/ Olive Park East
Stick*	Blood Stone Villians/Sa Town Bloods
T-Note	Tray-Five-Seven Crip (3-5-7)/ Dayton St. Posse (Newark, NJ)
Twista	Blood associate
Wizard	Ruthless Kings
Non-SA Gang Members in SA	*Gang/Location*
Azul	107 Hoover Crip/Tulsa, OK
Hound	Kurk Town Piru /Albuquerque, NM
Sinister	Big Time Surenos/LA, CA
Sky (F)	Puro Segundo Varrio Crip/Houston, TX
Southpaw	Florencia 13/Los Angeles, CA

*Indicates two separate interviews, 5-years apart.

Acknowledgments

There are many people to thank for making this work possible, but I want to start with my wife, Dr. Rae Taylor, who has been my rock and my rock star throughout. Thank you for reading countless drafts and always maintaining a critical and honest perspective. You were my biggest and most important cheerleader. I can never thank you enough. To my brother, Ian Bolden, thank you for also reading draft after draft, and correcting my inaccuracies. To my mother, Debra Masey, thank you for never giving up on me, even when I was at my lowest levels. You have always stood by me and pulled me through. A special thanks goes to my beautiful baby boy, Julian, who was born as this book was written. I held you in one arm, while I wrote this book with the other. The joy you brought me helped me through many of the dark moments I had to write about. I hope you bring the same healing to the world that you brought to me.

I cannot give enough thanks to my acquiring editor, Peter Mickulas, for believing in this project and giving it a chance. This work also could not have happened without the diligence of my reviewers. Mike Tapia, I hope to follow in the tradition you set in researching gang history. Tim Lauger, you are truly the most professional, thorough, helpful, and thoughtful reviewer, anyone could ever hope for. I look forward to working with you again in the future. A special thanks goes to Luke Pruett for bringing the cover artwork to life.

This project was many years in the making, and it took a village to bring it to fruition. I am thankful to the legion of research assistants who completed transcription work. Lanier Clement, Laura Fletcher, Kristin Pepper Ginsberg, Emma Grauerholz-Fisher, Valerie Leblanc, Leanna Maasarani, Colleen Powers, and Milan Ray, thank you for the transcription work. I am extremely grateful to all of the interview respondents who shared their stories with me, and my utmost gratitude goes to Phoebe Joel Martinez for helping me complete my interview research.

On the writing end, there are many beta readers who suffered through early drafts of the work. I am very grateful for the patience, critiques, design sketches and advice from Camille Didelot-Hearn, Ashley Howard, Carol

Ann MacGregor, Molly Mulroy, and Laura Murphy, My eternal gratitude goes to Hillary Eklund, whose line-by-line editing and organizational advice were critical for the transformation of free-flowing information into readable narrative. A special thank-you goes to Victoria Elmwood, Jason Ezell, and Melissa Tetzlaff-Bemiller for saving my hide with technical assistance. I also want to thank Diane Ersepke for the outstanding and meticulous copyediting, Cheryl Hirsch for the kind, professional, and efficient production editing that refined the final product, and Becky Hornyak for intuitive indexing.

I want to give my heartfelt gratitude to those who believed in me and created the paths I needed to succeed. For those who supported me during my darkest hours, there are no words to express what I owe you. Jay Holland Jr. and Mary S. Wynn, your guidance and words of encouragement helped shape who I am today. Earl Moseley, there is always a hole in my heart due to your absence. You are forever missed.

I have a profound reverence for the Texas State and University of Central Florida sociology faculty, who educated me and nurtured me. Audwin Anderson, Donna Barnes (Howard University), Harold Dorton (Spring Hill College), Patti Guiffre, Debarun Majumdar, Kelly Mosel-Talavera, Barbara Trepagnier, Toni Watt, and Mike Whitehawk, I cherish all of you. I have to reserve an extra-special thanks for Jay Corzine, Susan Day, Lin Huff-Corzine, and Jody Miller. All of you were the gatekeepers that allowed me to succeed. I hope that I have done right by you. What you have done has certainly meant the world to me. Thank you!

NOTES

PROLOGUE

1. Robert S. Pynoos and Spencer Eth, "Children Traumatized by Witnessing Acts of Personal Violence: Homicide, Rape, and Suicide Behavior," in *Post-traumatic Stress Disorder in Children*, eds. Robert S. Pynoos and Spencer Eth (Washington, DC: American Psychiatric Press), 17–43.
2. Jane L. Wood, Constantinos Kallis, and Jeremy W. Koid, "Differentiating Gang Members, Gang Affiliates, and Violent Men on Their Psychiatric Morbidity and Traumatic Experiences," *Psychiatry: Interpersonal and Biological Process* 80, no. 3 (2017): 221–235.

INTRODUCTION

1. David Skarbek, *The Social Order of the Underworld: How Prison Gangs Govern the American Penal System* (New York: Oxford University Press, 2014).
2. Loïc Wacquant, "The Curious Eclipse of Prison Ethnography in the Age of Mass Incarceration," *Ethnography* 3, no. 4 (2002): 371–397.
3. John H. Laub and Robert J. Sampson, *Shared Beginnings, Divergent Lives: Delinquent Boys to Age 70* (Cambridge: Harvard University Press, 2003).
4. A notable exception is Randol Contreras, *The Stickup Kids: Race, Drugs, Violence, and the American Dream* (Los Angeles: University of California Press, 2012).
5. See Stanley Cohen, *Folk Devils and Moral Panics: The Creation of the Mods and Rockers* (London: Routledge, 1972).

CHAPTER 1—POVERTY

1. James C. Howell and Arlen Egley Jr., "Moving Risk Factors into Developmental Theories of Gang Membership," *Youth Violence and Juvenile Justice* 3, no. 4 (October 2005): 334–354.
2. Cardell K. Jacobson and Tim B. Heaton, "Inter-group Marriage and United States Military," *Journal of Political and Military Sociology* 31, no. 1 (2003): 1–22.
3. Richard A. Pride, "Public Opinion and the End of Busing: (Mis)Perceptions of Policy Failure," *Sociological Quarterly* 41, no. 2 (Spring 2000): 207–225.
4. Beverly L. Stiles, Liu Xiarou, and Howard B. Kaplan, "Relative Deprivation and Deviant Adaptations: The Mediating Effects of Negative Self-Feelings," *Journal of Research in Crime and Delinquency* 37, no. 1 (February 2000): 64–90.
5. Kevin Moran, "Social Structure and Bonhomie: Emotions in the Youth Street Gang," *British Journal of Criminology* 55, no. 3 (May 2015): 566–577.
6. Robert Agnew, "Building on the Foundation of General Strain Theory: Specifying the Types of Strain Most Likely to Lead to Crime and Delinquency," *Journal of Research in Crime and Delinquency* 38, no. 4 (November 2001): 319–361.

CHAPTER 2—ADULTISM

1. A study of gangs in Cleveland and Columbus, Ohio, found that busing created the unintended consequence of exacerbating turf-oriented gang conflict and recruitment of members from distant areas. C. Ronald Huff, "Youth Gangs and Public Policy," *Crime and Delinquency* 35, no. 4 (October 1989): 524–537.
2. Robert Agnew, "Foundation for a General Strain Theory of Crime and Delinquency," *Criminology* 30, no. 1 (February 1992): 47–88.
3. Elijah Anderson, *Code of the Street: Decency, Violence, and the Moral Life of the Inner City* (New York: W. W. Norton and Company, 1999).
4. See Timothy R. Lauger, *Real Gangstas: Legitimacy, Reputation, and Violence in the Intergang Environment* (New Brunswick: Rutgers University Press, 2012).
5. Jack Flasher, "Adultism," *Adolescence* 13, no. 51 (Fall 1978): 517–523.
6. Jessica McCrory Calarco, "Coached for the Classroom: Parents' Cultural Transmission and Children's Reproduction of Educational Inequalities," *American Sociological Review* 79, no. 5 (October 2014): 1015–1037.
7. Howell and Egley, "Moving Risk Factors."
8. Texas Education Code Title 2, Sec 37.0011. See Elizabeth T. Gershoff and Sarah A. Font, "Corporal Punishment in U.S. Public Schools: Prevalence, Disparities in Use, and Status in State and Federal Policy," *Social Policy Report* 30, no. 1 (September 2016): 1–26.
9. Elizabeth T. Gershoff, "More Harm Than Good: A Summary of Scientific Research on the Unintended Effects of Corporal Punishment on Children," *Law and Contemporary Social Problems* 73, no. 2 (Spring 2010): 31–56.
10. Albert K. Cohen, *Delinquent Boys: The Culture of a Gang* (Glencoe, IL: The Free Press, 1955).
11. Thomas Mowen and John Brent, "School Discipline as a Turning Point: The Cumulative Effect of Suspension on Arrest," *Journal of Research in Crime and Delinquency* 53, no. 5 (August 2016): 628–653.

CHAPTER 3—NEIGHBORHOODS

1. See Pierre Bourdieu, *Distinction: A Social Critique of the Judgement of Taste* (Cambridge: Harvard University Press, 1984).
2. Penelope Eckert, *Jocks and Burnouts: Social Categories and Identity in High School* (New York: Teachers College Press, 1989).
3. See Martín Sánchez Jankowski, *Islands in the Street: Gangs and American Urban Society* (Berkeley: University of California Press, 1991).
4. Jankowski, *Islands in the Street.*
5. Lauger, *Real Gangstas.*
6. Christian L. Bolden, "Tales from the Hood: An Emic Perspective on Gang Joining and Gang Desistance," *Criminal Justice Review* 38, no. 4 (October 2013): 473–490; Scott H. Decker, "Collective and Normative Features of Gang Violence," *Justice Quarterly* 13, no. 2 (June 1996): 243–264.
7. Mike Tapia, "San Antonio's Barrio Gangs: Size, Scope, and Other Characteristics," *Deviant Behavior* 36, no. 9 (September 2015): 691–704.
8. Robert E. Park, Ernest W. Burgess, and Roderick Duncan Mackenzie, *The City* (Chicago: University of Chicago Press, 1925); Clifford Shaw and Henry D. McKay, *Juvenile Delinquency and Urban Areas: A Study of Rates of Delinquents in Relation to Differential Characteristics of Local Communities in American Cities* (Chicago: University of Chicago Press, 1942).
9. For a detailed history of gang development in the Cassiano Courts, San Juan Homes, Victoria Courts, Villa Veramendi, Lincoln Heights, Menchaca Courts,

and the Mirasol Homes, see Mike Tapia, *The Barrio Gangs of San Antonio: 1915–2015* (Fort Worth: Texas Christian University Press, 2017).

10. David Montejano, *Quixote's Soldiers: A Local History of the Chicano Movement, 1966–1981* (Austin: University of Texas Press, 2010).
11. Montejano, *Quixote's Soldiers.*
12. Montejano, *Quixote's Soldiers.*
13. Montejano, *Quixote's Soldiers.*
14. Robert Vargas, "Criminal Group Embeddedness and the Adverse Effects of Arresting a Gang's Leader: A Comparative Case Study," *Criminology* 52, no. 2 (May 2014): 143–168.
15. Ruth Triplett, "Youth Gangs in Texas Part II," *Texas Law Enforcement Management and Administrative Statistics Program* 4, no 4 (1997): 2.
16. James B. Jacobs, "Street Gangs behind Bars," *Social Problems* 21, no. 3 (1974): 395–409.
17. Tapia, *The Barrio Gangs.*
18. Patrick Lopez-Aguado, "I Would Be a Bulldog: Tracing the Spillover of Carceral Identity," *Social Problems* 63, no. 2 (May 2016): 203–221.
19. Audrey Duff, "We Get All Hyped Up. We Do a Drive-By," *Texas Monthly*, October 1994. https://www.texasmonthly.com/articles/we-get-all-hyped-up-we-do-a-drive-by/.
20. Alejandro A. Alonso, "Racialized Identities and the Formation of Black Gangs in Los Angeles," *Urban Geography* 25, no. 7 (November 2004): 658–674.
21. Stacy Peralta, Baron Davis, Dan Halsted, Jesse Dylan, Gus Roxburgh, Shaun Murphy, Cash Warren, Sam George, and Forest Whitaker, *Crips and Bloods: Made in America* (New York: Docurama Films: Distributed by New Video, 2009).
22. Gregory Christopher Brown, James Diego Vigil, and Eric Robert Taylor, "The Ghettoization of Blacks in Los Angeles: The Emergence of Street Gangs," *Journal of African American Studies* 16, no. 2 (June 2012): 209–225.
23. Cheryl Maxson, "Gang Members on the Move," *Juvenile Justice Bulletin* (Washington, DC: Office of Juvenile Justice and Delinquency Prevention: United States Department of Justice, October 1998): 3–14.
24. Christian L. Bolden, "Liquid Soldiers: Fluidity and Gang Membership," *Deviant Behavior* 33, no. 3 (February 2012): 207–222.
25. Walter B. Miller, "Lower Class Culture as a Generating Milieu of Gang Delinquency, *Journal of Social Issues* 14, no. 3 (Summer 1958): 5–19.

CHAPTER 4—BANGIN' IN SAN ANTONE

1. Terence P. Thornberry, Marvin D. Krohn, Alan J. Lizotte, and Deborah Chard-Wierschem, "The Role of Juvenile Gangs in Facilitating Delinquent Behavior," *Journal of Research in Crime and Delinquency* 30, no. 1 (February 1993): 55–87.
2. For example, Uberto Gatti, Richard E. Tremblay, Frank Vitaro, and Peirre McDuff, "Youth Gangs, Delinquency, and Drug Use: A Test of the Selection, Facilitation, and Enhancement Hypotheses," *Journal of Child Psychology and Psychiatry* 46, no. 11 (November 2005): 1178–1190; Rachel A. Gordon, Benjamin B. Lahey, Eriko Kawai, Rolf Loeber, Magda Stouthamer-Loeber, and David P. Farrington, "Antisocial Behavior and Youth Gang Membership: Selection and Socialization," *Criminology* 42, no. 1 (February 2004): 55–88; Terence P. Thornberry, Marvin D. Krohn, Alan J. Lizotte, Carolyn A. Smith, and Kimberly Tobin, *Gangs and Delinquency in Developmental Perspective* (Cambridge: Cambridge University Press, 2003).

3. Edwin H. Sutherland, Donald Cressey, and David F. Luckenbill. *Principles of Criminology*, 11th ed. (Oxford: General Hall, 1992).
4. See Victor Rios, *Punished: Policing the Lives of Black and Latino Boys* (New York: New York University Press, 2011).
5. Agnew, "Building on the Foundation," 319–361.
6. James Diego Vigil, *A Rainbow of Gangs: Street Cultures in the Mega-City* (Austin: University of Texas Press, 2002).
7. Cohen, *Delinquent Boys*.
8. William B. Sanders, *Gangbangs and Drive-Bys: Grounded Culture and Juvenile Gang Violence* (New York: De Gruyter, 1994).
9. Howard S. Becker, *Outsiders: Studies in the Sociology of Deviance* (New York: Free Press, 1963).
10. See Rios, *Punished*.
11. Katrina A. Rufino, Kathleen Talbot, and Glen A. Kercher, "Gang Membership and Crime Victimization among Prison Inmates," *American Journal of Criminal Justice* 37, no. 3 (September 2012): 321–337.
12. Anderson, *Code of the Street*.
13. Albert Cortez and Josie Danini Cortez, "Disciplinary Alternative Education Programs in Texas," Intercultural Development Research Association, 2009. https://files.eric.ed.gov/fulltext/ED509896.pdf.
14. Alexander Riley, "The Rebirth of Tragedy Out of the Spirit of Hip Hop: A Cultural Sociology of Gangster Rap Music," *Journal of Youth Studies* 8, no. 3 (September 2005): 297–311.
15. Kaitlyn J. Selman, "Imprisoning 'Those' Kids: Neoliberal Logics and the Disciplinary Alternative School," *Youth Justice* 17, no. 3 (December 2017): 213–231.
16. Joan Moore, Diego Vigil, and Robert Garcia, "Residence and Territoriality in Chicano Gangs," *Social Problems* 31, no. 2 (December 1983): 182–194.
17. Daniel J. Monti, "Origins and Problems of Gang Research in the United States," in *Gangs: The Origins and Impact of Contemporary Youth Gangs in the United States*, eds. Scott Cummings and Daniel. J. Monti (Albany: State University of New York Press, 1993), 3–25.
18. Beth Bjerregaard and Alan J. Lizotte, "Gun Ownership and Gang Membership." *Journal of Criminal Law and Criminology* 86, no. 1 (Autumn 1995): 37–58.
19. Robert Garot, "'Where You from!': Gang Identity as Performance," *Journal of Contemporary Ethnography* 36, no. 1 (February 2007): 50–84.
20. George E. Tita, Jacqueline Cohen, and John Engberg, "An Ecological Study of the Location of Gang 'Set Space,'" *Social Problems* 52, no. 2 (May 2005): 272–299.
21. Bruce A. Jacobs and Richard Wright, "Bounded Rationality, Retaliation, and the Spread of Urban Violence," *Journal of Interpersonal Violence* 25, no. 10 (October 2010): 1739–1766.
22. Nonresident gang members are much more likely to face continual questioning and are apt to aggressively overcompensate in response. Moore, Vigil, and Garcia, "Residence and Territoriality," 182–194.
23. Avelardo Valdez, Charles D. Kaplan, and Edward Codina, "Psychopathy among Mexican American Gang Members: A Comparative Study," *International Journal of Offender Therapy and Comparative Criminology* 44, no. 1 (February 2000): 46–58.
24. Malcolm W. Klein, *The American Street Gang: Its Nature, Prevalence, and Control* (New York: Oxford University Press, 1995).
25. Klein, *The American Street Gang*; C. Ronald Huff, "The Criminal Behavior of Gang Members and Nongang At-Risk Youth," in C. R. Huff, *Gangs in America*, 2nd ed., ed. C. Ronald Huff (Thousand Oaks: Sage, 1996), 75–102.

26. Jeffrey Fagan, "The Social Organization of Drug Use and Drug Dealing among Urban Gangs," *Criminology* 27, no. 4 (November 1989): 633–669.

27. Richard A. Cloward and Lloyd E. Ohlin, *Delinquency and Opportunity: A Theory of Delinquent Gangs* (New York: Free Press, 1960).

28. James Diego Vigil, *Barrio Gangs: Street Life and Identity in Southern California* (Long Grove, IL: Waveland Press, 1988), 160.

29. Joan W. Moore, *Going Down to the Barrio: Homeboys and Homegirls in Change* (Philadelphia: Temple University Press, 1991), 62–64.

30. Deanna L. Wilkinson, "Violent Events and Social Identity: Specifying the Relationship between Respect and Masculinity in Inner-City Violence," *Sociological Studies of Children and Youth* 8 (2001): 235–269.

31. Chris Melde and Finn-Aage Esbensen, "Gangs and Violence: Disentangling the Impact of Gang Membership on the Level and Nature of Offending," *Journal of Quantitative Criminology* 29, no. 2 (June 2013): 143–166.

32. See Robert Garot, *Who You Claim: Performing Gang Identity in School and on the Streets* (New York: New York University Press, 2010).

33. Klein, *The American Street Gang*, 11.

34. See Scott H. Decker and Barrik Van Winkle, *Life in the Gang: Family, Friends, and Violence* (New York: Cambridge University Press, 1996); Walter B. Miller, "Violent Crimes in City Gangs," *Annals of the American Academy of Political and Social Science* 364, no. 1 (March 1966): 96–112; Lauger, *Real Gangstas*.

35. David Matza, *Delinquency and Drift*. (New Brunswick, NJ: Transaction Publishers, 1990).

Chapter 5—Escalation

1. Matza, *Delinquency and Drift*.

2. Vigil, *A Rainbow of Gangs*; Decker and Van Winkle, *Life in the Gang*.

3. Malcolm W. Klein and Cheryl Maxson, "The Escalation Hypothesis: Street Gang Violence," in *Violent Crime, Violent Criminals*, eds. Neil Alan Wiener and Marvin E. Wolfgang (Beverly Hills: Sage, 1989), 219; Decker, "Collective and Normative," 243–264; Andrew V. Papachristos, "Murder by Structure: Dominance Relations and the Social Structure of Gang Homicide," *American Journal of Sociology* 115, no. 1 (July 2009): 74–128.

4. Brian G. Sellers and Bruce A. Arrigo, "Zero Tolerance, Social Control, and Marginalized Youth in U.S. Schools: A Critical Reappraisal of Neoliberalism's Theoretical Foundations and Epistemological Assumptions," *Contemporary Justice Review* 21, no. 1 (February 2018): 60–79.

5. Michael Rocque and Ray Paternoster, "Understanding the Antecedents of the 'School-to-Jail' Link: The Relationship between Race and School Discipline," *Journal of Criminal Law and Criminology* 101, no. 2 (March 2011): 633–665.

6. See Catherine Y. Kim, Daniel J. Losen, and Damon T. Hewitt, *The School to Prison Pipeline: Structuring Legal Reform* (New York: New York University Press, 2010).

7. Scott H. Decker and G. David Curry, "Gangs, Gang Homicides, and Gang Loyalty: Organized Crimes or Disorganized Criminals," *Journal of Criminal Justice* 30, no. 4 (February 2002): 343–352.

8. Paul B. Stretesky and Mark R. Pobregin, "Gang-Related Gun Violence: Socialization, Identity, and Self," *Journal of Contemporary Ethnography* 36, no. 1 (February 2007): 85–114.

9. Paul D. Harms and Howard N. Snyder, "Trends in the Murder of Juveniles: 1980–2000," *Juvenile Justice Bulletin* (Washington, DC: U.S. Department of Justice, Office of Juvenile Justice and Delinquency Programs, September 2004). https://www.ncjrs.gov/pdffiles1/ojjdp/194609.pdf,

10. Moore, Vigil, and Garcia, "Residence and Territoriality," 182–194.
11. Michela Lenzi, Jill D. Sharkey, Alessio Vieno, Ashley M. Mayworm, Danielle Dougherty, and Karen Nylund-Gibson, "Adolescent Gang Involvement: The Role of Individual, Family, Peer, and School Factors in a Multilevel Perspective," *Aggressive Behavior* 41, no. 4 (July–August 2015): 386–397.
12. Stretesky and Pobregin, "Gang-Related," 65–114.
13. Laub and Sampson, *Shared Beginnings*.
14. See David Dawley, *A Nation of Lords: The Autobiography of the Vice Lords*, 2nd ed. (Long Grove, IL: Waveland Press, 1993); R. Lincoln Keiser, *The Vice Lords: Warriors of the Streets* (New York: Holt, Rinehart, and Winston, 1969); George W. Knox, *An Introduction to Gangs* (Chicago: New Chicago School Press, 2006).
15. Geoffrey P. Hunt and Karen J. Laidler, "Alcohol and Violence in the Lives of Gang Members," *Alcohol Research and Health: The Journal of the National Institute on Alcohol Abuse and Alcoholism* 25, no. 1 (February 2001): 68–71.
16. Sanders, *Gangbangs*, 65–84.

CHAPTER 6—PURGATORY

1. Michele Peterson-Badali, Stephanie Care, and Julia Broeking, "Young People's Perceptions and Experiences of the Lawyer-Client Relationship," *Canadian Journal of Criminology and Criminal Justice* 49, no. 3 (July 2007): 375–401.
2. Herbert Packer, *The Limits of the Criminal Sanction* (Stanford: Stanford University Press, 1968).
3. See Adam Dunbar, Charis E. Kubrin, and Nicholas Skurich, "The Threatening Nature of "Rap" Music," *Psychology, Public Policy, and Law* 22, no. 3 (August 2016): 280–292.
4. See Timothy R. Lauger and James A. Densley, "Broadcasting Badness: Violence, Identity, and Performance in the Online Gang Rap Scene," *Justice Quarterly* 35, no. 5 (August 2018): 816–841.
5. Charis E. Kubrin and Erik Nielson, "Rap on Trial," *Race and Justice* 4, no. 3 (March 2014): 185–211.
6. David S. Abrams, "Is Pleading Really a Bargain?" *Journal of Empirical Legal Studies* 8, s1 (December 2011): 200–221.
7. Stephen J. Schulhofer, "Plea Bargaining as Disaster," *Yale Law Journal* 101, no. 8 (June 1992): 1979–2010.
8. Christian L. Bolden, "Charismatic Role Theory: Towards a Theory of Gang Dissipation," *The Journal of Gang Research* 17, no. 4 (Summer 2010): 39–70.
9. Federal Bureau of Investigation, "Crime in the United States" (Washington DC: U. S. Department of Justice, 1996); Michael Marks, "Drive-By City: Remembering San Antonio Gang Violence in the 1990s," *San Antonio Current*, February 24, 2016. https://www.sacurrent.com/sanantonio/drive-by-city-remembering -san-antonio-gang-violence-in-the-1990s/Content?oid=2509008&showFull Text=true
10. Thomas A. Myers, "The Unconstitutionality, Ineffectiveness, and Alternatives of Gang Injunctions," *Michigan Journal of Race and Law* 14. No. 2 (2009): 285–305.

CHAPTER 7—TEXAS HOLD'EM

1. Thomas A. Loughran, Edward P. Mulvey, Carol A. Schubert, Jeffrey Fagan, Alex R. Piquero, and Sandra H. Losoya, "Estimating a Dose–Response

Relationship between Length of Stay and Future Recidivism in Serious Juvenile Offenders," *Criminology* 47, no. 3 (August 2009): 699–740.

2. An idea passed down from classical social theorist, Jeremy Bentham, in which all interior parts of a building would be visible from a single location—the central guard station.

3. Erving Goffman, *Asylums: Essays on the Social Situation of Mental Patients and Other Inmates* (Garden City, NY: Anchor Books, 1961).

4. Lawrence L. Bench and Terry D. Allen, "Investigating the Stigma of Prison Classification: An Experimental Design," *Prison Journal* 83, no. 4 (December 2003): 367–382.

5. Ethan Watters, "The Love Story That Upended the Texas Prison System," *Texas Monthly*, October 18, 2018. https://www.texasmonthly.com/articles/love-story-upended-texas-prison-system/.

6. Susanne Mason, prod., *Writ Writer* (Newburgh, NY: New Day Films, 2008).

7. Robert S. Fong, "The Organizational Structure of Prison Gangs: A Texas Case Study, *Federal Probation* 54, no. 1 (March 1990): 36–43.

8. Fong, "The Organizational Structure."

9. Ben M. Crouch and James W. Marquart, *An Appeal to Justice: Litigated Reform of Texas Prisons* (Austin: University of Texas Press, 1989); Paige H. Ralph and James W. Marquart, "Gang Violence in Texas Prisons," *Prison Journal* 71, no. 2 (September 1991): 38–49.

10. Robert Perkinson, *Texas Tough: The Rise of America's Prison Empire* (New York: Picador, 2010).

11. Matthew T. Clarke, "Texas Federal District Judge Throws Out Vita Pro Convictions," *Prison Legal News*, July 2006, 34. https://www.prisonlegalnews.org/news/2006/jul/15/texas-federal-district-judge-throws-out-vitapro-convictions/.

12. Kathleen E. Maguire, Timothy J. Flanagan, and Terence P. Thornberry, "Prison Labor and Recidivism," *Journal of Quantitative Criminology* 4, no. 1 (March 1988): 3–18.

CHAPTER 8—FELLOWSHIP

1. Vigil, *Barrio Gangs*.

2. Scott H. Decker and Janet L. Lauritsen, "Leaving the Gang," in *Gangs in America III*, ed. C. R. Huff (Thousand Oaks, CA: Sage, 2002), 51–67.

3. Bolden, "Tales from the Hood," 473–490.

4. Avelardo Valdez and Raquel Flores, "A Situational Analysis of Dating Violence among Mexican American Females Associated with Street Gangs," *Sociological Focus* 38, no. 2 (May 2005): 95–114.

5. Robert Brenneman, *Homies and Hermanos: God and Gangs in Central America* (New York: Oxford University Press, 2012).

6. Donald Clemmer, *The Prison Community* (New Braunfels, TX: Christopher Publishing House, 1940).

7. Salvador Buentello, Robert S. Fong, and Ronald E. Vogel, "Prison Gang Development: A Theoretical Model," *Prison Journal* 71, no. 2 (September 1991): 3–14.

8. Scott H. Decker, David C. Pyrooz, and Richard K. Moule Jr., "Disengagement form Gangs as Role Transitions," *Journal of Research on Adolescence* 24, no. 2 (June 2014): 268–283.

9. Todd R. Clear, Patricia L. Hardyman, Bruce Stout, Karol Lucken, and Harry R. Dammer, "The Value of Religion in Prison: An Inmate Perspective," *Journal of Contemporary Criminal Justice* 16, no. 1 (February 2000): 53–74.

10. Edward O. Flores, *God's Gangs: Barrio Ministry, Masculinity, and Gang Recover* (New York: New York University Press, 2014).

11. Shadd Maruna, Louise Wilson, and Kathryn Curran, "Why God Is Often Found Behind Bars: Prison Conversions and the Crisis of Self-Narrative," *Research in Human Development* 3, no. 2 (September 2006): 161–184.

12. Shadd Maruna, *Making Good: How Ex-Convicts Reform and Rebuild Their Lives* (Washington, DC: American Psychological Association Books, 2001).

13. David C. Pyrooz and Scott H. Decker, *Competing for Control: Gangs and the Social Order of Prisons* (Cambridge, UK: Cambridge University Press, 2019): 228–244.

14. Pyrooz and Decker, *Competing for Control,* 228–244.

15. Brenneman, *Homies and Hermanos.*

16. Christopher J. Mumola and Allen J. Beck, "Prisoners in 1996," Bureau of Justice Statistics Bulletin (Washington, DC: U.S. Department of Justice: Office of Justice, June 1997). https://www.bjs.gov/content/pub/pdf/p96.pdf.

17. Frances T. Cullen, "Social Support as an Organizing Concept for Criminology: Presidential Address to the Academy of Criminal Justice Sciences," *Justice Quarterly* 11, no. 4 (December 1994): 527–559 Andy Hochstetler, Matt DeLisi, and Travis C. Pratt, "Social Support and Feelings of Hostility among Released Inmates," *Crime and Delinquency* 56, no. 4 (October 2010): 588–607.

CHAPTER 9—BETWEEN THE LINES

1. Gresham M. Sykes, *The Society of Captives: A Study of a Maximum Security Prison* (Princeton: Princeton University Press, 1958).

2. Christian L. Bolden, "Gang Organization and Gang Types," in the *Oxford Research Encyclopedia of Criminology and Criminal Justice*, ed. Henry Pontell (New York: Oxford University Press, March 2018): 1–23.

3. David C. Pyrooz, Scott H. Decker, and Mark Fleisher, "From the Street to the Prison, from the Prison to the Street: Understanding and Responding to Prison Gangs," *Journal of Aggression, Conflict, and Peace Research* 3, no. 1 (January 2011): 12–24.

4. Pyrooz and Decker, *Competing for Control*, 94–121.

5. See Skarbek, *The Social Order.*

6. Perkinson, *Texas Tough.*

7. Mason, *Writ Writer.*

8. Montejano, *Quixote's Soldiers*, 214.

9. Mike Tapia, "Barrio Criminal Networks and Prison Gang Formation in Texas," *Journal of Gang Research* 25, no. 4 (September 2018): 45–63.

10. Tapia, "Barrio Criminal Networks."

11. Tapia, "Barrio Criminal Networks."

12. Wilson McKinney, *Fred Carrasco: The Heroin Merchant* (Austin: Heidelberg Publishers, 1975).

13. McKinney, *Fred Carrasco.*

14. McKinney, *Fred Carrasco.*

15. Juan Santana and Gabriel Morales, *Don't Mess with Texas: Gangs in the Lone Star State* (Columbia, SC: CreateSpace, 2014).

16. Santana and Morales, *Don't Mess with Texas.*

17. Tapia, "Barrio Criminal Networks," 45–63.

18. Avelardo Valdez, "Mexican American Youth and Adult Prison Gangs in a Changing Heroin Market," *Journal of Drug Issues* 35, no. 4 (October 2005): 843–867.

19. Mike Tapia, Corey S. Sparks, and J. Mitchell Miller, "Texas Latino Prison Gangs: An Exploration of Generational Shift and Rebellion," *Prison Journal* 94, no. 2 (June 2014): 159–179.

20. R. V. Gundur, "Negotiating Violence and Protection in Prison and on the Outside: The Organizational Evolution of the Transnational Prison Gang Barrio Azteca," *International Criminal Justice Review* (March 2019). https://doi.org/10.1177/1057567719836466.

CHAPTER 10—TRANSITIONS

1. Christian Henrichson and Ruth Delaney, "The Price of Prisons: What Incarceration Costs Taxpayers" (New York: Vera Institute of Justice, January 2012). https://www.vera.org/downloads/Publications/price-of-prisons-what-incarceration-costs-taxpayers/legacy_downloads/price-of-prisons-updated-version-021914.pdf.
2. Michelle Alexander, *The New Jim Crow: Mass Incarceration in the Age of Colorblindness* (New York: Free Press, 2011).
3. John F. Pfaff, *Locked In: The True Causes of Mass Incarceration and How to Achieve Real Reform* (New York: Basic Books, 2017).
4. Texas State Library and Archives Commission, "An Inventory of Youth Commission Historical Records at the Texas State Archives, 1886–1892, 1902, 1909–2003, Undated, Bulk 1949–2000." https://legacy.lib.utexas.edu/taro/tslac/20124/tsl-20124.html#series5.
5. William S. Bush, Isela Gutiérrez, and Kim Wilks, *Protecting Texas' Most Precious Resource: A History of Juvenile Justice Policy in Texas, Part II, The TYC Era: Between Rehabilitation and Punishment, 1949–2008* (Austin: Texas Criminal Justice Coalition, 2009). https://www.texascjc.org/system/files/publications/A%20History%20of%20JJ%20Policy%20in%20TX%20-%20Part%202%20%28Jan%202009%29.pdf.
6. Bush, Gutiérrez, and Wilks, *Protecting Texas' Most Precious Resource.*
7. Elizabeth T. Buhmann and Roberto San Miguel, *Gangs in Texas Cities: Background, Survey Results, and State-Level Policy Options* (Austin: Office of the Attorney General, 1991). https://www.ncjrs.gov/pdffiles1/Digitization/137580NCJRS.pdf.
8. Buhmann and San Miguel, *Gangs in Texas Cities.*
9. Texas Juvenile Justice Department, *TJJD Strategic Plan 2015–2019.* http://www.tjjd.texas.gov/index.php/doc-library/send/145-strategic-plans/359-texas-juvenile-justice-department-strategic-plan-for-2015-2019-july-2014.
10. Michele Deitch, *Juveniles in the Adult Criminal Justice System in Texas*, Special Project Report (Austin: The University of Texas at Austin, LBJ School of Public Affairs, March 2011). https://lbj.utexas.edu/sites/default/files/file/news/juvenilestexas--final.pdf.
11. Marilyn D. McShane and Frank P. Williams III, "The Prison Adjustment of Juvenile Offenders," *Crime & Delinquency* 35 no. 2 (April 1989): 254–269.
12. Donna M. Bishop, "Juvenile Offenders in the Adult Criminal Justice System," *Crime and Justice* 27 (2000): 81–167.

CHAPTER 11—WALLY WORLD

1. See Christopher E. Smith, "Black Muslims and the Development of Prisoners' Rights," *Journal of Black Studies* 24, no. 2 (December 1993): 131–146.
2. Ralph and Marquart, "Gang Violence," 38–49.
3. Mark S. Hamm, *The Spectacular Few: Prisoner Radicalization and the Evolving Terrorist Threat* (New York: New York University Press, 2013).
4. Gordon A. Crews, Reid H. Montgomery, and W. Ralph Garris, *Faces of Violence in America* (Needham Heights, MA: Simon and Schuster, 1996).

5. TDCJ was not considered compliant with desegregation orders until 1991 and was not fully desegregated until 1999. Consistent with the reform-litigation literature, desegregation of Texas prisons saw a brief increase in interracial violence, followed by a significant decline. Chad R. Trulson and James W. Marquart, "Racial Desegregation and Violence in the Texas Prison System," *Criminal Justice Review* 27, no. 2 (September 2002): 233–255.
6. Mary E. (Beth) Pelz, James W. Marquart, and C. Terry Pelz, "Right-Wing Extremism in the Texas Prisons: The Rise and Fall of the Aryan Brotherhood of Texas," *Prison Journal* 71, no. 2 (September 1991): 23–37.
7. Brentin Mock, "Vicious Circle: Aryan Circle Blamed for Two Cop Killings," in *North American Criminal Gangs*, ed. Tom Barker, (Durham, NC: Carolina Academic Press, 2007), 151–156 >
8. Prison Legal News, "Guard Raped, Entire Texas Prison System Locked Down," May 1999. https://www.prisonlegalnews.org/news/1999/may/15/guard-raped-entire-texas-prison-system-locked-down/.
9. While most outlaw motorcycle clubs are White only, the Bandidos, one of the "Big 5" biker clubs in the United States, were integrated with Whites and Latinos.
10. V. Wolfe Mahfood, Wendi Pollock, and Dennis Longmire, "Leave It at the Gate: Job Stress and Satisfaction in Correctional Staff," *Criminal Justice Studies* 26, no. 3 (September 2013): 308–325.
11. Kelsey Kauffman, *Prison Officers and Their World* (Cambridge: Harvard University Press, 1988); Robert M. Worley and Vidisha Barua Worley, "Guards Gone Wild: A Self-Report Study of Correctional Officer Misconduct and the Effect of Institutional Deviance on 'Care' within the Texas Prison System," *Deviant Behavior* 32, no. 4 (April 2011): 293–319.

CHAPTER 12—STARTING FROM THE BOTTOM

1. Clear et al. "The Value of Religion in Prison," 53–74.
2. Sung Joon Jang, Byron R. Johnson, Joshua Hays, Michael Hallett, and Grant Duwe, "Religion and Misconduct in 'Angola' Prison: Conversion, Congregational Participation, Religiosity, and Self-Identities," *Justice Quarterly* 35, no. 3 (May 2018): 412–442.
3. Brenneman, *Homies and Hermanos*.

CHAPTER 13—LETTERS

1. Visitation both anecdotally and empirically reduces rates of recidivism. William D. Bales and Daniel P. Mears, "Inmate Social Ties and the Transition to Society: Does Visitation Reduce Recidivism?" *Journal of Research in Crime and Delinquency* 45, no. 3 (August 2008): 287–321.
2. Alexis Watts, Edward E. Rhine, Mariel Apler, and Cecilia Klingele, *Profiles in Parole Release and Revocation: Examining the Legal Framework in the United States—Texas* (University of Minnesota: Robina Institute of Criminal Law and Criminal Justice, 2016. https://robinainstitute.umn.edu/sites/robinainstitute.umn.edu/files/602501_texas_legal_parole_profile_final.pdf.
3. Lois M. Davis, Jennifer L. Steele, Robert Bozick, Malcolm V. Williams, Susan Turner, Jeremy N. V. Miles, Jessica Saunders, and Paul S. Steinberg, *How Effective Is Correctional Education, and Where Do We Go from Here? The Results of a Comprehensive Evaluation* (Santa Monica, CA: Rand Corporation, 2014). https://www.rand.org/pubs/research_reports/RR564.html.

4. Tony Fabelo, "The Impact of Prison Education on Community Reintegration of Inmates: The Texas Case," *Journal of Correctional Education* 53, no. 3 (September 2002): 106–110.
5. Jamie Watson, Amy L. Solomon, Nancy G. La Vigne, Jeremy Travis, Meagan Funches, and Barbara Parthasarathy, *A Portrait of Prisoner Reentry in Texas* (Washington, DC: Urban Institute Justice Policy Center, March 2004). https://www.urban.org/research/publication/portrait-prisoner-reentry-texas.
6. John O'Brien, John Newton, Anita Zinnecker, and Bill Parr, *Statewide Criminal Justice Recidivism and Revocation Rates* (Austin: State of Texas, Legislative Budget Board, January 2005). http://www.lbb.state.tx.us/documents/publications/policy_report/4914_recividism_revocation_rates_jan2019.pdf; Pew Center on the States, *State of Recidivism: The Revolving Door of America's Prisons* (Washington, DC: Pew Charitable Trusts, April 2011). https://www.pewtrusts.org/~/media/legacy/uploadedfiles/pcs_assets/2011/pewstateofrecidivismpdf.pdf.
7. See Jill A. McCorkel, *Breaking Women: Gender, Race, and the New Politics of Imprisonment* (New York: New York University Press, 2013).
8. Douglas N. Evans, Emily Pelletier, and Jason Szokla, "Education in Prison and the Self-Stigma: Empowerment Continuum," *Crime and Delinquency* 64, no. 2 (February 2018): 255–280.
9. Watson et al., *A Portrait of Prisoner Reentry.*
10. Dana Kaplan, Vincent Schiraldi, and Jason Zeidenberg, *Texas Tough: An Analysis of Incarceration and Crime Trends in the Lone Star State* (Washington, DC: Justice Policy Institute, October 2000). http://www.justicepolicy.org/research/2062.
11. Tapia, Sparks, and Miller, "Texas Latino," 159–179.
12. R. V. Gundur, "The Changing Social Organization of Prison Protection Markets: When Prisoners Choose to Organize Horizontally Rather than Vertically," *Trends in Organized Crime* (February 2018). DOI: 10.1007/s12117-018-9332-0.

Chapter 14—Outcast

1. Laurence Steinberg, He Len Chung, and Michelle Little, "Reentry of Young Offenders from the Justice System: A Developmental Perspective," *Youth Violence and Juvenile Justice* 2, no. 1 (January 2004): 21–38.
2. Rebecca L. Naser and Nancy G. La Vigne, "Family Support in the Prisoner Reentry Process: Expectations and Realities," *Journal of Offender Rehabilitation* 43, no. 1 (2006): 93–106.
3. Watson et al., *A Portrait of Prisoner Reentry.*
4. Alyssa W. Chamberlain, Matthew Gricius, Danielle M. Wallace, Diana Borjas, and Vincent M. Ware, "Parolee–Parole Officer Rapport: Does It Impact Recidivism?" *International Journal of Offender Therapy and Comparative Criminology* 62, no. 11 (August 2018): 3581–3602.
5. Christy A. Visher, Sara A. Debus-Sherrill, and Jennifer Yahner, "Employment after Prison: A Longitudinal Study of Former Prisoners," *Justice Quarterly* 28, no. 5 (October 2011): 698–718.
6. Marie Pryor and Douglas E. Thompkins, "The Disconnect between Education and Social Opportunity for the Formerly Incarcerated," *American Journal of Criminal Justice* 38, no. 3 (September 2013): 457–479.
7. Stephen J. Tripodi, "The Influence of Social Bonds on Recidivism: A Study of Texas Male Prisoners," *Victims and Offenders: An International Journal of Evidence-Based Research, Policy and Practice* 5, no. 4 (October 2010): 354–370.

8. Mark T. Berg and Beth M. Huebner, "Reentry and the Ties That Bind: An Examination of Social Ties, Employment, and Recidivism," *Justice Quarterly* 28, no. 2 (April 2011): 382–410.

9. Peggy C. Giordano, Ryan D. Schroeder, and Stephen A. Cernkovich, "Emotions and Crime over the Life Course: A Neo-Meadian Perspective on Criminal Continuity and Change," *American Journal of Sociology* 112, no. 6 (May 2007): 1603–1661.

10. See Keesha M. Middlemas, *Convicted and Condemned: The Politics and Policies of Prisoner Reentry* (New York: New York University Press, 2017).

11. Carrie Pettus-Davis, Elaine Eggleston Doherty, Christopher Veeh, and Christina Drymon, "Deterioration of Postincarceration Social Support for Emerging Adults," *Criminal Justice and Behavior* 44, no. 10 (October 2017): 1317–1339.

12. In 2005 (earliest data available), African Americans made up 7 percent of the twenty-three thousand undergraduate students at Texas State University. My attendance there began four years earlier. http://www.ir.txstate.edu/ir-self -service/self-service. The university would later make great efforts to diversify and ultimately earned the federal designation as a Hispanic-serving institution.

13. Travis Hirschi, *Causes of Delinquency* (Berkeley: University of California Press, 1969).

Chapter 15—Freedom

1. Pryor and Thompkins, "The Disconnect," 457–479.

2. Maruna, *Making Good*.

3. Michael Rocque, Chad Posick, and Ray Paternoster, "Identities through Time: An Exploration of Identity Change as a Cause of Desistance," *Justice Quarterly* 33, no. 1 (2016): 45–72.

Chapter 16—Pinnacles

1. Thomas P. LeBel, "Invisible Stripes? Formerly Incarcerated Persons' Perceptions of Stigma," *Deviant Behavior* 33, no. 2 (February 2012): 89–107.

2. See Amanda Geller and Marah A. Curtis, "A Sort of Homecoming: Incarceration and the Housing Security of Urban Men," *Social Science Research* 40, no. 4 (July 2011): 1196–1213.

3. In 2016, UCF ranked as having the largest student population in the United States, with over sixty-three thousand students.

4. Malcolm W. Klein, "Resolving the Eurogang Paradox," in *The Eurogang Paradox: Street Gangs in the U.S. and Europe*, eds. Malcolm W. Klein, Hans-Jürgen Kerner, Cheryl L. Maxson, and Elmar G. M. Weitekamp (Berlin: Springer Science + Business Media B. V., 2001), 7–20.

5. http://www.homeboyindustries.org.

6. See Darell Dones, Christian Bolden, and Michael Buerger, "Terrorism, Gangs, and Weapons of Mass Destruction: A Futures Assessment of a Potential Nexus" (Futures Working Group White Paper Series, University of Central Florida, Orlando, FL, November 2013). http://sciences.ucf.edu/fwg/wp-content/uploads /sites/157/2016/11/Terrorism.pdf.

Appendix A

1. Denver Heights Gangster (DHG) Crips contested the neighborhood, but it was mostly known for its Blood affiliation.

2. Skyline initially had Crip and Independent factions but then became Blood.

3. Formerly Wheatley Court Gangster (WCG) Crips.

4. DOG and Acme Park were neutral, favoring Crips. UNLV DOG favored Bloods.

5. Special thanks to Mike Tapia and former gang member respondents for their assistance in constructing this list.
6. For an exploration of gay gangs and gay gang members, see Vanessa R. Panfil, *The Gang's All Queer: The Lives of Gay Gang Members* (New York: New York University Press, 2017).
7. See Gini Sikes, *8 Ball Chicks* (New York: Anchor Books, 1997).
8. See Tapia, *The Barrio Gangs*.

BIBLIOGRAPHY

Abrams, David S. "Is Pleading Really a Bargain?" *Journal of Empirical Legal Studies* 8, S1 (December 2011): 200–221.

Agnew, Robert. "Building on the Foundation of General Strain Theory: Specifying the Types of Strain Most Likely to Lead to Crime and Delinquency." *Journal of Research in Crime and Delinquency* 38, no. 4 (November 2001): 319–361.

———. "Foundation for a General Strain Theory of Crime and Delinquency." *Criminology* 30, no. 1 (February 1992): 47–88.

Alexander, Michelle. *The New Jim Crow: Mass Incarceration in the Age of Colorblindness.* New York: Free Press, 2011.

Alonso, Alejandro A. "Racialized Identities and the Formation of Black Gangs in Los Angeles." *Urban Geography* 25, no. 7 (November 2004): 658–674.

Anderson, Elijah. *Code of the Street: Decency, Violence, and the Moral Life of the Inner City.* New York: W. W. Norton and Company, 1999.

Bales, William D., and Daniel P. Mears. "Inmate Social Ties and the Transition to Society: Does Visitation Reduce Recidivism?" *Journal of Research in Crime and Delinquency* 45, no. 3 (August 2008): 287–321.

Becker, Howard S. *Outsiders: Studies in the Sociology of Deviance.* New York: Free Press, 1963.

Bench, Lawrence L., and Terry D. Allen. "Investigating the Stigma of Prison Classification: An Experimental Design." *Prison Journal* 83, no. 4 (December 2003): 367–382.

Berg, Mark T., and Beth M. Huebner. "Reentry and the Ties That Bind: An Examination of Social Ties, Employment, and Recidivism." *Justice Quarterly* 28, no. 2 (April 2011): 382–410.

Bishop, Donna M. "Juvenile Offenders in the Adult Criminal Justice System." *Crime and Justice* 27 (2000): 81–167.

Bjerregaard, Beth, and Alan J. Lizotte. "Gun Ownership and Gang Membership." *Journal of Criminal Law and Criminology* 86, no. 1 (Autumn 1995): 37–58.

Bolden, Christian L. "Charismatic Role Theory: Towards a Theory of Gang Dissipation." *Journal of Gang Research* 17, no. 4 (Summer 2010): 39–70.

———. "Gang Organization and Gang Types." In the *Oxford Research Encyclopedia of Criminology and Criminal Justice*, edited by Henry Pontell. New York: Oxford University Press, March 2018: 1–23.

———. "Liquid Soldiers: Fluidity and Gang Membership." *Deviant Behavior* 33, no. 3 (February 2012): 207–222.

———. "Tales from the Hood: An Emic Perspective on Gang Joining and Gang Desistance." *Criminal Justice Review* 38, no. 4 (October 2013): 473–490.

Bourdieu, Pierre. Distinction: *A Social Critique of the Judgement of Taste.* Cambridge: Harvard University Press, 1984.

Brenneman, Robert. *Homies and Hermanos: God and Gangs in Central America.* New York: Oxford University Press, 2012.

Brown, Gregory Christopher, James Diego Vigil, and Eric Robert Taylor. "The Ghettoization of Blacks in Los Angeles: The Emergence of Street Gangs." *Journal of African American Studies* 16, no. 2 (June 2012): 209–225.

Buentello, Salvador, Robert S. Fong, and Ronald E. Vogel. "Prison Gang Development: A Theoretical Model." *Prison Journal* 71, no. 2 (September 1991): 3–14.

Buhmann, Elizabeth T., and Roberto San Miguel. *Gangs in Texas Cities: Background, Survey Results, and State-Level Policy Options.* Austin: Office of the Attorney General, 1991. https://www.ncjrs.gov/pdffiles1/Digitization/137580NCJRS.pdf.

Bush, William S., Isela Gutiérrez, and Kim Wilks. *Protecting Texas' Most Precious Resource: A History of Juvenile Justice Policy in Texas: Part II, The TYC Era: Between Rehabilitation and Punishment 1949–2008.* Austin: Texas Criminal Justice Coalition, 2009. https://www.texascjc.org/system/files/publications/A%20History%20of%20JJ%20Policy%20in%20TX%20-%20Part%202%20%28Jan%202009%29.pdf.

Calarco, Jessica McCrory. "Coached for the Classroom: Parents' Cultural Transmission and Children's Reproduction of Educational Inequalities." *American Sociological Review* 79, no. 5 (October 2014): 1015–1037.

Chamberlain, Alyssa W., Matthew Gricius, Danielle M. Wallace, Diana Borjas, and Vincent M. Ware. "Parolee–Parole Officer Rapport: Does It Impact Recidivism?" *International Journal of Offender Therapy and Comparative Criminology* 62, no. 11 (August 2018): 3581–3602.

Clarke, Matthew T. "Texas Federal District Judge Throws Out Vita Pro Convictions." *Prison Legal* News, July 2006, 34. https://www.prisonlegalnews.org/news/2006/jul/15/texas-federal-district-judge-throws-out-vitapro-convictions/.

Clear, Todd R., Patricia L. Hardyman, Bruce Stout, Karol Lucken, and Harry R. Dammer." The Value of Religion in Prison: An Inmate Perspective." *Journal of Contemporary Criminal Justice* 16, no. 1 (February 2000): 53–74.

Clemmer, Donald. *The Prison Community.* New Braunfels, TX: Christopher Publishing House, 1940.

Cloward, Richard A., and Lloyd E. Ohlin. *Delinquency and Opportunity: A Theory of Delinquent Gangs.* New York: Free Press, 1960.

Cohen, Albert K. *Delinquent Boys: The Culture of a Gang.* Glencoe, IL: Free Press, 1955.

Cohen, Stanley. *Folk Devils and Moral Panics: The Creation of the Mods and Rockers.* London: Routledge, 1972.

Contreras, Randol. *The Stickup Kids: Race, Drugs, Violence, and the American Dream.* Los Angeles: University of California Press, 2012.

Cortez, Albert, and Josie Danini Cortez. "Disciplinary Alternative Education Programs in Texas." Intercultural Development Research Association, 2009. https://files.eric.ed.gov/fulltext/ED509896.pdf.

Crews, Gordon A., Reid H. Montgomery, and W. Ralph Garris. *Faces of Violence in America.* Needham Heights, MA: Simon and Schuster, 1996.

Crouch, Ben M., and James W. Marquart. *An Appeal to Justice: Litigated Reform of Texas Prisons.* Austin: University of Texas Press, 1989.

Cullen, Francis T. "Social Support as an Organizing Concept for Criminology: Presidential Address to the Academy of Criminal Justice Science." *Justice Quarterly* 11, no. 4 (December 1994): 527–559.

Davis, Lois M., Jennifer L. Steele, Robert Bozick, Malcolm V. Williams, Susan Turner, Jeremy N. V. Miles, Jessica Saunders, and Paul S. Steinberg. *How Effective Is Correctional Education, and Where Do We Go from Here? The Results of a Comprehensive Evaluation.* Santa Monica, CA: Rand Corporation, 2014. https://www.rand.org/pubs/research_reports/RR564.html.

Dawley, David. *A Nation of Lords: The Autobiography of the Vice Lords,* 2nd ed. Long Grove, IL: Waveland Press, 1993.

Decker, Scott H. "Collective and Normative Features of Gang Violence." *Justice Quarterly* 13, no. 2 (June 1996): 242–264.

Decker, Scott H., and G. David Curry. "Gangs, Gang Homicides, and Gang Loyalty: Organized Crimes or Disorganized Criminals." *Journal of Criminal Justice* 30, no. 4 (February 2002): 343–352.

Decker, Scott H., and Janet L. Lauritsen. "Leaving the Gang." In *Gangs in America III,* edited by C. Ronald Huff, 51–76. Thousand Oaks: Sage, 2002.

Decker, Scott H., and Barrik Van Winkle. *Life in the Gang: Family, Friends, and Violence.* New York: Cambridge University Press, 1996.

Decker, Scott H., David C. Pyrooz, and Richard K. Moule, Jr. "Disengagement from Gangs as Role Transitions." *Journal of Research on Adolescence* 24, no. 2 (June 2014): 268–283.

Deitch, Michele. *Juveniles in the Adult Criminal Justice System in Texas.* Special Project Report. Austin: University of Texas at Austin, LBJ School of Public Affairs, March 2011. https://lbj.utexas.edu/sites/default/files/file/news/juvenilestexas--final.pdf.

Dones, Darell, Christian Bolden, and Michael Buerger. "Terrorism, Gangs, and Weapons of Mass Destruction: A Futures Assessment of a Potential Nexus." Futures Working Group White Paper Series, University of Central Florida, Orlando, FL, November 2013. http://sciences.ucf.edu/fwg/wp-content/uploads/sites/157/2016/11/Terrorism.pdf.

Duff, Audrey. "We Get All Hyped Up. We Do a Drive-By." *Texas Monthly,* October 1994. https://www.texasmonthly.com/articles/we-get-all-hyped-up-we-do-a-drive-by/.

Dunbar, Adam, Charis E. Kubrin, and Nicholas Scurich. "The Threatening Nature of "Rap" Music." *Psychology, Public Policy, and Law* 22, no. 3 (August 2016): 280–292.

Eckert, Penelope. *Jocks and Burnouts: Social Categories and Identity in High School.* New York: Teachers College Press, 1989.

Evans, Douglas N., Emily Pelletier, and Jason Szkola. "Education in Prison and the Self-Stigma: Empowerment Continuum." *Crime and Delinquency* 64, no. 2 (February 2018): 255–280.

Fabelo, Tony. "The Impact of Prison Education on Community Reintegration of Inmates: The Texas Case." *Journal of Correctional Education* 53, no. 3 (September 2002): 106–110.

Fagan, Jeffrey. "The Social Organization of Drug Use and Drug Dealing among Urban Gangs." *Criminology* 27, no. 4 (November 1989): 633–670.

Federal Bureau of Investigation. "Crime in the United States." Washington, DC: U.S. Department of Justice, 1996.

Flasher, Jack. "Adultism." *Adolescence* 13, no. 51 (Fall 1978): 517–523.

Flores, Edward O. *God's Gangs: Barrio Ministry, Masculinity, and Gang Recovery.* New York: New York University Press, 2014.

Fong, Robert S. "The Organizational Structure of Prison Gangs: A Texas Case Study." *Federal Probation* 54, no. 1 (March 1990): 36–43.

Garot, Robert. "'Where You from!': Gang Identity as Performance." *Journal of Contemporary Ethnography* 36, no. 1 (February 2007): 50–84.

———. *Who You Claim: Performing Gang Identity in School and on the Streets.* New York: New York University Press, 2010.

Gatti, Uberto, Richard E. Tremblay, Frank Vitaro, and Pierre McDuff. "Youth Gangs, Delinquency, and Drug Use: A Test of the Selection, Facilitation, and Enhancement Hypothesis." *Journal of Child Psychology and Psychiatry* 46, no. 11 (November 2005): 1178–1190.

Geller, Amanda, and Marah A. Curtis. "A Sort of Homecoming: Incarceration and Housing Security of Urban Men." *Social Science Research* 40, no. 4 (July 2011): 1196–1213.

Gershoff, Elizabeth T. "More Harm Than Good: A Summary of Scientific Research on the Intended and Unintended Effects of Corporal Punishment on Children." *Law and Contemporary Social Problems* 73, no. 2 (Spring 2010): 31–56.

Gershoff, Elizabeth T., and Sarah A. Font. "Corporal Punishment in U.S. Public Schools: Prevalence, Disparities in Use, and Status in State and Federal Policy." *Social Policy Report* 30, no. 1 (September 2016): 1–26.

Giordano, Peggy C., Ryan D. Schroeder, and Stephen A. Cernkovich. "Emotions and Crime over the Life Course: A Neo-Meadian Perspective on Criminal Continuity and Change." *American Journal of Sociology* 112, no. 6 (May 2007): 1603–1661.

Goffman, Erving. *Asylums: Essays on the Social Situation of Mental Patients and Other Inmates.* Garden City, NY: Anchor Books, 1961.

Gordon, Rachel A., Benjamin B. Lahey, Eriko Kawai, Rolf Loeber, Magda Stouthamer-Loeber, and David P. Farrington. "Antisocial Behavior and Youth Gang Membership: Selection and Socialization." *Criminology* 42, no. 1 (February 2004): 55–88.

Gundur, R. V. "The Changing Social Organization of Prison Protection Markets: When Prisoners Choose to Organize Horizontally Rather than Vertically." *Trends in Organized Crime* (February 2018). DOI: 10.1007/s12117-018-9332-0.

———. "Negotiating Violence and Protection in Prison and on the Outside: The Organizational Evolution of the Transnational Prison Gang Barrio Azteca." *International Criminal Justice Review* (March 2019). https://doi.org/10.1177/1057567 719836466.

Hamm, Mark S. *The Spectacular Few: Prisoner Radicalization and the Evolving Terrorist Threat.* New York: New York University Press, 2013.

Harms, Paul D., and Howard N. Snyder. *Trends in the Murder of Juveniles: 1980–2000.* Juvenile Justice Bulletin. Washington, DC: Office of Juvenile Justice and Delinquency Prevention, U.S. Department of Justice, September 2004. https://www.ncjrs.gov/pdffiles1/ojjdp/194609.pdf.

Henrichson, Christian, and Ruth Delaney. "The Price of Prisons: What Incarceration Costs Taxpayers." New York: Vera Institute of Justice, January 2012. https://www.vera.org/downloads/Publications/price-of-prisons-what-incarceration-costs-taxpayers/legacy_downloads/price-of-prisons-updated-version-021914.pdf.

Hirschi, Travis. *Causes of Delinquency.* Berkeley: University of California Press, 1969.

Hochstetler, Andy, Matt DeLisi, and Travis C. Pratt. "Social Support and Feelings of Hostility among Released Inmates." *Crime & Delinquency* 56, no. 4 (October 2010): 588–607.

Howell, James C., and Arlen Egley Jr. "Moving Risk Factors into Developmental Theories of Gang Membership." *Youth Violence and Juvenile Justice* 3, no. 4 (October 2005): 334–354.

Huff, C. Ronald. "The Criminal Behavior of Gang Members and Nongang At-Risk Youth." In *Gangs in America*, 2nd ed., edited by C. Ronald Huff, 75–102. Thousand Oaks: Sage, 1996.

———. "Youth Gangs and Public Policy." *Crime & Delinquency* 35, no. 4 (October 1989): 524–537.

Hunt, Geoffrey P., and Karen J. Laidler. "Alcohol and Violence in the Lives of Gang Members." *Alcohol Research and Health: The Journal of the National Institute on Alcohol Abuse and Alcoholism* 25, no. 1 (February 2001): 66–71.

Jacobs, Bruce A., and Richard Wright. "Bounded Rationality, Retaliation, and the Spread of Urban Violence." *Journal of Interpersonal Violence* 25, no. 10 (October 2010): 1739–1766.

Jacobs, James B. "Street Gangs behind Bars." *Social Problems* 21, no. 3 (January 1974): 359–409.

Jacobson, Cardell K., and Heaton, Tim B. "Inter-group Marriage and United States Military Service." *Journal of Political and Military Sociology* 31, no. 1 (2003): 1–22.
Jang, Sung Joon, Byron R. Johnson, Joshua Hays, Michael Hallett, and Grant Duwe. "Religion and Misconduct in 'Angola' Prison: Conversion, Congregational Participation, Religiosity, and Self-Identities." *Justice Quarterly* 35, no. 3 (May 2018): 412–442.

Jankowski, Martín Sánchez. *Islands in the Street: Gangs and American Urban Society.* Berkeley: University of California Press, 1991.

Kaplan, Dana, Vincent Schiraldi, and Jason Zeidenberg. *Texas Tough: An Analysis of Incarceration and Crime Trends in the Lone Star State.* Washington, DC: Justice Policy Institute, October 2000. http://www.justicepolicy.org/research/2062.

Kauffman, Kelsey. *Prison Officers and Their World.* Cambridge: Harvard University Press, 1988.

Keiser, R. Lincoln. *The Vice Lords: Warriors of the Streets.* New York: Holt, Rinehart, and Winston, 1969.

Kim, Catherine Y., Daniel J. Losen, and Damon T. Hewitt. *The School to Prison Pipeline: Structuring Legal Reform.* New York: New York University Press, 2010.

Klein, Malcolm W. *The American Street Gang: Its Nature, Prevalence, and Control.* New York: Oxford University Press, 1995.

———. "Resolving the Eurogang Paradox." In *The Eurogang Paradox: Street Gangs in the U.S. and Europe*, edited by Malcolm W. Klein, Hans-Jürgen Kerner, Cheryl L. Maxson, and Elmar G. M. Weitekamp, 7–20. Berlin: Springer Science + Business Media B. V., 2001.

Klein, Malcolm W., and Cheryl Maxson. "The Escalation Hypothesis: Street Gang Violence. In *Violent Crime, Violent Criminals*, edited by Neil Alan Weiner and Marvin E. Wolfgang, 219. Beverly Hills: Sage, 1989.

Knox, George W. *An Introduction to Gangs.* Chicago: New Chicago School Press, 2006.

Kubrin, Charis E., and Erik Nielson. "Rap on Trial." *Race and Justice* 4, no. 3 (March 2014): 185–211.

Laub, John H., and Robert S. Sampson. *Shared Beginnings, Divergent Lives: Delinquent Boys to Age 70.* Cambridge: Harvard University Press, 2003.

Lauger, Timothy R. *Real Gangstas: Legitimacy, Reputation, and Violence in the Intergang Environment.* New Brunswick, Rutgers University Press, 2012.

Lauger, Timothy R., and James A. Densley. "Broadcasting Badness: Violence, Identity, and Performance in the Online Gang Rap Scene." *Justice Quarterly* 35, no. 5 (August 2018): 816–841.

LeBel, Thomas P. "Invisible Stripes? Formerly Incarcerated Persons' Perceptions of Stigma." *Deviant Behavior* 33, no. 2 (February 2012): 89–107.

Lenzi, Michela, Jill D. Sharkey, Alessio Vieno, Ashley M. Mayworm, Danielle Dougherty, and Karen Nylund-Gibson. "Adolescent Gang Involvement: The Role of Individual, Family, Peer, and School Factors in a Multilevel Perspective." *Aggressive Behavior* 41, no. 4 (July–August 2015): 386–397.

Lopez-Aguado, Patrick. "I Would Be a Bulldog: Tracing the Spillover of Carceral Identity." *Social Problems* 63, no. 2 (May 2016): 203–221.

Loughran, Thomas A., Edward P. Mulvey, Carol A. Schubert, Jeffrey Fagan, Alex R. Piquero, and Sandra H. Losoya. "Estimating a Dose–Response Relationship between Length of Stay and Future Recidivism in Serious Juvenile Offenders." *Criminology* 47, no. 3 (August 2009): 699–740.

Maguire, Kathleen E., Timothy J. Flanagan, and Terence P. Thornberry. "Prison Labor and Recidivism." *Journal of Quantitative Criminology* 4, no. 1 (March 1988): 3–18.

Mahfood, V. Wolfe, Wendi Pollock, and Dennis Longmire. "Leave It at the Gate: Job Stress and Satisfaction in Correctional Staff." *Criminal Justice Studies: A Critical Journal of Crime, Law, and Society* 26, no. 3 (September 2013): 308–325.

Marks, Michael. "Drive-By City: Remembering San Antonio Gang Violence in the 1990s." *San Antonio Current*, February 24, 2016. https://www.sacurrent.com/sananto nio/drive-by-city-remembering-san-antonio-gang-violence-in-the-1990s/Content ?oid=2509008&showFullText=true.

Maruna, Shadd. *Making Good: How Ex-Convicts Reform and Rebuild Their Lives.* Washington, DC: American Psychological Association Books, 2001.

Maruna, Shadd, Louise Wilson, and Kathryn Curran. "Why God Is Often Found Behind Bars: Prison Conversions and the Crisis of Self-Narrative." *Research in Human Development* 3, no. 2 (September 2006): 161–184.

Mason, Suzanne, prod. *Writ Writer.* Newburgh, NY: New Day Films, 2008.

Matza, David. *Delinquency and Drift.* New Brunswick, NJ: Transaction Publishers, 1990.

Maxson, Cheryl. "Gang Members on the Move." *Juvenile Justice Bulletin.* Washington, DC: Office of Juvenile Justice and Delinquency Prevention: U.S. Department of Justice, October 1998: 3–14.

McCorkel, Jill A. *Breaking Women: Gender, Race, and the New Politics of Imprisonment.* New York: New York University Press, 2013.

McKinney, Wilson. *Fred Carrasco: The Heroin Merchant.* Austin: Heidelberg Publishers, 1975.

McShane, Marilyn D., and Frank P. Williams III. "The Prison Adjustment of Juvenile Offenders." *Crime & Delinquency* 35, no. 2 (April 1989): 254–269.

Melde, Chris, and Finn-Aage Esbensen. "Gangs and Violence: Disentangling the Impact of Gang Membership on the Level and Nature of Offending." *Journal of Quantitative Criminology* 29, no. 2 (June 2013): 143–166.

Middlemass, Keesha M. *Convicted and Condemned: The Politics and Policies of Prisoner Reentry.* New York: New York University Press, 2017.

Miller, Walter B. "Lower Class Culture as a Generating Milieu of Gang Delinquency." *Journal of Social Issues* 14, no. 3 (Summer 1958): 5–19.

———. "Violent Crimes in City Gangs." *Annals of the American Academy of Political and Social Science* 364, no. 1 (March 1966): 96–112.

Mock, Brentin. "Vicious Circle: Aryan Circle Blamed for Two Cop Killings." In *North American Criminal Gangs*, edited by Tom Barker, 151–156. Durham, NC: Carolina Academic Press, 2007.

Montejano, David. *Quixote's Soldiers: A Local History of the Chicano Movement, 1966–1981.* Austin: University of Texas Press, 2010.

Monti, Daniel J. "Origins and Problems of Gang Research in the United States." In *Gangs: The Origins and Impact of Contemporary Youth Gangs in the United States,* edited by Scott Cummings and Daniel J. Monti, 3–25. Albany: State University of New York Press, 1993.

Moore, Joan W. *Going Down to the Barrio: Homeboys and Homegirls in Change.* Philadelphia: Temple University Press, 1991.

Moore, Joan, Diego Vigil, and Robert Garcia. "Residence and Territoriality in Chicano Gangs." *Social Problems* 31, no. 2 (December 1983): 182–194.

Moran, Kevin. "Social Structure and Bonhomie: Emotions in the Youth Street Gang." *British Journal of Criminology* 55, no. 3 (May 2015): 556–577.

Mowen, Thomas, and John Brent. "School Discipline as a Turning Point: The Cumulative Effect of Suspension on Arrest." *Journal of Research in Crime and Delinquency* 53, no. 5 (August 2016): 628–653.

Mumola, Christopher J., and Allen J. Beck. "Prisoners in 1996." Bureau of Justice Statistics Bulletin. Washington, DC: U.S. Department of Justice: Office of Justice Programs, June 1997. https://www.bjs.gov/content/pub/pdf/p96.pdf.

Myers, Thomas A. "The Unconstitutionality, Ineffectiveness, and Alternatives of Gang Injunctions." *Michigan Journal of Race and Law* 14, no. 2 (2009): 285–305.

Naser, Rebecca L., and Nancy G. La Vigne. "Family Support in the Prisoner Reentry Process." *Journal of Offender Rehabilitation* 43, no. 1 (2006): 93–106.

O'Brien, John, John Newton, Anita Zinnecker, and Bill Parr. *Statewide Criminal Justice Recidivism and Revocation Rates.* Austin: State of Texas, Legislative Budget Board, January 2005. http://www.lbb.state.tx.us/documents/publications/policy_report/4914_recividism_revocation_rates_jan2019.pdf.

Packer, Herbert. *The Limits of the Criminal Sanction.* Stanford: Stanford University Press, 1968.

Panfil, Vanessa R. *The Gang's All Queer: The Lives of Gay Gang Members.* New York, New York University Press, 2017.

Papachristos, Andrew V. "Murder by Structure: Dominance Relations and the Social Structure of Gang Homicide." *American Journal of Sociology* 115, no. 1 (July 2009): 74–128.

Park, Robert E., Ernest W. Burgess, and Roderick Duncan McKenzie. *The City.* Chicago: University of Chicago Press, 1925.

Pelz, Mary E. (Beth), James W. Marquart, and C. Terry Pelz. "Right-Wing Extremism in the Texas Prisons: The Rise and Fall of the Aryan Brotherhood of Texas." *Prison Journal* 71, no. 2 (September 1991): 23–37.

Peralta, Stacy, Baron Davis, Dan Halsted, Jesse Dylan, Gus Roxburgh, Shaun Murphy, Cash Warren, Sam George, and Forest Whitaker. *Crips and Bloods: Made in America.* New York: Docurama Films: Distributed by New Video, 2009.

Perkinson, Robert. *Texas Tough: The Rise of America's Prison Empire.* New York: Picador, 2010.

Peterson-Badali, Michele, Stephanie Care, and Julia Broeking. "Young People's Perceptions and Experiences of the Lawyer–Client Relationship." *Canadian Journal of Criminology and Criminal Justice* 49, no. 3 (July 2007): 375–401.

Pettus-Davis, Carrie, Elaine Eggleston Doherty, Christopher Veeh, and Christina Drymon. "Deterioration of Postincarceration Social Support for Emerging Adults." *Criminal Justice and Behavior* 44, no. 10 (October 2017): 1317–1339.

Pew Center on the States. "*State of Recidivism: The Revolving Door of America's Prisons.*" Washington, DC: The Pew Charitable Trusts, April 2011. https://www.pewtrusts .org/~/media/legacy/uploadedfiles/pcs_assets/2011/pewstateofrecidivismpdf.pdf.

Pfaff, John F. *Locked In: The True Causes of Mass Incarceration-And How to Achieve Real Reform.* New York: Basic Books, 2017.

Pride, Richard A. "Public Opinion and the End of Busing: (Mis)Perceptions of Policy Failure." *Sociological Quarterly* 41, no. 2 (Spring 2000): 207–225.

Prison Legal News. "Guard Raped, Entire Texas Prison System Locked Down." May 1999. https://www.prisonlegalnews.org/news/1999/may/15/guard-raped-entire -texas-prison-system-locked-down/.

Pryor, Marie, and Douglas E. Thompkins. "The Disconnect between Education and Social Opportunity for the Formerly Incarcerated." *American Journal of Criminal Justice* 38, no. 3 (September 2013): 457–479.

Pynoos, Robert. S, and Spencer Eth. "Children Traumatized by Witnessing Acts of Personal Violence: Homicide, Rape, and Suicide Behavior." In *Post-Traumatic Stress Disorder in Children*, edited by Spencer Eth and Robert S. Pynoos, 17–43. Washington, DC: American Psychiatric Press, 1985.

Pyrooz, David C. and Scott H. Decker. *Competing for Control: Gangs and the Social Order of Prisons.* Cambridge, UK: Cambridge University Press, 2019.

Pyrooz, David C., Scott H. Decker, and Mark Fleisher. "From the Street to the Prison, from the Prison to the Street: Understanding and Responding to Prison Gangs." *Journal of Aggression, Conflict, and Peace Research* 3, no. 1 (January 2011): 12–24.

Ralph, Paige H., and James W. Marquart. "Gang Violence in Texas Prisons." *Prison Journal* 71, no. 2 (September 1991): 38–49.

Riley, Alexander. "The Rebirth of Tragedy Out of the Spirit of Hip Hop: A Cultural Sociology of Gangsta Rap Music." *Journal of Youth Studies* 8, no. 3 (September 2005): 297–311.

Rios, Victor. *Punished: Policing the Lives of Black and Latino Boys.* New York: New York University Press, 2011.

Rocque, Michael, and Ray Paternoster. "Understanding the Antecedents of the 'School-to-Jail' Link: The Relationship between Race and School Discipline." *Journal of Criminal Law and Criminology* 101, no. 2 (March 2011): 633–665.

Rocque, Michael, Chad Posick, and Ray Paternoster. "Identities through Time: An Exploration of Identity Change as a Cause of Desistance." *Justice Quarterly* 33, no. 1 (2016): 45–72.

Rufino, Katrina A., Kathleen Talbot, and Glen A. Kercher. "Gang Membership and Crime Victimization among Prison Inmates." *American Journal of Criminal Justice* 37, no. 3 (September 2002): 321–337.

Sanders, William B. *Gangbangs and Drive-Bys: Grounded Culture and Juvenile Gang Violence.* New York: De Gruyter, 1994.

Santana, Juan, and Gabriel Morales. *Don't Mess with Texas! Gangs in the Lone Star State.* Columbia, SC: CreateSpace, 2014.

Schulhofer, Stephen J. "Plea Bargaining as Disaster." *Yale Law Journal* 101, no. 8 (June 1992): 1979–2010.

Sellers, Brian G., and Bruce A. Arrigo. "Zero Tolerance, Social Control, and Marginalized Youth in U.S. Schools: A Critical Reappraisal of Neoliberalism's Theoretical Foundations and Epistemological Assumptions." *Contemporary Justice Review* 21, no. 1 (February 2018): 60–79.

Selman, Kaitlyn J. "Imprisoning 'Those' Kids: Neoliberal Logics and the Disciplinary Alternative School." *Youth Justice* 17, no. 3 (December 2017): 213–231.

Shaw, Clifford, and Henry H. McKay. *Juvenile Delinquency in Urban Areas: A Study of Rates of Delinquents in Relation to Differential Characteristics of Local Communities in American Cities*. Chicago: University of Chicago Press, 1942.

Sikes, Gini. *8 Ball Chicks*. New York: Anchor Books, 1997.

Skarbek, David. *The Social Order of the Underworld: How Prison Gangs Govern the American Penal System*. New York: Oxford University Press, 2014.

Smith, Christopher E. "Black Muslims and the Development of Prisoners' Rights." *Journal of Black Studies* 24, no. 2 (December 1993): 131–146.

Steinberg, Laurence, He Len Chung, and Michelle Little. "Reentry of Young Offenders from the Justice System: A Developmental Perspective." *Youth Violence and Juvenile Justice* 2, no. 1 (January 2004): 21–38.

Stiles, Beverly L., Xiaoru Liu, and Howard B. Kaplan. "Relative Deprivation and Deviant Adaptations: The Mediating Effects of Negative Self-Feelings." *Journal of Research in Crime and Delinquency* 37, no. 1 (February 2000): 64–90.

Stretesky, Paul B., and Mark R. Pogrebin. "Gang-Related Gun Violence: Socialization, Identity, and Self." *Journal of Contemporary Ethnography* 36, no. 1 (February 2007): 85–114.

Sutherland, Edwin H, Donald Cressey, and David F. Luckenbill. *Principles of Criminology*, 11th ed. Oxford: General Hall, 1992.

Sykes, Gresham M. *The Society of Captives: A Study of a Maximum Security Prison*. Princeton: Princeton University Press, 1958.

Tapia, Mike. "Barrio Criminal Networks and Prison Gang Formation in Texas." *Journal of Gang Research* 25, no. 4 (September 2018): 45–63.

———. *The Barrio Gangs of San Antonio: 1915–2015*. Fort Worth: Texas Christian University Press, 2017.

———. "San Antonio's Barrio Gangs: Size, Scope, and Other Characteristics." *Deviant Behavior* 36, no. 9 (September 2015): 691–704.

———. "Texas Latino Gangs and Large Urban Jails: Intergenerational Conflicts and Issues in Management." *Journal of Crime and Justice* 37, no. 2 (February 2013): 256–274.

Tapia, Mike., Corey S. Sparks, and J. Mitchell Miller. "Texas Latino Prison Gangs: An Exploration of Generational Shift and Rebellion." *Prison Journal* 94, no. 2 (June 2014): 159–179.

Texas Fusion Center. "*Texas Gang Threat Assessment: 2012/2018.*" Austin, Texas: Fusion Center, Intelligence and Counterterrorism Division, Texas Department of Public Safety, 2013/2018. https://www.dps.texas.gov/director_staff/media_and_communications/2018/txGangThreatAssessment201811.pdf.

Texas Juvenile Justice Department. *TJJD Strategic Plan 2015–2019*. https://www.tjjd.texas.gov/publications/reports/RPTSTRAT201401.pdf.

Texas State Library and Archives Commission. "An Inventory of Youth Commission Historical Records at the Texas State Archives, 1886–1892, 1902, 1909–2003, Undated, Bulk 1949–2000." https://legacy.lib.utexas.edu/taro/tslac/20124/tsl-20124.html#series5.

Thornberry, Terence P., Marvin D. Krohn, Alan J. Lizotte, and Deborah Chard-Wierschem. "The Role of Juvenile Gangs in Facilitating Delinquent Behavior." *Journal of Research in Crime and Delinquency* 30, no. 1 (February 1993): 55–87.

Thornberry, Terence P., Marvin D. Krohn, Alan J. Lizotte, Carolyn A. Smith, and Kimberly Tobin. *Gangs and Delinquency in Developmental Perspective*. Cambridge: Cambridge University Press, 2003.

Tita, George E., Jacqueline Cohen, and John Engberg. "An Ecological Study of the Location of Gang 'Set Space.'" *Social Problems* 52, no. 2 (May 2005): 272–299.

Triplett, Ruth. "Youth Gangs in Texas Part II." *Texas Law Enforcement Management and Administrative Statistics Program* 4, no. 4 (1997): 2.

Tripodi, Stephen J. "The Influence of Social Bonds on Recidivism: A Study of Texas Male Prisoners." *Victims and Offenders: An International Journal of Evidence-Based Research, Policy, and Practice* 5, no. 4 (October 2010): 354–370.

Trulson, Chad R., and James W. Marquart. "Racial Desegregation and Violence in the Texas Prison System." *Criminal Justice Review* 27, no. 2 (September 2002): 233–255.

Valdez, Avelardo. "Mexican American Youth and Adult Prison Gangs in a Changing Heroin Market." *Journal of Drug Issues* 35, no. 4 (October 2005): 843–867.

Valdez, Avelardo, and Raquel Flores. "A Situational Analysis of Dating Violence among Mexican American Females Associated with Street Gangs." *Sociological Focus* 38, no. 2 (May 2005): 95–114.

Valdez, Avelardo, Charles D. Kaplan, and Edward Codina. "Psychopathy among Mexican American Gang Members: A Comparative Study." *International Journal of Offender Therapy and Comparative Criminology* 44, no. 1 (February 2000): 46–58.

Vargas, Robert. "Criminal Group Embeddedness and the Adverse Effects of Arresting a Gang's Leader: A Comparative Case Study." *Criminology* 52, no. 2 (May 2014): 143–168.

Vigil, James Diego. *Barrio Gangs: Street Life and Identity in Southern California.* Long Grove, IL: Waveland Press, 1988.

———. *A Rainbow of Gangs: Street Cultures in the Mega-City.* Austin: University of Texas Press, 2002.

Visher, Christy A., Sara A. Debus-Sherrill, and Jennifer Yahner. "Employment after Prison: A Longitudinal Study of Former Prisoners." *Justice Quarterly* 28, no. 5 (October 2011): 698–718.

Wacquant, Loïc. "The Curious Eclipse of Prison Ethnography in the Age of Mass Incarceration." *Ethnography* 3, no. 4 (2002): 371–397.

Watson, Jamie, Amy L. Solomon, Nancy G. La Vigne, Jeremy Travis, Meagan Funches, and Barbara Parthasarthy. *A Portrait of Prisoner Reentry in Texas.* Washington, DC: Urban Institute Justice Policy Center, March 2004. https://www.urban .org/research/publication/portrait-prisoner-reentry-texas.

Watters, Ethan. "The Love Story That Upended the Texas Prison System." *Texas Monthly*, October 11, 2018. https://www.texasmonthly.com/articles/love-story -upended-texas-prison-system/.

Watts, Alexis, Edward E. Rhine, Mariel Alper, and Cecilia Klingele. *Profiles in Parole Release and Revocation: Examining the Legal Framework in the United States—Texas.* University of Minnesota: Robina Institute of Criminal Law and Criminal Justice, 2016. https://robinainstitute.umn.edu/sites/robinainstitute.umn.edu/files/602501 _texas_legal_parole_profile_final.pdf.

Wilkinson, Deanna L. "Violent Events and Social Identity: Specifying the Relationship Between Respect and Masculinity in Inner-City Youth Violence." *Sociological Studies of Children and Youth* 8 (2001): 235–269.

Wood, Jane, L., Constantinos Kallis, and Jeremy W. Coid. "Differentiating Gang Members, Gang Affiliates, and Violent Men on Their Psychiatric Morbidity and Traumatic Experiences." *Psychiatry: Interpersonal and Biological Process* 80, no. 3 (2017): 221–235.

Worley, Robert M., and Vidisha Barua Worley. "Guards Gone Wild: A Self-Report Study of Correctional Officer Misconduct and the Effect of Institutional Deviance on 'Care' within the Texas Prison System." *Deviant Behavior* 32, no. 4 (April 2011): 293–319.

Index

Page numbers in *italics* indicate photos and figures.

ABOUT THE AUTHOR

CHRISTIAN L. BOLDEN is an associate professor of criminology and justice at Loyola University New Orleans. He earned his undergraduate and master's degrees from Texas State University–San Marcos, and his PhD in sociology from the University of Central Florida. From 2012 to 2013, he was the Futurist in Residence research fellow for the FBI Behavioral Sciences Unit. His research focuses on gang social networks, gang organizational processes, and human trafficking.

Available titles in the Critical Issues in Crime and Society series: